1KBW on Trusts in Matrimonial Finance Proceedings

1KBW on Trusts in Matrimonial Finance Proceedings

Richard Harrison QC
Harry Oliver
Laura Moys
Charlotte Hartley
Thomas Dance
Max Turnell

Bloomsbury Professional
LONDON • DUBLIN • EDINBURGH • NEW YORK • NEW DELHI • SYDNEY

Bloomsbury Professional
Bloomsbury Publishing Plc

41–43 Boltro Road, Haywards Heath, RH16 1BJ, UK

BLOOMSBURY and the Diana logo are trademarks of Bloomsbury Publishing Plc

First published in Great Britain 2019

British Library Cataloguing-in-Publication Data

A catalogue record for this book is available from the British Library.

ISBN:	PB:	978 1 52650 805 8
	ePDF:	978 1 52650 807 2
	ePub:	978 1 52650 806 5

Typeset by Evolution Design and Digital Ltd (Kent)

Preface

This book is intended to be a practical guide to trust issues for lawyers who deal with or become involved in divorce and financial remedies proceedings in England and Wales. The book is written from our perspective as litigators operating in this field and our emphasis has been on practice as much as principle. We hope that the book will provide a useful and accessible guide to other practitioners.

There are many people we should thank for the shared pool of knowledge we have acquired over the years. The list is a long one, running from our parents to our pupil supervisors and not forgetting the many judges who have provided us with judicial – if not always judicious – encouragement in response to our submissions. In particular we must thank James Turner QC and Charles Howard QC who, between them, have led all of us on numerous occasions in very substantial financial and trust cases, some of which have been instrumental in the development of the law.

We would also like to thank the publishing team at Bloomsbury for their expertise, encouragement and professional support.

RH, HO, LM, CH, TD and MT
January 2019
1 King's Bench Walk

Contents

Table of Cases

[All references are to paragraph numbers]

Q

R

S

T

Table of Statutes

[All references are to paragraph numbers]

Table of Statutory Instruments

[*All references are to paragraph numbers*]

Table of European Legislation

[*All references are to paragraph numbers*]

Table of International Legislation

[*All references are to paragraph numbers*]

CHAPTER 1

Introduction

SCOPE OF THE BOOK

1.1 This book is intended to be a practical guide for family law practitioners who deal with applications for financial remedies which involve trusts.

1.2 **Chapter 2** contains a detailed overview of the general principles applicable to the determination of financial claims in matrimonial cases. It is no more than an overview, as this book is not intended to provide an in depth analysis of all of the many legal issues which may arise in such cases; its focus is upon the trust issues that may arise in this context.

1.3 **Chapters 3** and **4** cover issues relating to the court's jurisdiction to make orders in relation to trusts and their assets. **Chapter 4** is devoted solely to the important question of submission to the jurisdiction by trustees; whether or not trustees have submitted may well determine a spouse's ability to enforce a financial order against them.

1.4 **Chapter 5** focuses upon the rules relating to service and joinder; it deals mainly with issues of procedure. **Chapter 6** deals with powers of the court to make orders for disclosure and the limits of those powers; it also addresses the entitlement of beneficiaries to obtain disclosure of trust documents.

1.5 **Chapter 7** contains a section explaining fundamental trust principles with which family practitioners need to be familiar. The chapter deals with the circumstances in which a trust will be validly created either expressly or impliedly and explores how practitioners may seek to uncover the reality of ownership of assets ostensibly held in trust or in the names of third parties.

1.6 **Chapter 8** is devoted to the crucial issue of ante-nuptial and post-nuptial settlements. Establishing that a trust or other arrangement amounts to a nuptial settlement enables the court to exercise wide powers to vary the trust for the benefit of one of the spouses; such powers do not exist absent a determination of nuptiality and thus the issue is often one of critical importance.

1.7 **Chapter 9** is concerned with the question of when non-nuptial trusts will be treated as a resource of one of the parties for the purposes of assessing their net worth. The best known authority in which this issue is considered is *Thomas v Thomas*[1].

1 [1995] 2 FLR 668, [1996] 2 FCR 544, CA.

1.8 **Chapters 10** and **11** are both concerned with aspects of enforcement. **Chapter 10** covers the avoidance of dispositions and explains how important steps can be taken to prevent or undo attempts by unscrupulous litigants to defeat their spouses' claims by placing their assets in the names of third parties. **Chapter 11** examines some of the steps that can be taken to enforce orders against trusts and limits of enforcement.

The family courts' approach to trusts in the 20th century

1.9 In the 20th century it was relatively uncommon for the family court to have to consider trust issues in any detail.

1.10 Although cases did arise involving trusts, it was rare to encounter situations in which it was appropriate for the trust assets to be *shared* between the parties.

1.11 The courts operated on the basis that the spouse who had created the family wealth was entitled to retain the wealth they had generated subject only to payment of a sum sufficient to meet the needs or, in more substantial cases, the 'reasonable requirements' of the other spouse[2].

1.12 In 'big money' cases there was a ceiling to the amount a wealth-generator would have to pay out. It might not matter whether a rich person was worth £50 million, £100 million or even £10 billion: their spouse was limited to claiming an amount sufficient to meet their needs, which usually comprised a suitable house, possibly a second home, some furniture, a car, perhaps a small contingency fund[3] and a *Duxbury*[4] fund to provide an income for life.

EXAMPLES OF 'REASONABLE REQUIREMENTS' AWARDS	
F v F [1995] 2 FLR 45	Eight year marriage; three children, one of whom had special needs; substantial pre-matrimonial wealth; H assets of £150m–200m. W received £9m (c.5%).
Dart [1996] 2 FLR 286	15 year marriage; two children; significant premarital wealth; also substantial accrual of wealth in marriage. W received £9m out of c£400m (2%).
Conran [1997] 2 FLR 615	30 year marriage; three children; wealth created during marriage by H. W received £10.5m (12%); H retained £74.5m (88%).

1.13 The limited ambit of potential claims would often mean that there was no need to conduct a detailed investigation of assets held in trust. Wealthy litigants could forestall such an investigation by relying on the so-called 'millionaire's

2 *Dart v Dart* [1996] 2 FLR 286, CA.
3 *Re Besterman, deceased; Besterman v Grusin* [1984] Ch 458, CA.
4 *Duxbury v Duxbury* [1992] Fam 62, CA.

defence': an open concession that they could meet any reasonable amount claimed by their spouse[5].

The changes after White v White

1.14 On 26 October 2000 the House of Lords decided the appeal in *White v White*[6] and the legal landscape changed. It was held to be discriminatory, and therefore impermissible, to attach greater importance to the contribution to a marriage of a breadwinner than that of a homemaker. The division of assets between spouses had to be checked against the '*yardstick of equal division*'. Equality should only be departed from if and to the extent that there was good reason for doing so.

1.15 The principles established in *White* were later reinforced by the House of Lords in *Miller v Miller; McFarlane v McFarlane*[7]. Since *Miller* was decided, assets accrued during the marriage are now normally divided equally between the spouses apart from in cases where the needs of one of the parties require an unequal division or there exists some other exceptional basis for an unequal division such as 'special contribution' or 'conduct'.

1.16 A consequence of the modern focus upon equal division is that it is now necessary for the courts to evaluate with far greater specificity the extent of the marital 'pot' in order to determine the value of a claimant spouse's entitlement to 50%. This has resulted in the courts having to conduct investigations into trust structures far more frequently than was previously the case in order to uncover the 'reality' underlying such structures and the true value of assets held within a trust. **Chapters 7** and **9** of this book deal with the approach of the courts to establishing the reality of ownership that may lie behind a legal structure.

1.17 The 21st century has thus seen a change of emphasis in the financial battles fought by warring spouses in 'big money' cases. The primary focus in most substantial cases is now upon establishing the extent of the parties' resources and how assets can be extracted from the vehicles through which they are held in order to meet the justice of the case.

1.18 The financial stakes in many cases have been raised exponentially post-*White* in comparison to equivalent cases heard in the last century. This in turn has increased the incentives for dishonest litigants to conceal their assets and behave obstructively. Obtaining a financial remedy is often merely the precursor to the real battle over enforcement, a topic covered in **Chapter 11** of this book.

1.19 The 'super-rich' typically have at their disposal a plethora of financial and legal advisers enabling them to structure their wealth in ways which are

5 *Thyssen-Bornemisza v Thyssen-Bornemisza (No 2)* [1986] Fam 1, CA.
6 [2001] 1 AC 596.
7 [2006] UKHL 24, [2006] 2 AC 618.

tax-efficient and which shield their assets from potential attack by third party creditors. It is legitimate to use all lawful means to save tax and protect assets in this way; but it is dishonest to use structures intended to mitigate tax as a means of denying the reality of ownership in financial proceedings.

1.20 The existence of tax-saving structures is commonly used by spouses minded to be less than frank as means of concealing the reality of their interest from the family courts. It is therefore essential for practitioners operating in this field to have a clear understanding of the ways in which trusts are formed and can operate (see **Chapter 7**) and of the process by which disclosure may be sought (see **Chapter 6**). Practitioners also need – at the outset of proceedings – to have a clear understanding of the means by which any order their client may obtain can be enforced and of the hurdles they may face in seeking enforcement (see **Chapter 11**).

1.21 Family justice is imperfect. There are a great many litigants who have succeeded in persuading a judge that their spouse is dishonest, but ultimately failed in their endeavours to enforce the resulting award made in their favour. It is important to understand the limitations in the system to be able to assess when it may be better for a client to cut their losses and accept the proverbial 'bird in the hand'.

CHAPTER 2

Overview of General Principles in Financial Remedy Proceedings

Content at a Glance:

A. INTRODUCTION

2.1 This chapter provides an overview of the general principles in financial remedy proceedings in England and Wales. The principal statute governing financial applications ancillary to divorce[1] is the Matrimonial Causes Act 1973 ('MCA 1973').

2.2 The courts of England and Wales are internationally renowned for their handling of complex and high value financial remedy proceedings between divorcing spouses and civil partners.

1 References to 'divorce' in this chapter should be taken to include dissolution/annulment of a civil partnership, nullity and judicial separation. Particularly, the Civil Partnership Act 2004, Sch 5 makes provision for financial relief in connection with civil partnerships that corresponds to provision made for financial relief in connection with marriages.

2.3 The attractions of the jurisdiction include:

1 The ability of parties to seise the jurisdiction: see **Chapter 3**.

2 The court's insistence upon full and frank disclosure from the parties: see **Chapter 6**.

3 The ability to join third parties to the proceedings and to seek disclosure from third parties (such as trustees): see **Chapters 5** and **6**.

4 The requirement for the court to take account of a wide range of income and capital resources available to the parties including resources held in trust, and assets held in the names of third parties: see **Chapter 9**.

5 The court's substantial powers to grant financial relief, including the statutory power to vary nuptial settlements: see **Chapter 8**.

6 The court's power to grant declarations of beneficial ownership and make orders in relation to assets held in the name(s) of others: see **Chapter 7**.

7 The perceived generosity in the distributive principles to financially weaker parties.

2.4 Broadly, the court follows a tri-partite process in determining an application for financial orders under the MCA 1973:

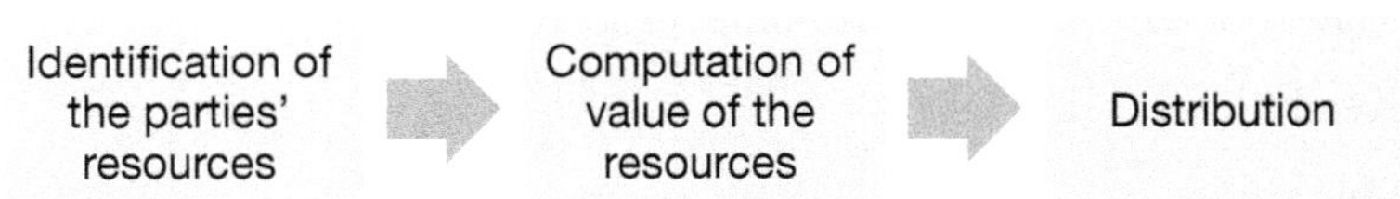

2.5 As discussed in **Chapter 6**, intrinsic to identification and allied to the court's responsibility to safeguard the interests of the parties, as well as the public interest, is the parties' duty to make full and frank disclosure of all relevant information to one another and to the court. As Lord Brandon of Oakbrook emphasised in *Livesey v Jenkins*[2] in a passage recently cited with approval by Baroness Hale in *Sharland v Sharland*[3]:

> '... unless a court is provided with correct, complete and up-to-date information on the matters to which, under section 25(1), it is required to have regard, it cannot lawfully or properly exercise its discretion in the manner ordained by that subsection.'

B. POWERS OF THE COURT

2.6 The courts have a wide discretion when making financial orders on divorce. The court's power is principally derived from the MCA 1973 under

2 [1985] AC 424 at 437.
3 [2015] UKSC 60, [2016] AC 871.

which it has the power upon the grant of a decree of divorce or at any time thereafter[4] to make one or more of the following orders[5]:

(a) Periodical Payments;

(b) Secured provision;

(c) Lump sums;

(d) The transfer of property;

(e) The settlement of property;

(f) The variation of ante-nuptial or post-nuptial settlements;

(g) Pension Sharing Orders; and

(h) Pension Attachment Orders.

C. THE STATUTORY DISCRETION

2.7 The court has a discretion as to the orders it may make but does not exercise that discretion in a vacuum. Section 25 of the MCA 1973 sets out the factors which the court is obliged to consider.

2.8 Section 25(1) requires the court to have regard to '*all the circumstances of the case*' but to give '*first consideration*' to the welfare of any child of the family who has not attained the age of 18.

2.9 Section 25(2) requires the court to have regard '*in particular*' to a list of eight factors from (a) to (h), namely:

(a) The income, earning capacity, property and other financial resources which each of the parties to the marriage has or is likely to have in the foreseeable future, including in the case of earning capacity any increase in that capacity which it would in the opinion of the court be reasonable to expect a party to the marriage to take steps to acquire.

(b) The financial needs, obligations and responsibilities which each of the parties to the marriage has or is likely to have in the foreseeable future.

(c) The standard of living enjoyed by the family before the breakdown of the marriage.

(d) The age of each party to the marriage and the duration of the marriage.

(e) Any physical or mental disability of either of the parties to the marriage.

4 It should, however, be noted that a spouse may not make an application for a financial remedy if he or she has remarried, although an application which was made prior to remarriage may be pursued: *Jackson v Jackson* [1973] Fam. 99, [1973] 2 WLR 735, Bagnall J.

5 The MCA 1973, ss 23–25D. It should be noted that Pension Sharing Orders are not available upon judicial separation.

(f) The contributions which each of the parties has made or is likely in the foreseeable future to make to the welfare of the family, including any contribution by looking after the home or caring for the family.

(g) The conduct of each of the parties, if that conduct is such that it would in the opinion of the court be inequitable to disregard it.

(h) In the case of proceedings for divorce or nullity of marriage, the value to each of the parties to the marriage of any benefit which, by reason of the dissolution or annulment of the marriage, that party will lose the chance of acquiring.

2.10 Section 25A contains what is known as the '*clean break*' principle. It requires the court to consider in every case whether it would be appropriate to exercise its powers so as to terminate the parties' financial obligations to each other as soon after the grant of decree absolute as is just and reasonable. Where a court makes an order for ongoing periodical payments it must consider whether it would be appropriate to require the payments to be made only for such term as would be sufficient to enable the receiving party to adjust '*without undue hardship*' to the termination of his or her financial dependence on the other party.

D. THE DISTRIBUTIVE PRINCIPLES

2.11 The MCA 1973 does not identify the objective of the courts or provide guidance as to the weight to be given to the different factors which the courts are required to take into account. It has been judicially stated that the implicit objective must be to achieve a fair outcome[6].

2.12 In *Miller v Miller, McFarlane v McFarlane*[7] both Baroness Hale and Lord Nicholls identified three main distributive principles to be discerned from the MCA 1973, s 25(2):

Need | Sharing | Compensation

2.13 Since *Miller*, however, the courts have sought to limit the ambit of the compensation principle[8] and so the large majority of cases are determined in accordance with the principles of need and sharing alone. These principles are applied in the light of the size and nature of all the computed resources which are usually heavily circumscribing factors.

6 See *White v White* [2001] 1 AC 596, HL at 604 per Lord Nicholls of Birkenhead.

7 [2006] UKHL 24, [2006] 2 AC 618, HL.

8 The principle is thought to be difficult to evidence and apply and can be subsumed within the court's consideration of generously-assessed needs and sharing: *RP v RP* [2006] EWHC 3409 (Fam), [2007] 1 FLR 2105, Coleridge J; *McFarlane v McFarlane* [2009] EWHC 891 (Fam), [2009] 2 FLR 1322, Charles J; *Hvorostovsky v Hvorostovsky* [2009] EWCA Civ 791, [2009] 2 FLR 1574, CA; *SA v PA (Pre-Marital Agreement: Compensation)* [2014] EWHC 392 (Fam), [2014] 2 FLR 1028, Mostyn J.

E. AUTONOMY AND AGREEMENTS

2.14 Respect for the parties' autonomy to enter into ante-nuptial and post-nuptial agreements may now be considered another core principle[9]. The court will give effect to a nuptial agreement that was freely entered into by each party with a full appreciation of its implications unless, in the circumstances, it would not be fair to hold the parties to their agreement[10]. For instance, it may not be fair to uphold an agreement if implementing it would leave one of the parties unable to meet their needs[11].

F. NON-DISCRIMINATION AND THE YARDSTICK OF EQUALITY

2.15 In *White v White*[12], the House of Lords agreed that fairness required there should be no discrimination between husband and wife in the respective roles that they played during the marriage. If they had both made an equal contribution to the welfare of the family, then it did not matter which party had specifically acquired the assets.

2.16 However, the invitation to formulate a principle that the assets should be divided equally in every case was rejected[13]. Instead, it was said that the equality of division was to be used as a check or yardstick by the judge against his or her provisional award to avoid discrimination and the provisional award could thereafter be adjusted to achieve fairness.

2.17 Since *White,* the yardstick of equal division has developed into a principle of equal sharing of those assets which are classed as 'matrimonial'. The Court of Appeal in *Charman v Charman (No 4)*[14], following *Miller v Miller; McFarlane v McFarlane,* moved towards the position of Lord Cooke in *White* in that the court should share matrimonial property in equal proportions unless there is good reason to depart from such proportions (the most common reason being 'need'). Thus, the court's consideration of the yardstick is no longer postponed until the end of the distributive exercise but takes place within the principle of sharing.

G. SPECIAL CONTRIBUTIONS

2.18 The principle of sharing has encouraged generators of substantial wealth to find reasons to justify an unequal division of matrimonial assets in their favour.

9 See *Radmacher (formerly Granatino) v Grantino (pre-nuptial contract)* [2010] UKSC 42, [2011] 1 AC 534, SC.

10 See above.

11 See above.

12 [2001] 1 AC 596, HL.

13 Lord Nicholls for instance stated at 606 that the 'presumption of equal division would be an impermissible judicial gloss on the statute.'

14 [2007] EWCA Civ 503, [2007] 1 FLR 1246.

One argument that is sometimes raised is 'special contributions', namely that the contribution the wealth generator has made to the marriage has been in some way stellar, either by virtue of individual genius or, more usually, due to the sheer amount of wealth they have generated [15]. As Lord Nicholls held in *Miller*:

> '... the principled answer in those cases where the earnings of one party, usually the husband, have been altogether exceptional. The question is whether earnings of this character can be regarded as a "special contribution", and thus as a good reason for departing from equality of division. The answer is that exceptional earnings are to be regarded as a factor pointing away from equality of division when, but only when, it would be inequitable to proceed otherwise. The wholly exceptional nature of the earnings must be, to borrow a phrase more familiar in a different context, obvious and gross.'

2.19 The doctrine has been criticised due to its potential to imperil an outcome of fairness by valuing a breadwinner's efforts over those of a homemaker[16] to the extent that it is now confined to cases involving a truly exceptional contribution and exorbitant wealth. There are thus only five reported cases in which the argument has succeeded[17].

2.20 The treatment of 'special contribution' was considered by the Court of Appeal in *Work v Gray*[18] where the wife's argument that there was no place for the concept was dismissed. Instead, the Court of Appeal approved, with one amendment, the summary of the law on special contributions set out by the first instance judge, Holman J:

(a) The characteristics or circumstances which would result in a departure from equality have to be of a wholly exceptional nature such that it would very obviously be inconsistent with the objective of achieving fairness for them to be ignored.

(b) Exceptional earnings are to be regarded as a factor pointing away from equality of division when, but only when, it would be inequitable to proceed otherwise.

(c) Only if there is such a disparity in their respective contributions to the welfare of the family that it would be inequitable to disregard it should this be taken into account in determining their shares.

(d) It is extremely important to avoid discrimination against the home-maker.

15 See *Cowan v Cowan* [2001] EWCA Civ 679, [2002] Fam 97, CA; *Charman*; *Cooper-Hohn v Cooper-Hohn* [2014] EWHC 4122 (Fam), [2015] 1 FLR 745, Roberts J.

16 See *Lambert v Lambert* [2002] EWCA Civ 1685, [2003] Fam. 103, CA.

17 *Cowan v Cowan* [2001] EWCA Civ 679, [2002] Fam. 97, CA; *Sorrell v Sorrell* [2005] EWHC 1717 (Fam), [2006] 1 FLR 497, Bennett J; *Charman v Charman (No 4)* [2007] EWCA Civ 503, [2007] 1 FLR 1246, CA; *Cooper-Hohn v Cooper-Hohn* [2014] EWHC 4122 (Fam), [2015] 1 FLR 745, Roberts J; *XW v XH* [2017] EWFC 76 (appeal outstanding).

18 [2017] EWCA Civ 270, [2018] Fam 35 at [102].

(e) The amount of the wealth alone may be so extraordinary as to make it easy for the party who generated it to claim an exceptional and individual quality which deserves special treatment. Often, however, he or she will need independently to establish such a quality, whether by genius in business or some other field. A windfall is not enough.

(f) There is no identified threshold for such a claim to succeed.

H. MATRIMONIAL AND NON-MATRIMONIAL PROPERTY

2.21 The court must consider *all* the property and financial resources of the parties, but draws a distinction between '*matrimonial*' and '*non-matrimonial*' property where it is possible to do so:

(a) Matrimonial property includes property acquired during the marriage[19] by the efforts of one or both of the parties[20] and normally other assets that are intended for joint use and enjoyment, regardless of source. It is, for instance, well-established that the matrimonial home stands in a special category, whatever its source, and should usually be treated as matrimonial property[21]. The source from which the home derives may, however, justify an unequal division[22].

(b) Non-matrimonial property broadly falls into three categories[23]:

Pre-marital property: property acquired or created before the commencement of the marriage.	**Extra-marital property:** property acquiring during the marriage by gift or inheritance.	**Post-marital property:** property acquired or created after separation.

2.22 The distinction between 'matrimonial' and 'non-matrimonial' property is not always clear-cut. In cases where it is difficult to draw the line, the courts have adopted different approaches in striving to meet the ultimate objective of fairness. The following graphic identifies some of the problems that have been identified in trying to draw a sharp distinction between matrimonial and non-matrimonial assets, and the courts' response to those problems.

19 For these purposes, the dominant view is that no distinction should be made between years of seamless pre-marital cohabitation and years of marriage: *GW v RW (Financial Provision – Department from Equality)* [2003] EWHC 611 (Fam), [2003] 2 FLR 108, Mostyn J; *M v M (Financial Relief – Substantial Earning Capacity)* [2004] EWHC 688 (Fam), [2004] 2 FLR 236, Baron J; *Miller* at [149] per Baroness Hale.

20 See *Miller*, at [22]–[25] per Lord Nicholls and *Charman*.

21 See *Miller*.

22 *K v L (Ancillary Relief: Inherited Wealth)* [2011] EWCA Civ 550, [2012] 1 WLR 306, CA.

23 See *Miller; S v S (Non-Matrimonial Property: Conduct)* [2006] EWHC 2793 (Fam), [2007] 1 FLR 1496, Burton J; *Charman*; *Rossi v Rossi* [2006] EWHC 1482 (Fam), [2007] 1 FLR 790, Mostyn J.

MINGLING Funds held before the marriage or received by one party during the marriage, i.e. by inheritance, are often not maintained in specie but are mixed with matrimonial property or otherwise utilised and enjoyed by the family such that it is impossible for the court to ring-fence them.	Where a party brings assets into a marriage which become part of the economic life of the marriage i.e. utilised, converted, sustained and enjoyed by the family, that property may become matrimonial. The longer the marriage or enjoyment, the more likely such assets will become mingled. However, even so, often the source of the money demands reflection in the award: *N v F* [2011] EWHC 586 (Fam), [2011] 2 FLR 533.
PASSIVE AND ACTIVE GROWTH Property owned prior to marriage often increases in value during the marriage. In some cases, the increase is 'organic' or 'passive', attributable to the fluctation in the market. In others, the growth is the product of the active endeavours of one or both of the parties.	Generally, the element of growth which fairly represents the fruits of non-matrimonial assets that accrue during marriage will be characterised as non-matrimonial, i.e. 'organic' or 'passive' growth. However, growth which is referable to endeavours within the marriage will be matrimonial : *Jones v Jones* [2011] EWCA Civ 41, [2012] Fam 1, [2011] 1 FLR 1723.
POST-SEPARATION ACCRUAL Assets held at the date of the parties' separation often accrue value by the time the court is considering how to distribute them. The accrual in value may be attributable to 'organic' growth or to the continued active involvement by a party.	The arrival of wealth post-separation generated within marriage will be characterised as matrimonial. However, where no direct or indirect contribution (such as use or passive growth of matrimonial property), to such property can be shown, it may fairly be characterised as non-matrimonial: *Cooper-Hohn v Hohn* [2014] EWHC 4122, [2015] 1 FLR 745.

I. NEEDS

2.23 The principle of 'need' is an elastic concept[24] but will usually be the *'factor of magnetic importance'*[25]. In assessing a party's needs the court takes into account a number of factors.

2.24 In most cases the available assets are insufficient to meet adequately the needs of two households. The statutory requirement to prioritise the needs of any children of the family will often result in the spouse who has the primary care of the children receiving a greater share (even in some cases 100%) of the available assets, or at least retaining the use of the assets to provide a home for the children during their minority[26].

24 *SS v NS (Spousal Maintenance)* [2014] EWHC 4183 (Fam), [2015] 2 FLR 1124, Mostyn J.

25 *McCartney v Mills-McCartney* [2008] EWHC 401 (Fam), [2008] 1 FLR 1508, Bennett J at [311].

26 See *Cordle v Cordle* [2001] EWCA Civ 1791, [2002] 1 WLR 1441, CA; *Marshall v Beckett* [1998] 1 FLR 53, CA; *B v B (Mesher Order)* [2002] EWHC 3106 (Fam), [2003] 2 FLR 285, Munby J.

2.25 In cases involving substantial resources the courts have been willing to hold that a party 'needs' sufficient income and capital to maintain a lifestyle of great luxury.

The applicant wife received over £25m to meet her 'needs' in *McCartney v Mills McCartney* [2008] EWHC 401 (Fam), [2008] 1 FLR 1508.	The applicant wife received £63m to meet her 'needs' in *Juffali v Juffali* [2016] EWHC 1684 (Fam), [2016] 4 WLR 119, [2017] 1 FLR 729.	The applicant wife's needs were assessed at £224m in *AAZ v BBZ (No 1)* [2016] EWHC 3234 (Fam), [2018] 1 FLR 153.

2.26 However, there is no requirement for a party to meet the other party's needs in all circumstances. Whilst needs may be the dominant or magnetic factor, it does not follow that the financially stronger party should inevitably be held responsible for *any* established needs. Save in a situation of real hardship, it has been said that 'needs' must be causally related to the marriage[27]. For instance, a party is not necessarily liable for needs created by the applicant's financial mismanagement, extravagance or irresponsibility[28]. In the Supreme Court decision of *Mills v Mills*[29], provision had already been made for the wife's housing needs in a capital settlement and it was held that the first instance court was entitled not to increase her periodical payments so as to cover her increased housing costs where she had made unwise decisions in relation to capital.

J. SHARING

2.27 The 'sharing' principle derives from the basic concept that both parties to the marriage are equal. It is wrong to discriminate between the parties on the basis of the roles which each of them have assumed during the marriage. In the vast majority of cases, the contributions of 'a homemaker' have the same value as those of 'a breadwinner'[30].

2.28 When a marital partnership ends, the court will normally determine that each spouse is entitled to an equal share of the assets of the partnership (the matrimonial property) unless there is a good reason to the contrary[31].

2.29 The most common reason for an unequal distribution of matrimonial property is that a greater share is needed to meet the *needs* of one of the parties[32].

27 *FF v KF* [2017] EWHC 1093 (Fam), [2017] 2 FCR 509, Mostyn J at [18].

28 *North v North* [2007] EWCA Civ 76, [2008] 1 FLR 158, CA.

29 [2018] UKSC 38, [2018] 1 WLR 3945, SC.

30 *White v White* [2001] 1 AC 596, HL.

31 *Charman v Charman (No 4)* [2007] EWCA Civ 503, [2007] 1 FLR 1246, CA; *K v L (Ancillary Relief: Inherited Wealth)* [2011] EWCA Civ 550, [2011] 2 FLR 980, CA.

32 *Charman v Charman (No 4)*; *K v L (Ancillary Relief: Inherited Wealth)*.

2.30 In exceptional cases the court may distribute matrimonial property unequally to take account of other factors, including[33]:

The existence of an ante-nuptial or post-nuptial agreement.	The 'special contributions' of one of the parties.	The conduct of one of the parties if 'it would be inequitable to disregard' it.

2.31 Notwithstanding the inclusion of non-matrimonial property within the sharing principle, a reported decision is awaited in which a party's non-matrimonial property is transferred to the other party other than by reference to needs or compensation. Thus, the non-matrimonial property of a party will not normally be 'shared' with the other party[34]. Such property should normally only be encroached upon to the extent that it is necessary to meet the needs of the economically weaker party.

2.32 The sharing principle is equally applicable to short marriages as to long marriages and inevitably the duration of a marriage will affect the quantum of the matrimonial property accrued. However, a combination of relevant factors such as a short marriage involving no children, dual incomes and separate finances may be sufficient to justify a departure from the equal sharing principle in order to achieve fairness[35].

K. THE RELATIONSHIP BETWEEN NEEDS AND SHARING

2.33 In an ordinary case, the courts tend to adopt a formulaic four-stage process for determining the division of capital in financial remedy claims[36].

33 Agreements and special contributions are considered above at paras **2.14** and **2.18** respectively. In relation to conduct, such conduct may be classified as financial, marital, litigation or criminal/violent but it is settled law that such conduct must be exceptional: see for example *Al Khatib v Masry* [2002] EWHC 108 (Fam), [2002] 1 FLR 1053, Munby J; *S v S* [2006] EWHC 2793 (Fam), [2007] 1 FLR 1496, Burton J; *Miller v Miller; McFarlane v McFarlane*; *MAP v MFP* [2015] EWHC 627 (Fam), [2016] 1 FLR 70, Moor J; and, *R v B and Capita Trustees* [2017] EWFC 33, [2017] 3 FCR 519, Moor J.

34 *K v L (Ancillary Relief: Inherited Wealth).*

35 *Sharp v Sharp* [2017] EWCA Civ 408, [2018] 2 WLR 1617, [2017] 2 FLR 1095, CA.

36 *Charman v Charman (No 4)*; *K v L (Ancillary Relief: Inherited Wealth)*; *Jones v Jones*; *Scatliffe v Scatliffe (British Virgin Islands)* [2016] UKPC 36, [2017] AC 93, PC.

1. Divide the identified and computed assets into two parts: one part reflecting the non-matrimonial property and the other reflecting the matrimonial.

2. Divide the matrimonial property equally.

3. Consider whether this division results in an appropriate overall disposal engendering fairness to the parties and in particular will meet needs.

4. If the outcome does not meet the parties' needs, then the remainder of the parties' resources should be encroached upon to the extent that it is necessary to meet the parties' needs.

L. COMPENSATION

2.34 The compensation principle is aimed at redressing any significant prospective economic disparity between the parties arising from the way in which they conducted the marriage. It is thus relevant where one party is able to demonstrate the loss of career income specifically due to the demands of the family. *McFarlane* was described as a 'paradigm' case for an award of compensation where the wife received a joint-lives periodical payments order for £250,000pa.

2.35 However, the principle is difficult to evidence[37], apply and quantify. Thus other than in big money cases, the principle is usually subsumed within the court's consideration of sharing and generously-assessed needs[38].

37 In *SA v PA (Pre-Marital Agreement: Compensation)* [2014] EWHC 392 (Fam), [2014] 2 FLR 1028, Mostyn J rejected the argument of compensation as the wife had no appreciable track record by the time she gave up practice as a solicitor to raise a family. See also *RP v RP* [2006] EWHC 3409 (Fam), [2007] 1 FLR 2105, Coleridge J.

38 *McFarlane v McFarlane* [2009] EWHC 891 (Fam), [2009] 2 FLR 1322, Charles J; V*B v JP* [2008] EWHC 112 (Fam), [2008] 1 FLR 742, Potter P; *Hvorostovsky v Hvorostovsky* [2009] EWCA Civ 791, [2009] 2 FLR 1574, CA.

M. INCOME AND PERIODICAL PAYMENTS

2.36 It has been held that once a marriage has ended, in ordinary circumstances, a party does not have the right or expectation of continuing economic parity, ie to share the income of the other party[39]. However, periodical payments may be awarded to the extent that needs or, in rarer cases, compensation so require[40].

2.37 In *SS v NS (Spousal Maintenance)*[41], Mostyn J held that the relevant principles to consider on an application for spousal maintenance were as follows:

> '(i) A spousal maintenance award is properly made where the evidence shows that choices made during the marriage have generated hard future needs on the part of the claimant. Here the duration of the marriage and the presence of children are pivotal factors.
>
> (ii) An award should only be made by reference to needs, save in a most exceptional case where it can be said that the sharing or compensation principle applies.
>
> (iii) Where the needs in question are not causally connected to the marriage the award should generally be aimed at alleviating significant hardship.
>
> (iv) In every case the court must consider a termination of spousal maintenance with a transition to independence as soon as it is just and reasonable. A term should be considered unless the payee would be unable to adjust without undue hardship to the ending of payments. A degree of (not undue) hardship in making the transition to independence is acceptable.
>
> (v) If the choice between an extendable term and a joint lives order is finely balanced the statutory steer should militate in favour of the former.
>
> (vi) The marital standard of living is relevant to the quantum of spousal maintenance but is not decisive. That standard should be carefully weighed against the desired objective of eventual independence.
>
> (vii) The essential task of the judge is not merely to examine the individual items in the claimant's income budget but also to stand back and to look at the global total and to ask if it represents a fair proportion of the respondent's available income that should go to the support of the claimant.
>
> (viii) Where the respondent's income comprises a base salary and a discretionary bonus the claimant's award may be equivalently partitioned, with needs of strict necessity being met from the base

39 *Waggott v Waggot* [2018] EWCA Civ 727, [2018] 2 FCR 61, CA.

40 *SS v NS (Spousal Maintenance)* [2014] EWHC (Fam) 4183, [2015] 2 FLR 1124, Mostyn J; *B v S* [2012] EWHC 265 (Fam), [2012] 2 FLR 502, Mostyn J; *VB v JP* [2008] EWHC 112 (Fam), [2008] 1 FLR 742.

41 [2014] EWHC 4183 (Fam), [2015] 2 FLR 1124 at [46].

salary and additional, discretionary, items being met from the bonus on a capped percentage basis.

(ix) There is no criterion of exceptionality on an application to extend a term order[42]. On such an application an examination should to be made of whether the implicit premise of the original order of the ability of the payee to achieve independence had been impossible to achieve and, if so, why.

(x) On an application to discharge a joint lives order an examination should be made of the original assumption that it was just too difficult to predict eventual independence.

(xi) If the choice between an extendable and a non-extendable term is finely balanced the decision should normally be in favour of the economically weaker party.'

42 This determination by Mostyn J is controversial as it is inconsistent with the decision of the Court of Appeal in *Fleming v Fleming* [2003] EWCA Civ 1841, [2004] 1 FLR 667.

CHAPTER 3

Jurisdiction

Content at a Glance:

A. Introduction
- Orders which may affect trusts
- English law
- Enforcement considerations

B. Jurisdiction: divorce
- Brussels II Revised Regulation ('BIIR')
- Habitual residence
- Residence
- First seised
- Non-EU countries

C. Jurisdiction: financial relief
- Divorce in England and Wales
- Overseas divorce

D. Establishing jurisdiction over foreign trustees
- Relevance of enforcement to jurisdiction
- Service of proceedings
- Joinder
- Location of trust property situs
- The relevance of the 1985 Hague Convention on Trusts
- Submission to the jurisdiction

A. INTRODUCTION

3.1 At first blush, whether the English court has jurisdiction to make orders affecting trusts (English or those with a foreign element) is not a particularly complicated question; as long as it has jurisdiction to grant a decree of divorce[1] it has jurisdiction to make the full cohort of financial orders available to it under the Matrimonial Causes Act 1973 ('MCA 1973') in respect of the parties' financial resources.

1 References to 'divorce' in this chapter should be taken to include dissolution/annulment of a civil partnership, nullity and judicial separation.

3.2 Exceptions to that simple statement are found in the EU Maintenance Regulation[2] and the Lugano Convention 2007[3], which prevent the English court from making orders relating to 'maintenance' connected to divorce proceedings where:

1 Another Member State is seised of the maintenance jurisdiction[4]; or

2 The jurisdiction for divorce proceedings is based solely on the nationality/domicile of one of the parties[5].

In either of those circumstances, the English court would not have jurisdiction to make maintenance orders and would be confined to making orders which fell outside of that definition[6].

Orders which may affect trusts

3.3 A court dealing with an application for financial orders ancillary to divorce has the power to make orders and to grant declarations. Those which may be relevant in cases involving trusts include[7]:

A declaration that the trust is a sham	A declaration that a spouse is the true beneficial owner of property held by a third party (e.g. company or a trustee)
An order for the payment of a lump sum, transfer of property or periodical payments on the basis that the payer or transferor is likely to be able to access resources held within a trust structure	An order varying an ante-nuptial or post-nuptial settlement

2 Council Regulation (EC) No 4/2009 of 18 December 2008 on jurisdiction, applicable law, recognition and enforcement of decisions and cooperation in matters relating to maintenance obligations.

3 Convention on jurisdiction and the recognition and enforcement of judgments in civil and commercial matters.

4 Article 12(1) Maintenance Regulation; Article 27 Lugano Convention.

5 Article 3(c) Maintenance Regulation; Article 5(2)(b) Lugano Convention.

6 For the definition of 'maintenance orders' under the Maintenance Regulation and the Lugano Convention see *Van den Boogaard v Laumen* (C-220/95) [1997] QB 759, ECJ and **Chapter 11** on Enforcement at para **11.14**.

7 See: **Chapter 7** for a discussion of general trust principles and 'sham'; **Chapter 8** for varying a nuptial settlement; and **Chapter 9** for trusts as resources (whether to pay an income or a lump sum). As to the situation when a spouse is held to be the absolute beneficial owner of trust property see *Prest v Petrodel Resources Ltd* [2013] UKSC 34, [2013] 2 AC 415, SC, followed in: *Johnson v Takieddine* [2016] EWHC 1895 (Fam), Moylan J; *MA v SK* [2015] EWHC 887 (Fam), [2016] 1 FLR 310, Moor J; *NR v AB (Financial Remedies)* [2017] 1 FLR 1030, Roberts J; *AAZ v BBZ* [2016] EWHC 3234 (Fam), [2018] 1 FLR 153, Haddon-Cave J; *Akhmedova v Akhmedov* [2018] EWFC 23, Haddon-Cave J.

English law

3.4 The law that the court will apply is English law. This was explained by Baroness Hale in *Radmacher v Granatino*[8]:

> 'In strict legal terms the so-called "foreign element" is irrelevant. If the proceedings take place in England and Wales, the applicable law is that of England and Wales, irrespective of where the parties come from, how long they have been here, or how close their connection is with this jurisdiction. Anyone who chooses to divorce here must be advised that the court will apply English law and not the law of the country which the parties have chosen or with which the marriage has the closest connection.'

Enforcement considerations

3.5 There are not, in theory, any restrictions in English law which prevent financial remedy orders being made against offshore trusts holding assets offshore. Applications involving such trusts have been considered by the family courts in many instances[9]. In *C v C (Variation of Post-nuptial Settlement: Company Shares)*[10], a case in which the husband's shareholding in a company was held through a Cayman Islands trust, Coleridge J made clear:

> 'I find that there is no impediment to the court dealing with this trust, either because it is foreign or discretionary. The question is not whether it can but whether it should be raised.'

3.6 The apparent simplicity of the jurisdictional position contrasts with the practical complexities that may arise in enforcing orders of the English court in respect of assets held offshore. It is all very well the English court asserting jurisdiction to make orders in respect of the parties, but if a trustee will most likely refuse to comply and the foreign court most likely uphold that refusal, that is of little practical help to the applicant spouse.

8 [2010] UKSC 42, [2011] 1 AC 534, SC. See also Lord Phillips at para 103.

9 There are innumerable examples throughout this book. See for instance: *TM v AH* [2016] EWHC 572 (Fam), [2016] 4 WLR 78, Moor J (BVI and Swiss trusts); *DR v GR* [2013] EWHC 1196 (Fam), [2013] 2 FLR 1534 (Jersey trust owned a Liberian company, which owned a UK company, which owned various other properties and assets).

10 [2003] EWHC 1222 (Fam), [2003] 2 FLR 493, FD.

3.7 In cases involving offshore trusts practitioners should consider:

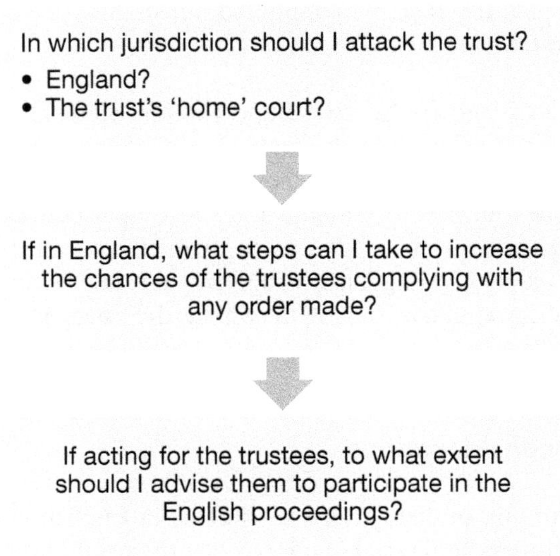

3.8 The scope of this book does not extend to the law of overseas jurisdictions in which offshore trusts may be based. In such cases, it is essential that practitioners should seek specialist advice as to the remedies that may be available in the jurisdictions in question.

3.9 Some of the issues which practitioners may need to consider prior to, or in some cases after, the issue of financial proceedings in cases involving offshore trusts include[11]:

11 See: **Chapter 4** for Submission to the Jurisdiction; **Chapter 5** for Service and Joinder; **Chapter 6** for Disclosure; and **Chapter 11** for Enforcement.

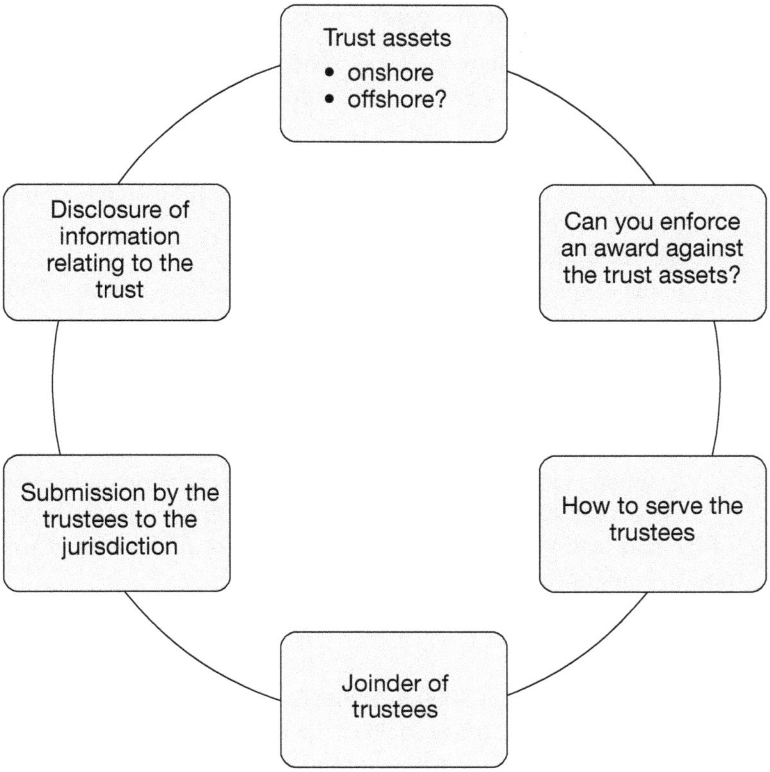

3.10 This Chapter begins with an overview of the English court's jurisdiction to entertain petitions for divorce. In the large majority of cases, if the court has jurisdiction in relation to the divorce it will also have jurisdiction to make ancillary financial orders including certain orders which may affect trusts[12].

B. JURISDICTION: DIVORCE

Brussels II Revised Regulation[13] ('BIIR')

3.11 BIIR came into force in March 2005 and replaced the previous Regulation[14] in its entirety. The Regulation applies to all Member States of the European Union, with the exception of Denmark, and has direct effect in their domestic laws. At the time of writing it has been determined that on 29 March 2019 the United Kingdom will leave the European Union and there is currently a great deal of uncertainty as to whether the provisions of BIIR will continue to apply beyond that date.

12 But see the exceptions under the EU Maintenance Regulation 4/2009 and the Lugano Convention 2007, referred to in para **3.2** above and the footnotes to para **3.20** below.

13 Council Regulation (EC) No 2201/2003 of 27 November 2003 concerning jurisdiction and the recognition and enforcement of judgments in matrimonial matters and the matters of parental responsibility, repealing Regulation (EC) No 1347/2000.

14 Council Regulation (EC) No 1347/2000.

3.12 Article 3 of BIIR governs 'general jurisdiction' and states that:

(1) In matters relating to divorce, legal separation or marriage annulment, jurisdiction shall lie with the courts of the Member State:

(a) in whose territory:

- the spouses are habitually resident, or
- the spouses were last habitually resident, insofar as one of them still resides there, or
- the respondent is habitually resident, or
- in the event of a joint application, either of the spouses is habitually resident, or
- the applicant is habitually resident if he or she resided there for at least a year immediately before the application was made, or
- the applicant is habitually resident if he or she resided there for at least six months immediately before the application was made and is either a national of the Member State in question or, in the case of the United Kingdom and Ireland, has his or her 'domicile' there;

(b) of the nationality of both spouses or, in the case of the United Kingdom and Ireland, of the 'domicile' of both spouses[15].

> Example
> The parties married in Italy in 2000 then moved to live and work in Malaysia. On the breakdown of the marriage in 2015 the wife and two teenage children moved to live in London. The husband remained in Malaysia. In 2017, after two years of living in London the wife issued a divorce petition in England. The husband contested jurisdiction and sought to litigate the divorce and subsequent financial proceedings in Malaysia.
>
> The English court has jurisdiction to entertain the wife's divorce petition under BIIR article 3(1)(a) indent five: she is habitually resident in England and has resided here for more than one year[16].

15 The concept of domicile denotes a party's connection with a particular legal system. A domicile of origin is akin to a party's nationality, but can be usurped by a domicile of choice, which is a factual question for the court (if it is disputed). It is possible to be habitually resident in one jurisdiction, but remain domiciled in another.

16 See the case of *Tan v Choy* [2014] EWCA Civ 251, [2015] 1 FLR 492, CA for similar facts. Crucially note that the court did not determine an issue concerning the meaning of the term 'residence' as opposed to 'habitual residence' for the purposes of Article 3(1)(a) indent five, as in that case the wife had been *habitually* resident in England for more than a year. It thus remains undecided whether an applicant has to have been *habitually resident* here for more than a year *or* simply to have *resided* here (but not necessarily habitually) for a year and only have acquired habitual residence at the time of the petition. The dispute as to interpretation dates back to *Marinos v Marinos* [2007] 2 FLR 1018, Munby J and *Munro v Munro* [2007] EWHC 3315 (Fam), [2008] 1 FLR 1613, Bennett J.

3.13 Article 7 provides a 'Residual Jurisdiction' under national law where no other Member State has jurisdiction under BIIR. Where this residual jurisdiction applies, it is possible to seek a divorce in England and Wales on the basis of the domicile of one of the parties at the date of the petition[17].

Habitual residence

3.14 The grounds for divorce in Article 3(2)(a) of BIIR all require consideration of the habitual residence of one or both of the spouses.

3.15 In *Marinos v Marinos*[18] Munby J analysed a number of decisions of the European Court of Justice as to the meaning of habitual residence under different European regulations and concluded at para 33:

> 'Accordingly, in my judgment, the phrase "habitually resident" in Article 3(1) has the meaning given to that phrase in the decisions of the ECJ…:
>
> "the place where the person had established, on a fixed basis, his permanent or habitual centre of interests, with all the relevant facts being taken into account for the purpose of determining such residence"'

This was approved by the Court of Appeal in *Tan v Choy*[19].

3.16 There is no minimum length of time for which a person must reside in a jurisdiction before acquiring habitual residence[20]. For the purposes of Article 3 of BIIR a party cannot be habitually resident in more than one jurisdiction[21].

17 Section 5(2)(b) of the Domicile and Matrimonial Proceedings Act 1973. However, please note the potential difficulties in seeking maintenance orders from the English court if jurisdiction is asserted only on the basis of domicile given the provisions of the EU Maintenance Regulation, discussed at para **3.2** above and the footnotes to para **3.20** below.

18 [2007] EWHC 2047 (Fam), [2007] 2 FLR 1018.

19 [2014] EWCA Civ 251, [2015] 1 FLR 492, CA at para 11. Ryder J also applied the same test in *V v V (Divorce: Jurisdiction)* [2011] EWHC 1190 (Fam), [2011] 2 FLR 778.

20 The Supreme Court in *re B (A Child) (Habitual Residence: Inherent Jurisdiction)* [2016] UKSC 4, [2016] AC 606 said any requirement for a person to spend an 'appreciable' period of time was too absolute and agreed with Munby J's comments at para 31 of *Marinos* in this regard.

21 See *Marinos*. Also see Munby LJ in *re L (A Child) (Recognition of Foreign Order)* [2012] EWCA Civ 1157, [2013] Fam 94 at para 75. The position in domestic law is the reverse and permits a party to be habitually resident in more than one country: see para 18 onwards in *Marinos* and the references to *Ikimi v Ikimi* [2001] EWCA Civ 873, [2002] Fam 72, CA.

Residence

3.17 If it is accepted that a person issuing a divorce petition was habitually resident in the jurisdiction at the date of issue, but there is a dispute as to precisely when that person became so habitually resident, then the meaning of the word 'resides' in indents 5 and 6 of Article 3(1)(a) BIIR becomes hugely relevant to the question of jurisdiction. Is there an elision between the concepts of residence and habitual residence, or are they separate concepts?

3.18 The answer, at least for now, is that they are separate concepts. In *Marinos v Marinos*[22] Munby J said the following at para 46–47:

> '[46] ...And [the words of indents 5 and 6 of article 3(1)(a) BIIR] as it seems to me, mean just what they say. What are required are two things: (i) habitual residence on a particular day and (i) residence, though not necessarily habitual residence, during the relevant immediately preceding period.
>
> [47] There is no need to read in, as it were, any qualification to the simple and unadorned word "resided"[23].'

Marinos v Marinos

[2007] EWHC 2047 (Fam), [2007] 2 FLR 1018
H was Greek and W was English. They met in England in 1988 and married here in 1992. They had two children. In 2002 they moved as a family for a 'trial' period to Greece which was extended a number of times. In 2007 W returned to England with the children. The parties had retained two properties in London, rented out, into which W moved with the children.
The day after her return to England, W petitioned for divorce here. She relied on BIIR Article 3(1)(a) indent 6, asserting she was habitually resident and domiciled in England and Wales, and had lived there for at least six months prior to the presentation of the petition. H disputed jurisdiction, asserting W to be habitually resident and domiciled in Greece. He applied for a stay.
Munby J refused H's application for a stay. He held on the facts of the case that:

(1) For at least the three years prior to the separation in 2007 W was *resident* in both Greece and England, spending roughly equal time in each country.

22 [2007] EWHC 2047 (Fam), [2007] 2 FLR 1018.

23 This dictum has been followed in *V v V (Divorce: Jurisdiction)* [2011] EWHC 1190 (Fam), [2011] 2 FLR 778, per Jackson J at para 47 and represents good law at the time of writing, although please note the judgment of Aitken LJ in *Tan v Choy* [2014] EWCA Civ 251, [2015] 1 FLR 492 at para 30 in which she identified a 'legitimate debate as to what is the precise construction of Article 3(1)(a) indent five' that it was not necessary to resolve in that case.

(2) It not being open to the judge to find her *habitually resident* in both countries, on balance W was habitually resident in England from about 2004 to her return in 2007.

(3) If he was wrong about (2), the judge held that W's habitual residence (if in Greece) would have been severed on her return to England on 31 January 2007 and that she had gained habitual residence in England almost immediately thereafter, just prior to the issue of her divorce petition.

As a result the court had jurisdiction under the final limb of BIIR Article 3(1)(a).

First seised

3.19 Article 19 of BIIR provides that where proceedings for divorce between the same parties are brought before courts of different Member States, the court second seised must stay its proceedings until such time as the jurisdiction of the court first seised is established. Once the jurisdiction of the court first seised is established, the court second seised must decline jurisdiction.

3.20 BIIR expressly excludes from its remit '*property consequences of the marriage or any other ancillary measures*'[24]. However, if an applicant seises the English court and establishes jurisdiction for divorce, he or she will in almost all cases also be able to establish jurisdiction under English law for the determination of financial claims[25]. Another Member State second seised will be obliged to stay its proceedings and ultimately decline jurisdiction[26].

24 Introductory Recital (8).

25 It is important, on issue of a divorce petition to include a 'prayer' for financial provision, in particular maintenance. Because England is subject to the EU Maintenance Regulation No 4/2009 and the Lugano Convention 2007, it would technically be possible for the court of another Member State to be first seised of the issue of maintenance, so limiting the claims in this jurisdiction to capital provision (that which could not be defined as for 'maintenance'). Obviously that would be undesirable, so should be avoided by seising the English court with jurisdiction to deal with *all forms* of financial provision at the earliest opportunity. See para **3.2** above and the following footnote.

26 If jurisdiction to grant the divorce is solely based on the nationality / domicile of one of the parties, the court granting the divorce does not have exclusive jurisdiction to make orders relating to maintenance under an exception to the EU Maintenance Regulation No 4/2009: Article 3(c).

Non-EU countries

3.21 Where there is a jurisdiction dispute between England and a country which is not bound by BIIR, different considerations arise as this diagram shows[27]:

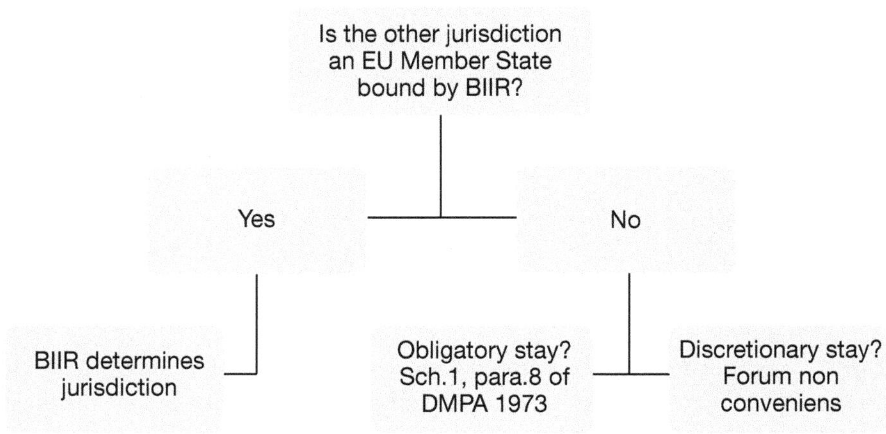

3.22 There was previously uncertainty as to whether the power under domestic law to grant a stay[28] survived the import of BIIR but that issue has now been resolved by the Court of Appeal in *Mittal v Mittal*[29].

> *Mittal v Mittal*
>
> [2014] Fam 102, CA
>
> W and H were Indian nationals. They married in India and moved to England in 2006 for H's work. On separation in 2009 W returned to India, H remained in England with indefinite leave to remain. There were no assets or income in England. H issued a divorce petition in India in 2009, W issued hers in England in 2011.
>
> The question was not whether the Indian court had jurisdiction to entertain H's proceedings (it did), but whether the English court had the jurisdiction to stay W's petition on *forum non conveniens* grounds.
>
> W argued that BIIR 'governed' all applications for a divorce and, thus, there was no residual power to grant a stay that the court could exercise under DMPA 1973[30]. The Court of Appeal disagreed. The following principles can be drawn out:

27 An obligatory stay is covered by the relatively limited provisions of Sch 1, para 8 of the Domicile and Matrimonial Proceedings Act 1973. A discretionary stay under the principle of *forum non conveniens* or *lis alibi pendens* is covered by Sch 1, para 9 of the Domicile and Matrimonial Proceedings Act 1973; see *Spiliada Maritime Corp v Consulex Ltd* [1987] AC 460, HL.

28 Under the Domicile and Matrimonial Proceedings Act 1973.

29 [2013] EWCA Civ 1255, [2014] Fam 102, [2014] 2 FCR 208, CA.

30 In this regard she sought to extend the reasoning of the ECJ in *Owusu v Jackson* [2005] QB 801.

(a) Proceedings are only 'governed' by BIIR if they fall within Article 19 (set out above);

(b) Article 7 of BIIR grants a residual jurisdiction to a Member State in accordance with the laws of that State if no court of another Member State has jurisdiction, which corresponded with the residual jurisdiction granted to the English court by s 5(2)(b) of the DMPA 1973; and

(c) The power to grant a stay in favour of proceedings in another jurisdiction more closely connected to the marriage under Sch 1, para 9 was part of the exercise of the residual jurisdiction given to the English court by virtue of the above.

C. JURISDICTION: FINANCIAL RELIEF

Divorce in England and Wales

3.23 In England and Wales, the power to make financial orders under the MCA 1973 stems from the power to grant the divorce itself. As soon as a spouse has filed a petition for divorce, he or she can issue an application for financial orders consequent upon the divorce.

3.24 If the English court has jurisdiction to grant the decree of divorce, it also has jurisdiction to exercise its discretionary redistributive powers in respect of the parties' finances[31]. The general principles governing financial applications are discussed in **Chapter 2**.

Overseas Divorce

3.25 After an overseas divorce, Part III of the Matrimonial and Family Proceedings Act 1984 ('MFPA 1984') potentially confers upon the court the power to make financial orders similar to those contained within the MCA 1973[32]. The circumstances in which the court may acquire jurisdiction under the MFPA 1984 are shown in following graphic[33]:

31 Subject of course to the exceptions discussed in relation to maintenance orders in para **3.2** above.

32 See MFPA 1984, s 17.

33 The conditions are in MFPA 1984, s 12(1) and (2), as to which see also *Sharbatly v Shagroon* [2012] EWCA Civ 1507, [2013] 1 FLR 1493, CA: not only does there have to be a valid divorce, but (as might sound obvious) there had to be a valid (or void) marriage for an application under MFPA 1984, Pt III. The grounds for jurisdiction are in MFPA 1984, s 15. If jurisdiction is founded on the existence of a dwelling house in England and Wales the court cannot make interim orders for maintenance (MFPA 1984, s 14(2)) and has restricted substantive powers under MFPA 1984, s 20.

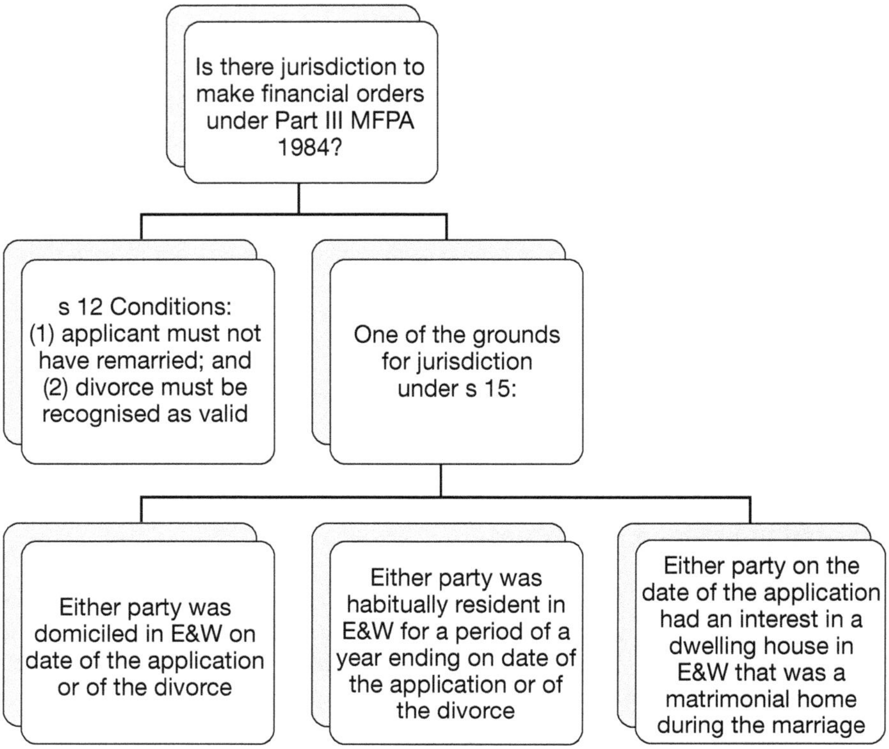

3.26 Leave of the court is required to make a Part III application. Such leave will not be granted unless the court considers there is a 'substantial ground' for making the application[34]. 'Substantial' has been held to mean 'solid', which is a higher threshold than 'good arguable case' or 'serious issue to be tried'[35].

3.27 The court is also obliged to consider whether in all the circumstances of the case it would be appropriate for an order to be made by a court in England and Wales and, if not, the application must be dismissed[36].

3.28 The leading authority on Part III is *Agbaje v Agbaje*[37]. A recent application of the relevant principles can be found in the Court of Appeal decision in *Zimina v Zimin*[38].

34 MFPA 1984, s 13(1).
35 See the decision of the Supreme Court in *Agbaje v Agbaje* [2010] UKSC 13, [2010] 1 AC 628, SC.
36 MFPA 1984, s 16.
37 [2010] UKSC 13, [2010] 1 AC 628, SC.
38 [2017] EWCA Civ 1429, [2018] 1 FCR 164.

D. ESTABLISHING JURISDICTION OVER FOREIGN TRUSTEES

3.29 The English court has wide powers to make orders under the MCA 1973 which may affect a trust either directly or indirectly. Most significantly, it has the power to vary a trust which is an ante-nuptial or post-nuptial settlement. This is discussed in **Chapter 8**.

3.30 If the trust is governed by English law, with assets, trustees and beneficiaries in England, then the court's ability to make orders relating to the substance of that trust will be closely aligned to considerations relevant to the fair distribution of assets between parties to a divorce[39].

3.31 A large number of the trusts with which the family court is concerned are not purely English trusts but instead have one or more foreign elements, which may include the following:

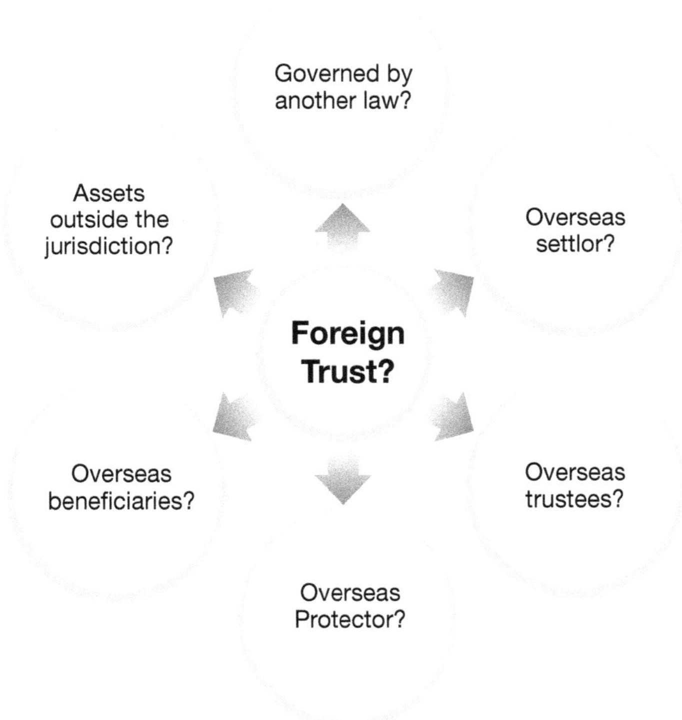

3.32 In cases involving overseas trusts it is necessary to consider issues of enforcement. There are two reasons for this:

39 See, for example, *AB v CB (Financial Remedies: Variation of Trust)* [2014] EWHC 2998 (Fam), [2015] 2 FLR 25, Mostyn J and [2015] EWCA Civ 447, [2016] 1 FLR 437, CA (upheld on appeal to the Court of Appeal).

1 The English court's assumption of jurisdiction to make orders affecting that foreign trust may be of little practical use if the trustees refuse to comply with the order and their local court refuses to enforce it. This is discussed in **Chapter 11**.

2 There is a line of authorities in which it has been held that the English court should decline to make orders against property sited in an overseas jurisdiction if such orders would not be enforced by the courts where the property is sited.

Relevance of enforcement to jurisdiction

3.33 It has long been established that even if the English court can assert jurisdiction to make orders in respect of foreign property or trusts with a foreign element it will not do so where those orders are incapable of enforcement in that foreign jurisdiction.

3.34 In *Goff v Goff*[40] Sir Boyd Merriman P refused to make an order varying a settlement of property in New York, not for lack of jurisdiction, but because the evidence showed that the order would not have been recognised or enforced by the American court.

3.35 In *Hamlin v Hamlin*[41] Kerr LJ emphasised the crucial difference between a jurisdiction to make orders[42] and whether the jurisdiction should be exercised in any given case:

> 'Thus it is a fundamental principle that, in the exercise of their discretion, our courts will not make orders which they cannot enforce. It follows, as shown by the cases, that in relation to property situated abroad, even if the parties are present within the jurisdiction, the courts will in general not make any order the effectiveness of which depends upon its recognition or enforcement by the courts or other authorities of the foreign locus if the evidence shows that these would be denied. However, such cases go to discretion and not to jurisdiction.'

3.36 More recently Mostyn J said in *BJ v MJ (Financial Order: Overseas Trust)*[43]:

> 'The variation powers extend to making outright provision to the applicant, and may even be exercised where the trust is offshore, although, following well-established principle, the court will be unlikely to make a variation order where both the trust and its assets are overseas unless it is satisfied

40 [1934] P107.

41 [1986] Fam. 11, CA. The case concerned a property situated in Spain.

42 At p 18 he said there was nothing indicating that Parliament intended to restrict the court's powers under the MCA 1973 to property situated in England and Wales.

43 [2011] EWHC 2708 (Fam), [2012] 1 FLR 667.

that the order would be implemented by the court exercising effective control over the trust (*Goff v Goff [1934] P 107*, *Hamlin v Hamlin [1986] Fam 11*). If, however, the Court is satisfied that the variation order will be effective against the husband *in personam*, then the order is more likely to be made (*Razelos v Razelos [1969] 3 All ER 929*).'

3.37 With these enforcement issues very much in mind, there are a number of ways in which it may be possible for the English court to seek to assert its jurisdiction to make orders in respect of foreign trusts and foreign trustees:

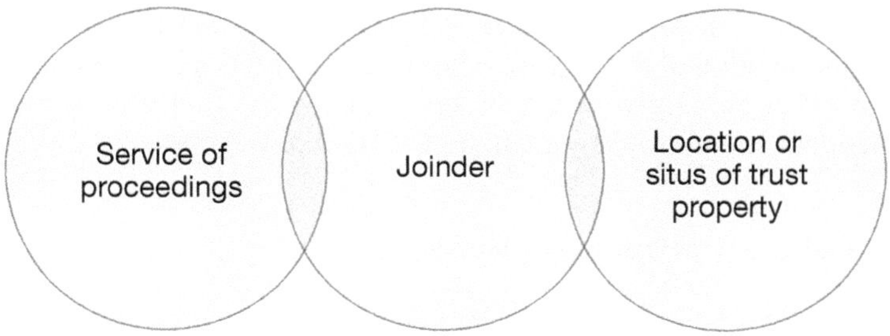

Service of proceedings

3.38 The general rules as to service under the common law provide that the jurisdiction of the English court depends on service of originating process on the respondent. By reason of the service of an application, the court has jurisdiction *in personam* over each of the respondents to that application in respect of the issues raised by the application. This principle applies to trusts and trustees served with matrimonial proceedings as much as it does in any other area of law[44]. Thus, as a result of the service of a Form A[45] and/or an application for joinder on a trustee the court assumes jurisdiction to make orders against that trustee *in personam*.

3.39 The service rules under Part 6 of the FPR 2010 are discussed in detail in **Chapter 5**.

3.40 The practical benefits of having served a trustee are obvious; if the trustee has not been served the court does not have jurisdiction to make orders *in personam* against the trustee, whether such orders take the form of an injunction or any other order. Thus, without service, a party will be unable to enforce an order against the trustee, for example by way of a committal application.

44 Dicey, Morris and Collins, *The Conflict of Laws* (15th edn) Vol 1, para 11R-001 onwards; see also *Chellaram v Chellaram* [1985] Ch. 409, Scott J at p 426–427.

45 The prescribed form used to commence financial remedy proceedings, headed 'Notice of intention to proceed with an application for a financial order.'

Joinder

3.41 Service of an application upon a trustee does not automatically result on them becoming a party to matrimonial proceedings[46]; it is necessary to obtain an order from the court which joins them as a party[47].

3.42 Joinder is discussed in detail in **Chapter 5**. Once made a party to the proceedings, the result of those proceedings and the orders made against them are in principle binding upon them[48]. The court is able to add or remove parties on an application or of its own volition under the FPR 2010[49].

3.43 Even if a trustee is joined as a party this does not mean that they will accept the jurisdiction of the English court to make orders against them or against the trust itself or comply with any orders made by the English court. A trustee may or may not submit to the jurisdiction of the English court[50].

Location of trust property: situs

3.44 The *situs* of property is the place where the property is located according to an established set of common law rules. In the vast majority of cases with which matrimonial finance practitioners are concerned, the law of *situs* will be easy to apply[51]:

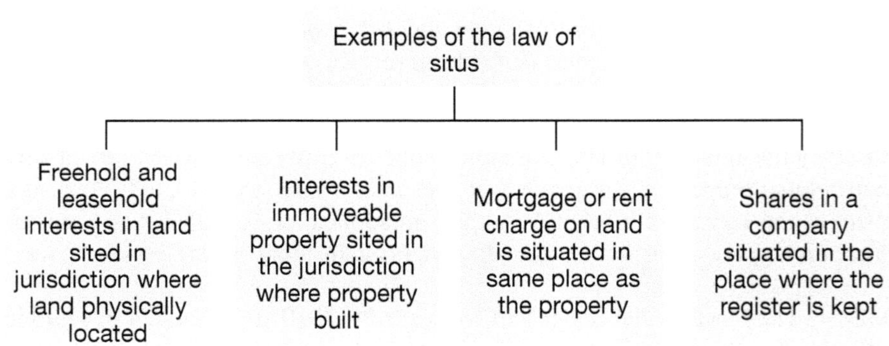

3.45 As a general rule, if the *situs* of the trust property is in England and Wales, the English court can assert jurisdiction in respect of that property and, subject to the jurisdictional requirements of the MCA 1973, may be able to make orders in respect of it[52]. It can thus do so in respect of a trust or against a trustee based out of the jurisdiction.

46 See Wilson J in *T v T and Others (Joinder of Third Parties)* [1996] 2 FLR 357, at 364.
47 See **Chapter 4** for a detailed discussion on joinder.
48 See for example Moor J at para 10 of *TM v AH* [2016] 4 WLR 78, FD.
49 FPR 2010, r 9.26B.
50 See **Chapter 4** on Submission to the jurisdiction.
51 See *re Hoyles* [1911] 1 Ch 179 and *Erie Beach Co Ltd v Attorney-General for Ontario* [1930] AC 161, PC.
52 Dicey, Morris and Collins, *The Conflict of Laws* (15th edn) Vol 1 para 11R-225.

The relevance the 1985 Hague Convention on Trusts

3.46 The 1985 Hague Convention on the Law Applicable to Trusts and on their Recognition ('the 1985 Convention') was incorporated as part of the law of the UK by way of the Recognition of Trusts Act 1987. It applies generally in an English court, irrespective of whether any competing state is a contracting state under the Convention.

3.47 At the time of writing the Convention has been ratified by a number of states[53]. The Bahamas and the Cayman Islands, notably, are not signatories. Further, although the UK extended the Convention to Jersey and Guernsey, they in fact have their own legislative provisions relating to the governing law of any trust based in their jurisdiction, discussed in **Chapter 11**[54].

3.48 Article 6 of the 1985 Hague Convention provides that a trust shall be governed by the law chosen by the settlor. If no applicable law has been chosen under Article 6, Article 7 provides that a trust shall be governed by the law with which it is '*most closely connected*' and requires the court to have regard to four factors shown in the following graphic.

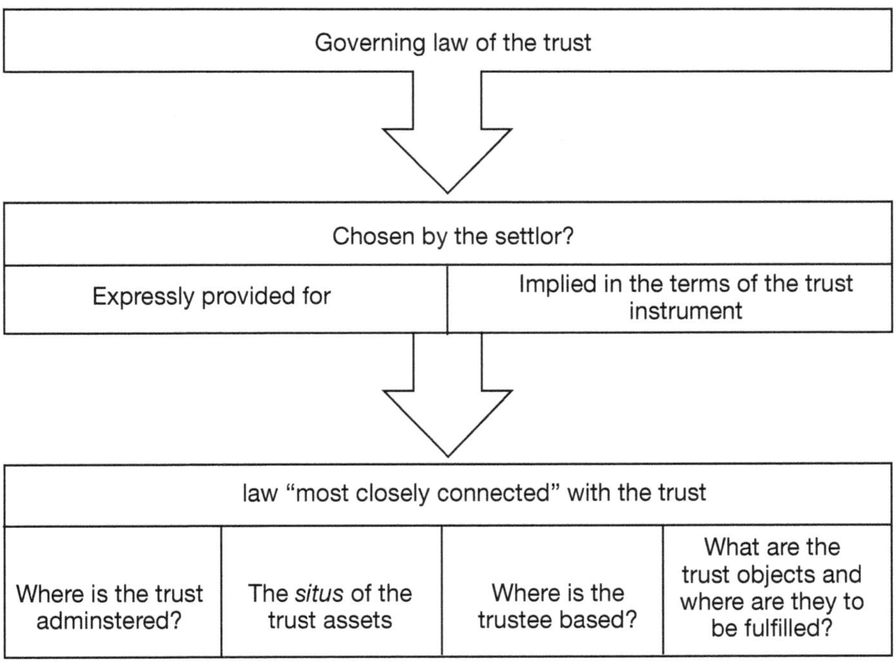

53 At the time of writing: Australia, Italy, Bermuda, British Antarctic Territory, the British Virgin Islands, Canada, Falkland Islands, Gibraltar, Hong King, Isle of Man, Jersey, Guernsey, Lichtenstein, Luxembourg, Mala, Monaco, Montserrat, the Netherlands, St Helena and Dependencies, San Marino, South Georgia, the Sovereign Base Areas of Akrotiri and Dhekelia, Switzerland, the Turks and Caicos Islands, Cyprus, France (signed but not ratified), Italy and the United States (signed but not ratified).

54 Trusts (Jersey) Law 1984 and Trusts (Guernsey) Law 2007 (repealed its 1989 forbear).

3.49 Article 8(h) of the Convention provides that the governing law of the trust shall govern 'the variation or termination of the trust'.

3.50 Despite the terms of the 1985 Hague Convention, it was held by the Court of Appeal in *Charalambous v Charalambous*[55] that the English courts can assert jurisdiction under the MCA 1973 in respect of a trust governed by foreign law; the power of variation comes from an English law statute and not from the settlement itself.

3.51 Despite the decision in *Charalambous*, the 1985 Hague Convention may be relevant to issues of enforcement in overseas jurisdictions. A foreign court considering the enforcement of an English order may apply the governing law of the trust rather than English law to its determination[56], especially in cases where the trustee has not submitted to the English jurisdiction[57].

Submission to the jurisdiction

3.52 Under the common law, a respondent trustee may preclude himself by his own conduct from objecting to the jurisdiction of the English court and thus give it the power to make orders *in personam* against him[58]. When this happens, a trustee (or any other respondent for that matter) is said to have submitted to the jurisdiction of the English court. Submission to the jurisdiction is dealt with in **Chapter 4.**

55 [2004] EWCA Civ 1030, [2005] Fam 250, per Arden LJ at paras 30–34.
56 As to which see **Chapter 11** on Enforcement.
57 See **Chapter 4** below.
58 Dicey, Morris and Collins, *The Conflict of Laws* (15th edn) Vol 1 para 11R-124.

CHAPTER 4

Submission to the Jurisdiction by Trustees

Content at a Glance:

A. INTRODUCTION

4.1 As discussed in **Chapter 3**, the English court may assert jurisdiction to make orders in respect of a 'foreign' trust (ie one where the trustees are resident outside England and Wales, and all or part of the trust property is also situated outside the jurisdiction) but that does not necessarily mean the orders it may make regarding the trust will be recognisable and enforceable in the trust's 'home' court.

4.2 When foreign trustees are served with an application for financial relief, or with an application for joinder[1] it is likely to create difficulties for them. Unlike the court's role under the MCA 1973, the duty of trustees is very different and they must balance the interests of spouses who may be beneficiaries under the trust, against their duties to other beneficiaries and their responsibility to uphold the terms of the trust. An attack on trust property, whether directly (eg, by means of an order varying the underlying terms of the trust as a nuptial settlement) or indirectly (eg, a lump sum order against one of the parties exerting pressure on the trustees to release trust assets[2]) could adversely affect other beneficiaries and expose the trustees to an action for breach of fiduciary duty for failing to act appropriately to preserve trust assets.

4.3 This leaves trustees of a foreign trust with a dilemma: do they involve themselves in the English financial remedy proceedings? If so, to what extent?

1 Service rules and joinder are discussed in **Chapter 5**.
2 As to which see **Chapter 11**.

4.4 Under the common law, trustees may preclude themselves by their own conduct from objecting to the jurisdiction of the English court and thus give it the power to make orders *in personam* against them[3]. When this happens, the trustees (or any other respondent for that matter) are said to have submitted to the jurisdiction of the English court.

B. WHAT IS 'SUBMISSION'?

4.5 Whether trustees have or have not submitted to the jurisdiction is sometimes a difficult question. It is ultimately a factual question to be ascertained by the trustees' conduct, whether in actively accepting jurisdiction, or in passively waiving their objection to it.

4.6 Examples of situations in which submission occurs include:

1 Where a respondent 'enters an appearance' in the court unless the appearance is to contest the jurisdiction of the court[4]; or

2 Where a respondent instructs a solicitor to accept service of an application in England, unless service is accepted subject to the express condition that the trustee disputes jurisdiction[5].

4.7 The common law rules relating to submission to the jurisdiction derive from the rules of civil procedure. There are clear differences between the CPR 1998 and the FPR 2010, but one key difference is that the there is no specific procedure under the FPR for disputing the court's jurisdiction that is equivalent to the procedure set out in CPR Part 11[6].

4.8 Joinder is discussed in **Chapter 5**, but it is important to note that the joinder of trustees as parties to proceedings does not mean that they have submitted to the jurisdiction of the court[7].

4.9 Trustees must be careful not to submit to the jurisdiction unwittingly by involving themselves in the proceedings. The following diagram shows the suggested procedure for trustees to ensure they do not do so:

3 Dicey, Morris and Collins, *The Conflict of Laws* (15th edn) Vol 1 para 11R-124.

4 In common law see *Sphere Drake Insurance plc v Gunes Sikorta* [1988] 1 Lloyd's Rep. 139, CA. This is also enshrined in European legislation: Brussels I Regulation (EC) No 44/2001, article 24; now replaced by the Brussels Regulation Recast (EU) no.1215/2012, article 26; and the Lugano Convention 2007, article 24.

5 See above.

6 For example, if in civil proceedings a defendant fails to make an application disputing jurisdiction within 14 days of filing an acknowledgment of service, he is treated as having accepted the English court's jurisdiction to try the claim: CPR rule 11(1)–(5).

7 As set out above, their joinder might found the basis of the court's assertion of jurisdiction to make orders *in personam* against the trustees, but this is to be distinguished from a jurisdiction based on submission.

Example 1

Foreign trustees notified of the wife's intention to declare the properties held in trust beneficially owned in their entirety by the husband and to seek an order against the trustees to transfer the legal and beneficial interest in certain properties to the wife.

The trustees instruct solicitors and counsel to represent them at the final hearing and assert through counsel that they 'will abide by any order/declaration made by the court'.

Have the trustees submitted to the jurisdiction?

Yes[8].

This can be contrasted with a more familiar example:

Example 2

Foreign trustees served with an application for joinder in respect of the wife's application to vary the offshore trust.

The trustees instructed solicitors in this jurisdiction, provided some disclosure in relation to the trust to the English court and were joined as parties to the proceedings by court order. The trustees made very clear that they were not submitting to the jurisdiction of the English court and would need to apply to their home courts (BVI and Switzerland) for guidance as to what they should do.

Have the trustees submitted to the jurisdiction?

No[9].

8 See *In the matter of the Fountain Trust* [2005] JLR 359. The Jersey court recognised and enforced the order of Singer J in *Minwalla v Minwalla* [2004] EWHC 2823 (Fam), [2005] 1 FLR 771, whilst noting that the trustees could be liable for breach of trust and that, had they not submitted to the jurisdiction, it might not have been fair to enforce the judgment against them.

9 See *TM v AH* [2016] 4 WLR 78, per Moor J, who described this situation as 'familiar'.

4.10 The tension between the need for co-operation and disclosure from trustees in any particular case and the potential danger to them of inadvertently submitting to the jurisdiction is clear. On the one hand the English court needs a full and clear picture of the trust structure in respect of which it is considering making orders; providing clarity might well benefit the trust and the beneficiaries of that trust. On the other hand the trustees might be understandably defensive and limited in their participation in the English court's inquiry through fear that anything else would be construed as submitting to its jurisdiction. Mostyn J considered this tension in *BJ v MJ*[10] and said[11]:

> 'I can therefore see why overseas trustees may not want to submit to the jurisdiction of the English Court. They may prefer to keep their powder dry and to wait to see what judgment emerges before deciding whether or not to resist enforcement proceedings in their local court. I have to say, however, that I find it hard to see why participation by the trustees in a helpful or meaningful way in this court's inquiry qua witness could be construed as a submission to the jurisdiction.[12]'

4.11 Mostyn J's observations may not be consistent with the rule that a respondent entering an appearance is taken to have submitted to the jurisdiction as set out above. In *BJ v MJ* the Jersey trustees partially complied with requests for disclosure but nothing more. A similar approach was adopted in *Joy v Joy-Marancho*[13] where the trustees (based in Hong Kong in respect of a BVI trust), through a named individual described as the 'human face and mind of the trustees' had 'made available some, and withheld much other, information and documentation.'

C. WHAT ARE THE CONSEQUENCES OF SUBMISSION FOR THE TRUSTEES?

4.12 Where the trustees of a trust with a foreign element submit to the jurisdiction of the English court they are accepting that the English court has jurisdiction over them *in personam* to make orders in respect of that trust. The Royal Court of Jersey made the following *obiter* comments in *re H Trust*[14] which summarise the position:

> 'Significant consequences may flow from a decision by a trustee of a Jersey trust to submit to the jurisdiction of the Family Division of the High Court or indeed any other court considering the matrimonial affairs of beneficiaries

10 [2011] EWHC 2708 (Fam), [2012] 1 FLR 667.

11 At para 21.

12 In *DR v GR (Financial Remedy: Variation of Overseas Trust)* [2013] EWHC 1196 (Fam), [2013] 2 FLR 1534, Mostyn J emphasised that: 'If trustees do not voluntarily participate as witnesses and give proper disclosure, they cannot complain if robust findings are made about the realities of control and the likelihood of benefit.'

13 [2015] EWHC 2507 (Fam), [2016] 1 FLR 815, Sir Peter Singer.

14 [2006] JLR 280 at paras 12–13.

of a trust. Any order subsequently made by the Family Division would be made in proceedings to which the trustee had voluntarily submitted and in which therefore it had full opportunity to put forward submissions on the order which the court should make. It follows that the trustee would be in some difficulty in arguing subsequently before this court against the proposition that any order of the Family Division relating to the trust should be enforced without reconsideration of the merits of such order.

Conversely, if the trustee has not submitted to the jurisdiction of the Family Division, any order of that court will not be enforceable in Jersey under the rules of private international law. On any subsequent application to this court to vary the trust so as to achieve the effect of any variation or other order made by the Family Division, this court would have complete discretion as to the course it should take.'

4.13 Similarly in *Mubarak v Mubarik*[15] Birt DB, sitting in the Royal Court of Jersey said:

'In the case of the variation or alteration of a trust, those affected are likely to include all the beneficiaries as well as the trustee. The effect of any variation order is not usually confined to the husband and wife. Other beneficiaries may be affected. Furthermore the trustee has legal title to the trust fund and is responsible for holding the trust assets in accordance with the terms of the trust deed. Quite apart from other beneficiaries, a trustee is clearly someone who will be substantially affected by an order of an English court altering a trust. Accordingly, **unless a trustee of a Jersey trust has submitted to the jurisdiction of the Family Division, it is very hard to see how any judgment of the Family Division varying or altering a Jersey trust can be enforced in Jersey under the ordinary rules of private international law**…'[Emphasis added]

4.14 Thus, the submission by a foreign trustee to the jurisdiction of the English court will likely result in the enforcement of any order by the English court. The corollary is that the absence of submission may render enforcement of the English order impossible (in the sense that enforcement means directly enforcing the terms of the English order itself).

4.15 The absence of submission and a consequent inability 'to enforce' an English order does not necessarily mean that an applicant will have no remedy in a foreign court. It may be possible to bring fresh proceedings and seek an equivalent order, but such an application will be subject to entirely different considerations. Applicants pursuing such a remedy are likely to be faced with

15 [2008] JRC 136, [2009] 1 FLR 664 at para 67.

'firewall' provisions which may prove insurmountable[16]. It is essential that practitioners should seek specialist advice in the relevant jurisdiction as to the potential remedies their clients may be able to pursue.

> *R Trust*
>
> [2015] JRC 267A – Jersey
>
> H and W divorce. Shortly before separation H settled a trust in Jersey naming the children of the marriage as beneficiaries. The trust document permitted the addition of beneficiaries. In financial relief proceedings the English court sets aside transfers by H into the trust and orders the Jersey trustee to remit the trust fund to H, for onward payment to W to meet her housing need.
>
> The trustee was not involved at all in the proceedings and had not submitted to the jurisdiction of the English court. However, considering the judgment the trustee considered it would be in the best interests of the beneficiaries of the trust (the children) for W to have access to the trust funds to maintain the home for the children. As a result, the trustee decided to add H as a beneficiary to the trust and distribute the whole of the trust assets to him so as to enable their onward payment to W.
>
> The Jersey Royal Court sanctioned the decision of the trustee as a legitimate exercise of his powers as a trustee, but explicitly *not* by way of enforcement or 'giving effect' to the English order (which would have been in breach of the Jersey firewall provisions).

D. DIRECTIONS FROM THE 'HOME' COURT

4.16 Trustees faced with financial relief proceedings in this jurisdiction and a probable application to join them or to provide disclosure[17] are likely to obtain directions from their 'home' court as to the extent to which they should engage with the proceedings given their position as trustee and their obligation to act in the interests of all the beneficiaries of the trust. They should almost always seek such directions before taking a positive decision to participate in foreign proceedings and/or submit to the jurisdiction of the foreign court.

4.17 An application of this type is commonly referred to as a *Beddoe* application.

16 See **Chapter 11** on Enforcement. See also the line of authority in Jersey stemming from *re H Trust* [2006] JLR 280, helpfully summarised in the recent decision of the Guernsey court in *A Limited FURBS* [2017] 21/2017 (re A Ltd) which adopted Jersey case law. Similarly, the Grand Court in the Cayman Islands considered a similar point in *RBS Coutts (Cayman) Ltd v W* (2010) 14 ITELR 557.

17 This is discussed in **Chapter 5**.

4.18 Strictly speaking a *Beddoe* application is where a trustee seeks permission from the court to incur costs in defending or engaging in proceedings concerning the trust and to be indemnified out of the trust fund in respect of those costs. However, the term is now used to include the wider ranging application by a trustee to the 'home' court for guidance and directions as to what course to take in any given case.

4.19 The practice stems from the principle set out in the judgment of Lindley LJ in *re Beddoe*[18] that a trustee is only indemnified against the costs of litigation which have been *properly* incurred:

> '... a trustee who, without the sanction of the Court, commences an action or defends an action unsuccessfully, does so at his own risk as regards the costs, even if he acts on counsel's opinion; and when the trustee seeks to obtain such costs out of his trust estate, he ought not to be allowed to charge them against his *cestui que trust* unless under very exceptional circumstances...
>
> I entirely agree that a trustee is entitled as of right to full indemnity out of his trust estate against all his costs, charges, and expenses properly incurred: such an indemnity is the price paid by *cestuis que trust* for the gratuitous and onerous services of trustees; and in all cases of doubt, costs incurred by a trustee ought to be borne by the trust estate and not by him personally. The words "properly incurred" in the ordinary form of order are equivalent to "not improperly incurred."'

4.20 In *TM v AH*[19] the trustees of BVI and Swiss trusts indicated they would seek directions from their home courts in the face of being joined. The practice is commonplace now in Jersey following *re H Trust*[20]. The case of *A and B Trusts*[21] – in which the Jersey court refused to grant retrospective approval to a trustee who had already been participating in English proceedings – illustrates the danger of failing to seek such guidance.

4.21 Whether the foreign court will sanction the trustee's submission to the jurisdiction of the English court must be approached on a case-by-case basis. In Jersey for example the court in *re H Trust*[22] said:

> 'It is unlikely to be in the interests of a Jersey trust for the trustee to submit to the jurisdiction of an overseas court which is hearing proceedings between a husband and wife, one or both of whom may be beneficiaries under the trust. To do so would be to confer an enforceable power upon the overseas court to act to the detriment of the beneficiaries of a trust when the primary focus of that court is the interests of the two spouses before it.

18 [1893] 1 Ch 547.
19 [2016] EWHC 572 (Fam), [2016] 4 WLR 78, Moor J.
20 [2006] JLR 280.
21 [2007] JLR 444.
22 [2006] JLR 280, at para 15.

It is more likely to be in the interests of a Jersey trust and the beneficiaries thereunder to preserve the freedom of action of both the trustee and this court to act as appropriate following and taking full account of the decision of the overseas court. We have said that this is likely to be the case in most circumstances. In some cases, *e.g.* where all the trust assets are in England, it may well be in the interests of a trustee to appear before the English court in order to put forward its point of view because, by reason of the location of the assets, that court will be able to enforce its order without regard to the trustee or this court.'

4.22 What follows are three case-law examples of the approach of the 'home' courts of a trust in Jersey, Guernsey and the Cayman Islands.

In re H Trust

[2006] JLR 280 – Jersey

H and W were married for 22 years. W issued divorce and financial proceedings in England in 2005.

The relevant trust was established in 1992 with a trustee in Jersey. The trust was a discretionary trust with the beneficiaries being H, W, H's two adult children from his first marriage, their spouses, H's grandchildren and any future issue. The trust assets consisted of an investment portfolio, land in Canada, a villa in Portugal and two flats in Scarborough.

In November 2005 (during the divorce proceedings) the trustee exercised his powers within the trust deed to change the governing law of the trust to Jersey law. Previously it had been English law.

The trustee sought directions. The Royal Court of Jersey decided:

(1) The trustee's change of the proper law of the trust was their decision and could not be challenged under the terms of the trust deed.

(2) The trust should not submit to the jurisdiction of the English court in the circumstances of the case, but that was distinct from the provision of information and the trustee should make the fullest information available.

(3) In a postscript the court noted that all the parties' assets were in the trust, the marriage had been a long one, the funds had been placed in trust during the marriage, the trustee had used the fund to maintain the parties at a high standard of living in recent years, and no payments had ever been made for other beneficiaries. The court felt it seemed entirely appropriate for the trustee to assist in giving effect to any reasonable arrangement reached.

4.23 The courts in Guernsey have recently adopted the approach of the Jersey court in *re A Ltd*[23].

> *Re A Ltd*
>
> [2017] 21/2017 – Guernsey
>
> W had sought to join the trustee of a Guernsey trust in English financial relief proceedings. The trust was a Funded Unapproved Retirement Benefits Scheme in Guernsey (like a workplace pension scheme) which held substantial assets, including properties, used by the divorcing parties.
>
> The trustee made an application to the Guernsey court for directions as to whether it should submit to the English jurisdiction in light of the Guernsey 'firewall' provisions.
>
> The Deputy Bailiff emphasised the importance of seeking such directions. He reviewed the case law flowing from Jersey as to whether a trustee should submit to the jurisdiction of a foreign court[24]. That case law pointed away from submission, but this case did not involve a 'standard' family discretionary trust with a class of beneficiaries extending beyond the divorcing parties (like that in *re H Trust*). Also, the FURBS trust instrument provided the trustee – in reality – with little or no discretion at all (the trustee's role was described as 'mechanistic').
>
> This was an 'exceptional' case where submission to the jurisdiction of the foreign court was permissible and appropriate.

4.24 In the Cayman Islands the position is arguably more stark. The leading case is *RBS Coutts (Cayman) Ltd v W*[25].

> *RBS Coutts (Cayman) Ltd v W*
>
> (2010) 14 ITELR 557 – Cayman Islands
>
> H, W and their three children were beneficiaries of a STAR trust[26] governed exclusively by the law of the Cayman Islands. The parties were going through financial relief proceedings in Hong Kong and W applied for an order varying

23 *In the matter of the A Limited FURBS and the B Employee Benefit Trust*, Judgment of the Royal Court of Guernsey No 21 of 2017 dated 24 April 2017.

24 See those cases referred to above: *re H Trust* [2007] JLR 280; *A and B Trusts* [2007] JLR 444; *R Trust* [2015] JRC 267A.

25 (2010) 14 ITELR 557.

26 STAR trusts are statutory trusts unique to the Cayman Islands and derive their name from the Special Trusts (Alternative Regime) Law 1997. They must have a Cayman Trust Corporation as one of the trustees, they have no perpetuity period, the governing law is always Cayman law, and they fit neatly within the Cayman firewall provisions established by the *Trusts Law (2017 Revision)* discussed in **Chapter 11**.

the trust such that certain assets held within the trust were transferred out to the parties. Notably, the primary asset held within the trust was a residential property in Hong Kong. The trustee applied for directions.

Henderson J was categorical in his rejection of the suggestion that the trustee might submit to the jurisdiction of Hong Kong. First, at paragraph 23 he noted that an order of the Hong Kong court purporting to vary a Cayman trust would not be recognised by the courts in the Cayman Islands, whether or not the trustee had submitted. Secondly, he was of the view that[27]:

> 'It would be unwise and inappropriate for a trustee to allow itself to be placed in a situation where its trust obligation comes into conflict or may come into conflict with an obligation to obey the order of a foreign court.'

4.25 It can be seen, therefore, that there is no general rule as to when a trustee will or will not submit to the jurisdiction of the English court, or indeed when their 'home' court will permit them to do so, or prevent them from doing so. It must be right though, from what has been said above, that a foreign 'home' court will be more likely to sanction the submission by the trustee where:

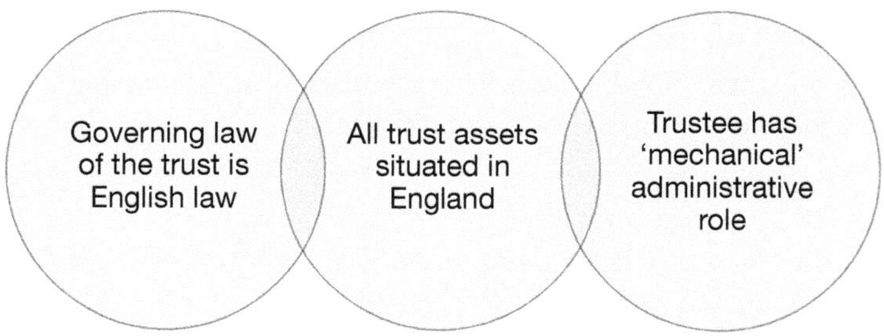

4.26 A good example of a case in which the trustees consciously submitted to the jurisdiction of the English court is *A v A & St George's Trustees Ltd.*

A v A & St George's Trustees Ltd

[2007] EWHC 99 (Fam), [2007] 2 FLR 467 – Munby J

H and W married for 17 years. They had adult children of previous marriages. The shareholding in company HDC was owned partially by the parties and partially by two trusts.

Each trust was explicitly governed by English law and a discretionary trust. The beneficiaries were the children and remoter issue of H's parents living or

27 At para 25.

born at any time before November 2064. Thus, as Munby J noted there was not a closed class of beneficiaries. The trustees had previously been English accountants, then the parties, but in 1991 they were replaced by professional trustees in Jersey.

W argued that (i) the trusts were shams; and (ii) the trust assets were, in any event, available to H as a financial resource.[28]

The trustees submitted to the jurisdiction of the English court and intervened in the proceedings so as to contest the allegations made by W. Munby J rejected both W's arguments.

4.27 If the trusts in *A v A* not been (a) governed by English law and (b) held assets all of which were in England, it is almost inevitable that the trustees would not have submitted to the jurisdiction pursuant to the *re H Trust* principles.

28 This is discussed in **Chapter 9**.

CHAPTER 5

Service and Joinder

Content at a Glance:

A. INTRODUCTION

5.1 In this Chapter we will consider:

- When and why it is necessary (or advantageous) to serve the financial remedies application (ie, Form A) on trustees and/or beneficiaries of a trust;
- When to make an application that trustees and/or beneficiaries should be *joined* as parties to the proceedings;
- The steps that should be taken to secure joinder including how service is to be effected; and
- The consequences of involving (or not involving) these third parties formally in the proceedings.

When should you consider involving trustees and/or beneficiaries?

5.2 At the outset of a financial remedies application, potential issues concerning trusts and trust assets may present themselves in a number of ways. In particular:

1 Where one party is asking the court to exercise its powers under s 24(1)(c) of the Matrimonial Causes Act 1973 ('MCA 1973') to vary the terms of the trust on the basis that it is a nuptial settlement (what constitutes a nuptial settlement is considered in **Chapter 8**).

2 Where a spouse is a beneficiary of a trust and the assets of the trust are said to be a financial 'resource' of that beneficiary that should be taken into account by the court pursuant to MCA 1973, s 25(2)(a) (following the authorities derived from *Thomas v Thomas*[1], considered in **Chapter 9**).

3 Where a spouse is alleging that a settlement of property made by one of the parties is a 'sham' and that the property has always remained the property of the spouse and that she/he never in fact divested themselves of it (the definition of a sham and its application to trusts is considered in **Chapter 7**).

4 Where a spouse is alleging that property held in the name of a third party such as a trustee is in fact beneficially owned by the other spouse (see **Chapter 7**).

5 Where it is necessary to join the trustees to enable enforcement of the court's orders (including interim orders freezing settled assets) or where joinder of trustees and/or beneficiaries may make enforcement easier (enforcement is considered at **Chapter 11**).

6 Where trustees and/or beneficiaries have in their power documents that are relevant to the issues in the proceedings, for example documents that go to the question of whether or not a trust is a nuptial settlement capable of variation and/or to obtain disclosure of information. Relevant documents may include:
   - 'Core' trust documents such as an original trust deed and any subsequent deeds of variation;
   - Documents relating to the value of assets held within the trust structure (eg, trust accounts); or
   - Documents pertaining to the way in which the trustees have exercised, or are likely to exercise, their discretion (for example, the settlor's letter of wishes, minutes of meetings of the trustees, or a request by a beneficiary for a formal explanation of the trustees' future intentions).

B. WHEN AND WHO TO SERVE

When must you serve?

5.3 In all cases in which a spouse has applied for a variation of settlement order r 9.13(1) of the Family Procedure Rules 2010 ('FPR') provides that it is mandatory to serve a copy of the application in Form A on three categories of person:

1 [1995] 2 FLR 668, [1996] 2 FCR 544, CA.

The trustee (in the case of complex and/or offshore trusts this may be a professional trustee or trust company).

/

The settlor of the trust, if living.

/

'Such other person as the court directs'. For example, a beneficiary residing in a property that forms part of the settlement.

5.4 Pursuant to FPR r 9.13(4), the person served then *may*, within 14 days beginning with the date of service, request that the court directs the disclosure to them of a copy of the applicant's financial statement in Form E or any relevant part of that Form E. That request has to be made in writing.

5.5 Under FPR r 9.13(5), where a person has been served with a copy of Form A in accordance with the provisions at either FPR r 9.13(1), (2) or (3) this then triggers a period of 14 days from service of either the application or the financial statement (or relevant part of the financial statement) within which the trustee/settlor/other person as directed by the court, has the opportunity to file a statement in answer the application or Form E, which must be verified by a statement of truth (FPR r 9.13(7)).

5.6 The Rules emphasise (at FPR r 9.13(6)) that in order to prove that they have complied with the requirement to serve under r 9.13, the applicant must file a certificate of service either at or before the first appointment.

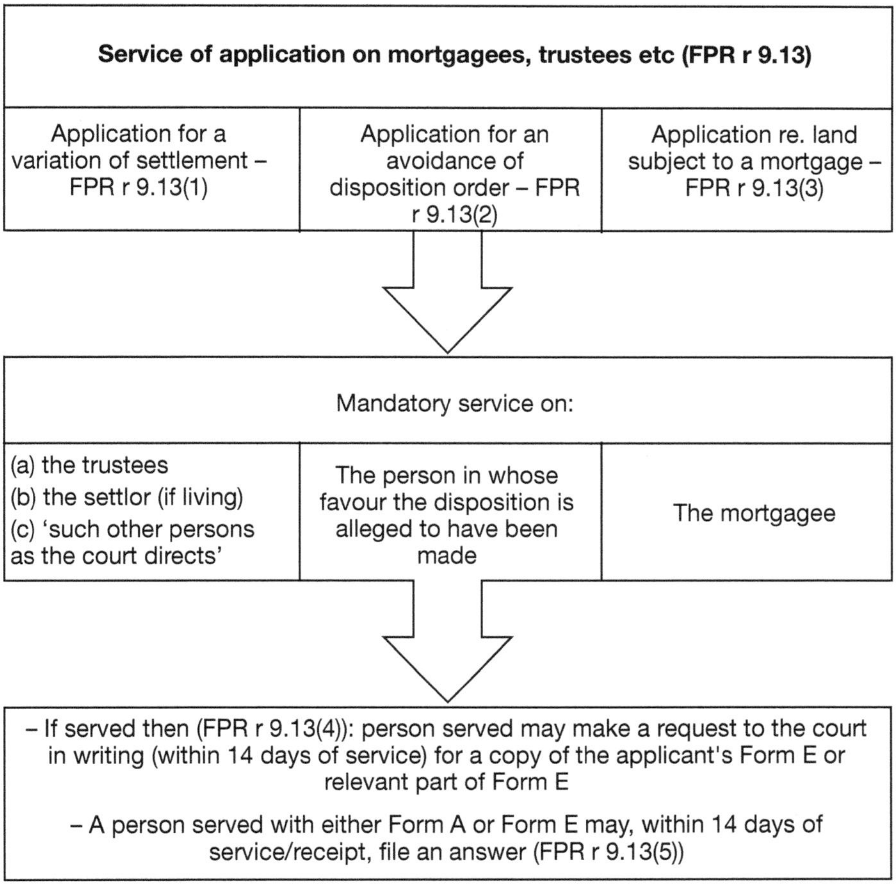

5.7 The requirement to serve Form A also applies if an application is made for an 'avoidance of disposition' order (eg, an order under MCA 1973, s 37 to prevent or set aside a disposition): FPR r 9.13(2).

Representation of minor children

5.8 Unless the court is satisfied that a proposed variation does not adversely affect the rights or interests of any child, the child must be *separately represented* on the application (FPR r 9.11(1)).

5.9 It is important to note that the definition of a '*child*' as being a person '*under the age of 18 years who is the subject of the application*' as set out in the definitions section at FPR r 2.3(1) does *not* apply to FPR r 9.11 and includes *any* minor child (who need not be a 'child of the family'). This is because the rule is intended to provide a right of representation to any minor who might be adversely affected by any proposed variation of settlement: *Tchenguiz-Imerman v Imerman (Application for Joinder)*[2].

5.10 It was also emphasised by the court in the *Tchenguiz-Imerman v Imerman* case that FPR r 9.11 does not have the effect of requiring that a child adversely affected by the variation of settlement application be *joined* as a party to the proceedings as a matter of course in every application. FPR r 9.11 is aimed at *representation* rather than joinder. The purpose of separate representation is to enable, by virtue of the separate representation, an opportunity to consider how the child's interests as a beneficiary of the trust might best be protected and observed. It may well be that the decision is then taken that nothing further needs to be done because all of the arguments that the child would want to have aired before the court will be aired by the existing parties[3].

Adult beneficiaries

5.11 In a situation in which trustees have been served with Form A (and joined to proceedings) but then choose not participate, there is a risk that arguments on behalf of the beneficiaries may go unheard. Mostyn J suggested in *BJ v MJ (Financial Remedy: Overseas Trusts)*[4], that it was the duty of an applicant to draw the claim to the attention of any significant beneficiaries explaining that they are at liberty to apply to intervene or otherwise make representations. At para 12 his Lordship said:

> 'I have mentioned above that on a variation application the trustees are entitled to be heard (FPR 2010 r 9.13(1) and (4)) and any children beneficiaries must be represented (r 9.11). I take the reference to 'a child' in r 9.11 to be a living minor child. The scheme of the rules assumes that the interests and views of adult children and the interests of the unborn will be represented by the trustees. However, those interests and views may not be best voiced if the trustees, as here, have, notwithstanding their joinder to the proceedings, refused to participate in the proceedings.'

5.12 As well as ensuring that the rights of significant beneficiaries are drawn to the court's attention by giving those beneficiaries notice of the proceedings, the court may wish to involve the beneficiaries for evidential reasons. The court emphasised in *BJ v MJ* that when deciding whether all or part of assets belonging to a non-nuptial trust could be attributed to a beneficiary spouse, the court was engaged in a fact-finding exercise as to whether the trustees would be likely to

2 [2012] EWHC 4277 (Fam), [2014] 1 FLR 865, Moylan J at 877–878.

3 Although Mostyn J in the later case of *DR v GR (Financial Remedy: Variation of Overseas Trust)* [2013] EWHC 1196 (Fam), [2013] 2 FLR 1534 appears to treat this provision as equating to mandatory joinder of minor beneficiaries in a way that conflicts with the decision in *Tchenguiz-Imerman.*

4 [2011] EWHC 2708 (Fam), [2012] 1 FLR 667 at 673.

benefit their beneficiary if called on to do so. In those circumstances the court will want to make its judgment based on all the available evidence, including that of the trustees. In the absence of that evidence being available by way of participation from the trustees, the court may wish to hear from beneficiaries as, in effect, the 'second best' option.

Need for disclosure

5.13 In circumstances where there is no application to vary a settlement but instead an argument is being run that a spouse is a discretionary beneficiary of trust assets that should be considered a future resource of that spouse, it may be desirable to serve Form A on the trustees. This is particularly important if the court will be asked to make orders which provide *'judicious encouragement'* to the trustees to distribute assets and/or is likely to at some stage make an application to join the trustees for the purpose of obtaining disclosure[5].

C. HOW TO SERVE

Methods of service in England and Wales

5.14 Service of a financial application in Form A on trustees who are in the jurisdiction of England and Wales may be by any of the following methods (FPR r 6.23):

Personal service (in accordance with FPR r 6.25)	+	First class post, document exchange or other service which provides for delivery on the next business day (in accordance with Practice Direction 6A).	+	Leaving it at a specified place (in accordance with FPR r 6.26).	+	By fax or email (in accordance with Practice Direction 6A).

Methods of service outside the jurisdiction

5.15 If service is to be on trustees *outside* the jurisdiction practitioners must consider the provisions of Chapter 4 of Part 6 of the FPR (r 6.40 onwards)

5 See para **9.1** of this book, and **Chapter 9** generally.

together with Practice Direction 6B. The following general provisions should be noted[6]:

No permission of the court is required to serve out of the jurisdiction under the FPR (r 6.41).

\+

Service should be in accordance with the law of the country in which service is to be effected, and may be made either:

(i) by the applicant his agent (if this is allowed under the local law of the country in which they are to be served), or

(ii) through the relevant foreign government or judicial authority.

\+

Where service is on a person resident in another member state of the European Union, the relevant provisions are currently contained in Council Regulation (EC) No 1393/2007 (the Service Regulation).

D. JOINDER

5.16 The act of *serving* an application on trustees (together with Form E if applicable) is not the same as *joining* the trustees as parties to the proceedings and does not have that effect: *T v T and others (Joinder of Third Parties)*[7]. A decision whether or not to apply to join trustees (or, indeed, the decision by trustees themselves to apply to intervene) will be case specific.

Who can apply?

5.17 An order for joinder (or discharging a party) can be made:

On an application by an existing party

\+

On an application by the proposed additional party (e.g. the trustee)

\+

By the court of its own initiative (FPR r 9.26B(4))

6 It remains to be seen whether, and to what extent, the Service Regulation will remain in force post-Brexit.

7 [1996] 2 FLR 357.

When should an application be made?

5.18 Joinder is likely to be required where the application being made *directly* affects third party property rights such as:

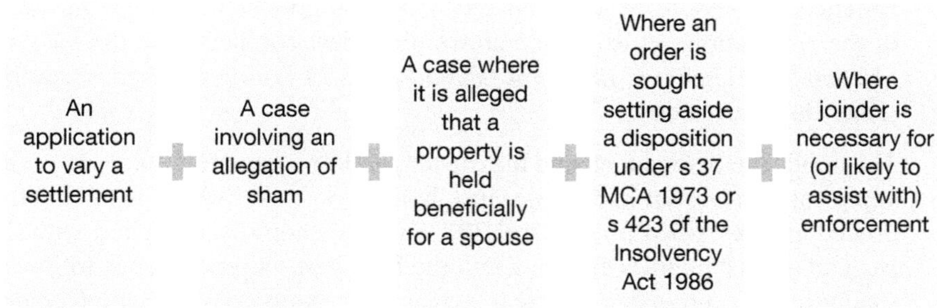

5.19 It has been emphasised that trustees do not need to be routinely joined in every single case simply because the case involves a trust. If, for example, a party is merely asserting that a spouse has potential 'resources' by way of a discretionary trust interest then it may not be necessary to apply for the trustees to be joined as parties and doing so may simply increase the cost and length of the proceedings unnecessarily; see, for example, the comments of Munby J in *A v A v St George Trustees Limited and others*[8].

5.20 If an application is made to vary a nuptial settlement it has been held by Moor J in *TM v AH*[9] that trustees should always be joined as '*it is hard to see how a court can make such an order without them being parties to the litigation, let alone to say that such a variation is binding on them in such circumstances*'. Moreover, Moor J questioned whether it would be a breach of Article 6 of the European Convention on Human Rights (ECHR) which guarantees the right to a fair trial if trustees were not joined before the court made an order varying the trust[10].

5.21 In *DR v GR (Financial Remedy: Variation of Overseas Trust*[11] Mostyn J gave guidance as to the principles relating to joinder as follows:

1 Joinder either of trustees or of the underlying companies is not an essential pre-condition for the validity of a variation of settlement order, as once the trustees have been served in accordance with FPR r 9.13 matters could then be determined without the need for them to be parties. As explained above, Moor J subsequently expressed a conflicting view in the later case of *TM v AH*[12].

8 [2007] EWHC 99 (Fam), [2007] 2 FLR 467.
9 [2016] EWHC 572, [2016] 4 WLR 78.
10 See also *T v T (joinder of third parties)* [1996] 2 FLR 357, [1997] 1 FCR 98.
11 [2013] EWHC 1196 (Fam), [2013] 2 FLR 1534.
12 [2016] 4 WLR 78.

2 It is mandatory for beneficiaries under the age of 18 to be joined unless the court can say that the proposed variation does not adversely affect the rights or interests of any such child. The court has power to modify this requirement but should be very sparing in its exercise. Failure to comply with this rule will not nullify any order later made. The application to join minor beneficiaries should be made at the first appointment following the issue of the application. As explained above, this view conflicts with the view of Moylan J in *Tchenguiz-Imerman*[13] that FPR r 9.11 is aimed at representation rather than party status.

3 The applicant, respondent, and the trustees and/or companies themselves can apply for joinder, but in each instance both the substantive terms of, and the procedure prescribed in, FPR r 9.26B must be carefully complied with. In particular, this includes ensuring that the FPR Part 18 procedure is followed (including the provision of clear evidence in support of the application) and that at least seven days' notice is given to the other party. Although, strictly speaking, the procedure requires 'notice' of the application rather than service of the application, Mostyn J's view is that 'it would be better in future if it were [served].'

Test for joinder

5.22 The applicant for joinder must show (under FPR r 9.26B) either:

That there is an existing matter in dispute which requires for its resolution the joinder of the new party.

/

That there is a matter in dispute between a party and the proposed new party which is connected to the main matters in dispute between the parties and that it is desirable to resolve all the issues together.

5.23 Under the first limb it must be clearly shown that an existing matter in dispute between the parties cannot be effectively and validly resolved without the joinder of the proposed new party.

5.24 Under the second limb it must be shown that there is a separate dispute between a party and the proposed new party and that it is desirable to hear the matters together. The question of whether it is desirable to hear the matters together extends to the commonality of evidence, as well as the saving of costs.

5.25 If better enforcement of an order in a foreign jurisdiction is relied on under either limb there must be evidence that joinder would *actually make a difference*. Mere assertion or statements of belief will not suffice.

13 [2014] 1 FLR 865.

5.26 The authors of *Detection and Preservation of Assets in Financial Remedy Claims* point out[14] that whereas the Civil Procedure Rules 1998 (CPR) contain, at CPR r 19.8, a specific power and procedure to make a judgment binding on any person who is not a party, but who is or may be affected by it, there is no equivalent provision in FPR 2010 and that r 9.13 relied upon in *DR v GR* contains no such enabling power. They suggest that to be sure of having an enforceable judgment against the trustees, the prudent course is to apply to join them as parties.

5.27 On the other hand, FPR r 33.2 applies CPR Part 70 to family applications for the enforcement of orders for the payment of money and CPR r 70.4 states '*If a judgment or order is given or made in favour of or against a person who is not a party to proceedings it may be enforced by or against that person by the same methods as if he were a party*'. This lends support to Mostyn J's view that provided trustees have been properly served with an application (and have simply declined the invitation to intervene) binding orders could be made against them.

Costs issues

5.28 It is important for a party applying to join a third party to bear in mind that if that third party then wins a satellite/preliminary issue between the parties (eg, an allegation that a trust is a sham) the third party can expect to recover his costs from the party who caused him to be joined. The 'no order for costs' regime in FPR r 28.3 does not apply as between an original party to the claim and a third party who intervenes in the claim: *KSO v MJO*[15].

5.29 In other words, if a party joins trustees to proceedings and then fails to establish their case against them (eg, a failed allegation of sham) then there may be adverse costs consequences.

14 Nigel Dyer QC, Juliet Chapman, *Detection and Preservation of Assets in Financial Remedy Claims* (LNUK, 2014) at para 15.43.
15 [2008] EWHC 3031 (Fam), [2009] 1 FLR 1036.

CHAPTER 6

Disclosure

Content at a Glance:

A. Introduction
- Parties to proceedings and the duty of full and frank disclosure

B. Obtaining disclosure from a party who is a beneficiary
- Trust documents that beneficiaries are entitled to obtain

C. Party status and disclosure

D. Orders for disclosure against non-parties
- Third parties resident in the jurisdiction
- Persons resident in the European Union (except Denmark)
- Letters of request – Non-EU states (and Denmark)
- Applications to the foreign court

A. INTRODUCTION

6.1 In matrimonial proceedings where either, (i) an application is made to vary a settlement, or (ii) it is advanced that a party has a beneficial interest under a trust, it will usually be necessary to obtain disclosure of information and documents relating to the trust, its assets, or the way in which trustees have or are likely to exercise their discretion.

6.2 Requests for such documents are frequently met with the response that the document is in the possession of a 'third party' or that the applicant has no right to obtain it.

6.3 This chapter summarises general principles that apply when dealing with requests and applications for disclosure in cases involving trusts.

Parties to proceedings and the duty of full and frank disclosure

6.4 A party who has a beneficial interest under a trust is under an obligation to disclose that interest, even where that interest is *discretionary* and the spouse is only one of a number of other discretionary beneficiaries.

6.5 In *AB v CD*[1] Roberts J emphasised that it is '... *not for a litigant to judge the ambit of the duty to disclose or the consequences of disclosure; any information which is relevant to outcome must be disclosed*'.

6.6 The court can compel a party to give disclosure of documents in his or her '*possession, custody or power*'[2]. This means a party can be ordered to disclose to the other party: (a) any trust documentation that he or she actually has in their possession or custody; or (b) trust documentation which is in their 'power', meaning that they have 'a presently enforceable legal right to obtain from whoever holds the document inspection of it without needing the consent of anyone else'[3]. It should be noted that the term 'possession' includes the right to possession[4], as well as actual physical control or ownership.

6.7 Secondly, a beneficiary (including a beneficiary who is simply in a class of discretionary beneficiaries), may request certain information and documentation relating to the trusts from the trustees. Indeed the court is likely to expect a spouse who is a beneficiary to make such requests and will assume that a number of 'core' trust documents such as the trust deeds will be readily obtainable by that beneficiary.

6.8 It should however be noted that there is a distinction between documents to which a beneficiary has an absolute entitlement (ie, documents that would be classed to be within the beneficiary's 'power') and documents which the trustees have a discretion either to disclose or to withhold.

6.9 Hughes J in *Mubarak v Mubarak*[5] held (in the context of company documentation, and referring to the decision in *Dubai Bank Ltd v Galdari and Others*[6]) '...*there is clear authority...that there is no power to order the husband to use all necessary endeavours to obtain documents which are not in his possession...*'. It could therefore be argued that a court ought not to require a beneficiary spouse to use their 'best endeavours' (or equivalent formulation) to obtain documents that they do not have an absolute entitlement to obtain from the trustees.

6.10 On the other hand, the position of a spouse beneficiary might be viewed as being in a different category to that of, say, a spouse who is a company director seeking company documents. If a beneficiary makes a request of trustees for disclosure of trust documents the trustees have to consider that request by exercising their discretion in accordance with their duties as trustees. Additionally, as referred to at para **6.14** (4) below, beneficiaries have a right to *request* disclosure about their interests under the trust (even if that request is not ultimately granted, or is granted in a more limited way). It is arguable therefore

1 [2016] EWHC 10 (Fam).
2 See *Lonrho Ltd v Shell Petroleum Co Ltd* [1980] 1 WLR 627, HL.
3 See above.
4 See *Mubarak v Mubarak* [2003] 2 FLR 553.
5 [2003] 2 FLR 553.
6 [1990] Ch 98.

that a court might draw adverse inferences from a refusal by a beneficiary even to *request* certain information from the trustees.

6.11 Section 2.14 of the financial statement (Form E) makes specific reference to trust interests and requires the party to estimate the value of the interest and when it is likely to become realisable. If the party alleges that the interest is not realisable then they are required to give reasons for that conclusion.

6.12 There are a number of authorities in which the English courts have emphasised their familiarity with offshore trusts in the context of financial remedy applications and emphasised their unwillingness to be 'bamboozled' by sophisticated structures. In *J v V (Disclosure: Offshore Corporations)*[7] Coleridge J stated:

> 'Respondents to such applications are required to be from the outset perhaps even fuller and franker in the exposure and explanation of their assets than in conventional onshore cases. Otherwise skulduggery is instantly presumed. Applicants justifiably believe that advantage is being taken to hide assets from view amongst complex corporate undergrowth.'

B. OBTAINING DISCLOSURE FROM PARTY WHO IS A BENEFICIARY

Trust documents that beneficiaries are entitled to obtain

6.13 In what circumstances is a spouse who is the beneficiary of a trust able to obtain trust documentation/information in their capacity as a beneficiary in order to satisfy the obligation to give full and frank disclosure of their 'resources'?

6.14

1 Trustees are under a duty of disclosure 'without demand' (essentially a duty to notify automatically) to communicate to adult beneficiaries the existence of their interest under a trust and the nature of their interest: *Brittlebank v Goodwin*[8].

2 The position is more complicated with adult beneficiaries with future interests/contingent interests and in the case of discretionary beneficiaries. In the case of discretionary beneficiaries, there may be a difference between those discretionary beneficiaries who are, in the circumstances, potential candidates for benefit in the proper exercise of the discretion under the trust or power and those who could be described as 'something of a remote beneficiary, or one beneficiary among a great many…': *Re Murphy's Settlements*[9].

3 The duty of disclosure 'without demand' is a duty to give general information about the nature of a beneficiary's interest under a trust. It does not extend

7 [2003] EWHC 3110 (Fam), [2004] 1 FLR 1042.
8 [1868] L.R 5 Eq 545 at 550.
9 [1998] 3 All ER 1; *Murphy v Murphy* [1999] 1 WLR 282.

to an automatic requirement to provide the beneficiary with copies of any accounts or trust documents. A beneficiary seeking further information or access to such accounts/documents will need to seek those documents from the trustees.

4 Beneficiaries are generally entitled to see the trust documents they need to hold the trustees to their fundamental duty to account for the proper administration of the trust and this applies whether or not the trust is a discretionary trust: *Schmidt v Rosewood Trust Ltd*[10]. However, whilst beneficiaries have a right *to seek* disclosure, a beneficiary does not have an automatic entitlement to disclosure of trust documents. Rather, disclosure will be ordered where appropriate as part of the court's inherent jurisdiction to supervise the administration of trusts. In deciding whether to exercise its discretion to order disclosure, a court may have to balance competing interests of different beneficiaries, the trustees and third parties. Disclosure may be limited or certain safeguards put in place.

5 When the court determines an application by a beneficiary for disclosure of trust documents in its supervisory jurisdiction it will be applying the principles in *Schmidt v Rosewood Trust Ltd* and will not generally order disclosure under its inherent supervisory jurisdiction of documents relating to reasons for the trustees' exercise of powers and discretion, or confidential documents such as internal trust correspondence and records. These may well be illuminating documents for a family court when considering the reality of a spouse's resources and so may instead need to be sought using the family court's disclosure powers (see para **6.20** onwards below).

C. PARTY STATUS AND DISCLOSURE

6.15 In *Tchenguiz-Imerman v Imerman (Application for Joinder)*[11] Moylan J considered it to be a significant factor when deciding whether to order (on their application) the joinder of adult beneficiaries that – on being joined – the beneficiaries would be subject to '*...direct disclosure obligations deriving from their status as parties.*'. He went as far as to suggest that on becoming parties, the beneficiaries would be under an (automatic) obligation to disclose:

> 'all documents relevant to the issues raised within these proceedings, which would include (a) whether the trusts are or are not nuptial settlements; (b) what are the resources held within the trusts; (c) the manner in which the trustees would be likely to exercise their discretion; and (d) any other issue going to the likely ability to enforce any order which this court might make.'

6.16 In contrast, in *DR v GR (Financial Remedy: Variation of Overseas Trust)*[12] Mostyn J commented:

10 [2003] UKPC 26, [2003] 2 AC 709, [2003] 2 WLR 1442, PC.
11 [2012] EWHC 4277 (Fam), [2014] 1 FLR 865.
12 [2013] EWHC 1196 (Fam), [2013] 2 FLR 1534.

'It may be said that the obtaining of information for the inquiry might be better achieved if the trustees are parties but as against that there is the fact that if they are not parties orders for disclosure against them as non-parties can be obtained under FPR 2010 rule 21.2 or, if the trustee is overseas, by means of the procedure in rule 24.12 (in a non-EU case) or rule 24.16 (in a EU case).'

D. ORDERS FOR DISCLOSURE AGAINST NON-PARTIES

Third parties resident in the jurisdiction

6.17 Where it has not been possible to obtain information about a trust directly from another party to the proceedings, an application can be made against third party trustees pursuant to FPR r 21.2 if the trustees are resident in the jurisdiction.

6.18 The power to order disclosure or inspection of documents against a third party trustee in this context derives from the Senior Courts Act 1981, s 34 and is contained within FPR Part 21. The test is that disclosure must be 'necessary to dispose fairly of the proceedings or to save costs' (FPR r 21.2(3)).

6.19 It is important to be aware of the definitions used:

'Disclosure' simply means stating a document exists or has existed (FPR r 21.1(1)).

+

'Inspection' means being permitted to see the document that has been disclosed. Inspection carries the right to take copies of the documents.

6.20 An application for a third party disclosure order under FPR Part 21 may be made without notice (in which case the usual principles applicable to without notice applications in family proceedings apply with force) and must be supported by evidence. The Part 18 procedure applies.

6.21 A third party against whom disclosure is sought has the right pursuant to FPR r 21.3 to apply for an order that they be permitted to withhold disclosure on the grounds that any disclosure would '*damage the public interest*' by stating in writing the right or duty claimed and the grounds on which it is claimed.

6.22 Under FPR r 24.2 the court can order the attendance of an individual resident within the jurisdiction to give evidence or produce documents via the witness summons procedure. Any such witness may apply to set side the order on the same ground as used to object to the inspection of documents under r 21.3.

6.23 The court can also order a third party witness to give 'evidence by deposition' (be examined under oath) by a judge, examiner of the court or 'such other person as the court appoints' (FPR r 24.7).

Persons resident in the European Union (except Denmark)

6.24 As Mostyn J observed in *DR v* GR[13] if the third party is resident in a 'Regulation State' (defined as being all member states of the European Union apart from Denmark – see FPR r 24.15) then Council Regulation (EC) No 1206/2001 of 28 May 2001 on co-operation between the courts of the Member States in the taking of evidence in civil and commercial matters ('the Regulation') enables evidence to be taken from a person in a Member State at the request of a designated court of a Member State. Each Member State has designated a central body to administer and oversee the operation of the scheme and in England and Wales, this is the Senior Master of the Queen's Bench Division: see FPR PD 24A para 8.2.

6.25 An application for an order for the issue of a request to the designated court in the member state should be made using Form D11, following the Part 18 Procedure (FPR PD 24A para 9.2).

6.26 The application should be accompanied by a draft letter of request (using a prescribed form called Form A annexed to the Regulation).

6.27 If the court makes an order that the request be issued, the party who obtained that order must then file the Form A and a translation of it (unless English is one of the official languages of the Regulation State where the examination is to take place, or the Regulation State has indicated that English is a language it will accept). The party must also file an undertaking to be responsible for certain costs and expenses set out at FPR r 24.16(3). The court then sends the form of request directly to the central body of the Regulation State.

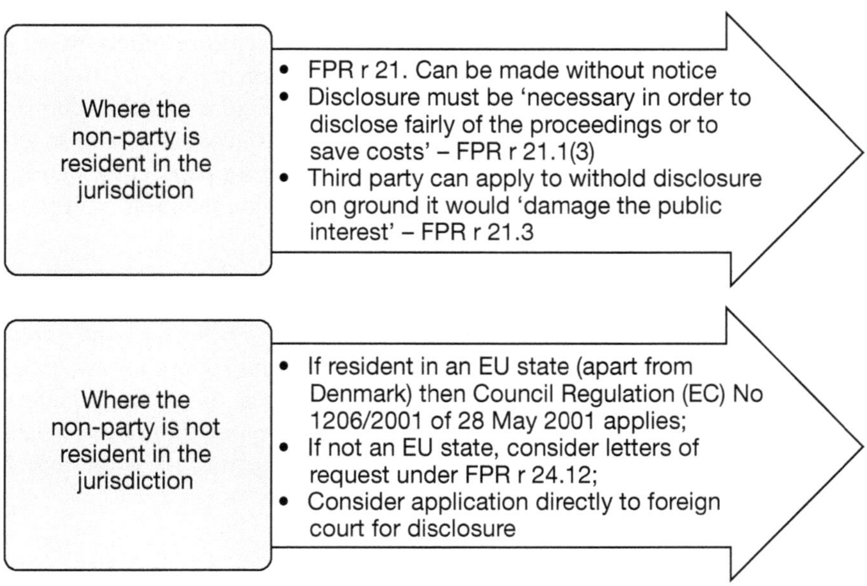

13 [2013] EWHC 1196 (Fam), [2013] 2 FLR 1534.

Letters of Request – Non-EU states (and Denmark)

6.28 If, as can often be the case in respect of the trustees of an offshore trust, the third party is resident abroad and not in a 'Regulation State' as described above, then recourse can be had to FPR r 24.12 which gives the High Court power to request assistance from a foreign court in obtaining evidence or documents from a third party based abroad using letters of request.

Applications to the foreign court

6.29 Finally, practitioners should not overlook the potential for applications to be made in the foreign court for disclosure of documents relevant to the financial remedy proceedings. This could happen in a number of ways:

Applications by trustees to their local court for guidance as to how to approach the financial remedy proceedings which can include directions in respect of disclosure of trust documentation.

\+

Applications by beneficiaries to the foreign court asking for orders against trustees to disclose documents to them.

\+

Applications for a 'Norwich Pharmacal order' (*Norwich Pharmacal v Customs & Excise Commissioners* [1974] AC 133).

6.30 *Norwich Pharmacal* orders are third party disclosure orders based on the principle that if a third party has facilitated or been involved (including innocently – no civil wrong or criminal behaviour is required) in the actions of a respondent (in this case a spouse who has failed to disclose his assets) so as to deny the applicant an effective remedy, that innocent third party comes under a duty to assist the person who has been wronged by giving then full information and disclosing the identity of the wrongdoers.

6.31 It may be possible to rely upon the *Norwich Pharmacal* principles to argue before the foreign court that a third party resident in the foreign jurisdiction has an obligation to disclose to the applicant spouse information in their possession so that the spouse's substantive claim can be properly pursued. However, in the context of trustees the foreign court would still need to balance the competing rights of the beneficiaries as a whole as part of the exercise of its discretion whether to order disclosure of the documents.

CHAPTER 7

Attacking trusts: formation, validity and 'sham'

Content at a Glance:

A. INTRODUCTION: VALID TRUSTS

Overview: Challenging validity

7.1 In some family cases, the very existence of a trust will be disputed. The outcome of such a contest may well be of fundamental importance in a matrimonial context. If, ultimately, the validity of an alleged trust is challenged successfully, the 'trust assets' may revert to the settlor's personal property and, if the settlor is a party to the marriage, such assets may become open to division[1].

7.2 It is therefore essential to have a basic understanding of how trusts are validly created, and conversely how, if they fail to fulfil the requisite formalities, they may be vulnerable to challenge in matrimonial proceedings.

1 See para **2.4** of this book for the sequential process performed by the court in determining an application for financial orders under the MCA 1973.

Trusts: Basic principles

7.3 At its very essence a trust is the relationship which arises wherever a person (a 'trustee') is compelled in equity to hold property for the benefit of some person or persons ('beneficiaries') or for some purpose, in such a way that the actual benefit of the trust property accrues not to the trustee but to the beneficiaries or objects of the trust.

7.4 In other words, a trust is a vehicle through which the control of property is separated from its enjoyment.

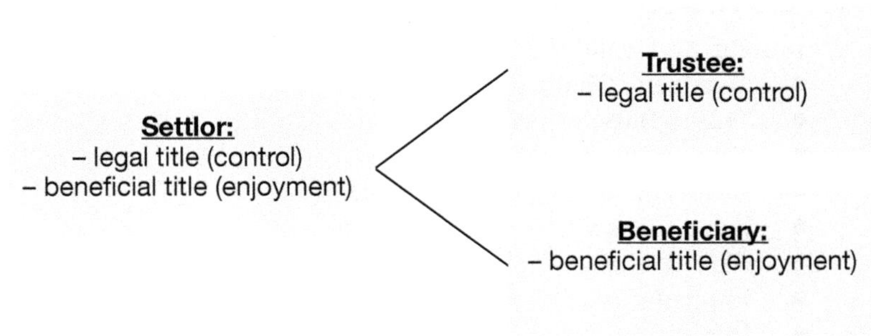

7.5 Trusts are recognised in English law, and similar concepts are an established part of the jurisprudence of a number of Commonwealth and other international jurisdictions.

7.6 The Convention of 1 July 1985 on the Law Applicable to Trusts and on their Recognition ('1985 Hague Convention') defines a trust as 'the legal relationship created – *inter vivos* or on death – by a person, the settlor, when assets have been placed under the control of a trustee for the benefit of a beneficiary or for a specified purpose'[2]. Any country that has ratified the 1985 Hague Convention (including the UK[3]) thus recognises the concept of trust ownership and is obliged to admit within the bounds of its own legal system a distinction between legal and beneficial interest in a property, recognising that through the establishment of a trust the settlor has divested him or herself of control of the property.

7.7 A trust does not have its own legal personality (unlike a company or incorporated association), so the possession of any trust assets must be held by the trustee subject to his or her fiduciary duties; duties implied by statute and common law and the terms of the trust.

7.8 The settlor may also be the trustee. Where this occurs, the settlor retains the legal title already held, and divests him or herself solely of the beneficial title, which is conferred upon another person or persons.

2 Article 2, 1985 Hague Convention.
3 See the Recognition of Trusts Act 1987.

7.9 There is nothing preventing the trustee from also being one of the beneficiaries (provided it does not conflict with his duties as trustee to perform this role), but if he or she is both the trustee and the only beneficiary, there is no trust.

7.10 The establishment of the trust automatically places the trustee under a binding fiduciary duty to preserve the property for the benefit of the beneficiary or the purpose of the trust, and to act in accordance with the trust deed. The settlor's purpose as expressed in any letter of wishes may be furthered by the trustees but, once the trust is validly created, the settlor loses control over the trust property and so the trustee takes ultimate responsibility for the management of the trust property.

Types of beneficial interest

7.11 The nature of beneficial entitlement will vary according to the terms of the trust. No two trusts are alike. In particular practitioners may wish to consider the following questions:

Is the beneficial interest vested or contingent?	Is the beneficial interest in posession or remainder?	Is the beneficial interest absolute or limited?

7.12 A beneficiary has a vested interest if he or she already exists and/or does not have to satisfy any conditions imposed by the trust to become entitled to the interest. The beneficial interest is contingent if the beneficiary is yet to come into existence or must satisfy conditions to be entitled to the property.

A beneficial interest in possession is one that can be enjoyed immediately. An interest in remainder is one that the beneficiary must wait for until another person's beneficial right to enjoyment of the property has first expired.

7.13 An absolute beneficial interest conveys full entitlement to enjoy the asset, capital and income. A limited beneficial interest may be restricted, for example to income only.

7.14 In circumstances where a beneficiary's interest is vested and in possession and not limited in enjoyment, the beneficiary is described as 'absolutely entitled'. Beneficiaries who are 'absolutely entitled' have a right to bring the trust to an end, provided the following conditions are satisfied:

The beneficiaries are all in existence and can be ascertained.	The beneficiaries are all over the age of 18 and are of sound mind.	The beneficiaries (where there is more than one) all consent.

Illustration: definitions in practice

Peter has chosen to leave the UK in favour of the Spanish Pyrenees. He has a large property in Shropshire and cash savings of £500,000, all of which he transfers to his former business partner Kate to hold on trust for his family members. He has a sister, Jenny and two children who are both at university, Alex and Matthew, aged 18 and 19. The terms of the trust provide:

1. Jenny may live in the house until her death, whereupon it will be held for the benefit of his children Alex and Matthew, who may choose to live there, rent it out, sell it or do whatever they want with it.

2. The savings are to be held on trust for any surviving children who have attained the age of 25 and completed a university degree. If there are no qualifying persons, it shall be donated to the local church to fix the roof.

- Peter is the settlor.
- Kate is the trustee.
- Jenny, Alex, Matthew and the church roof fund are all beneficiaries.
- Jenny's interest in the house is:
  - vested
  - in possession, and
  - limited.

  Jenny already satisfies all the conditions she needs in order to receive her benefit, she may enjoy the property immediately, but she is limited in the extent to which she may enjoy it. She may live there but not sell it.
- Alex and Matthew's interests in the house are:
  - vested,
  - in remainder, and
  - absolute.

  They already satisfy the conditions needed to receive their benefit, but they must first wait until Jenny's entitlement has expired, which will occur on her death. When that happens, they will be free to do with the property whatsoever they wish, including selling it and receiving the funds outright.
- Alex and Matthew's interests in the cash savings are:
  - contingent,
  - in possession, and
  - absolute.

  Neither has yet satisfied the two conditions required to receive the benefit. If and when they both do, they shall receive the funds without restrictions. If only one does, that person will receive the whole. If neither does, the interest will be lost to them.

- The church roof fund has an interest in the cash savings that is:
  - vested,
  - in remainder, and
  - absolute.

  The fund does not have to satisfy any conditions to become eligible, but no benefit will be conveyed until Alex and Matthew's contingent interests have been exhausted. If/when that occurs there will be no restriction on how the fund may use the trust property for its benefit.

Revocable trusts v Irrevocable trusts

7.15 A trust can be revocable or irrevocable. If it is revocable, the settlor retains a power to revoke the trust during the course of his or her lifetime, which would bring the trust to an end and cause any trust property to return to the settlor. The power of revocation must be plain from the inception of the trust: the settlor cannot award the power to him or herself once an irrevocable trust has been established.

7.16 An irrevocable trust is a trust which, once established, can only be disbanded by the trustee acting in accordance with his or her duties, and in respect of which the settlor retains no authority. A revocable trust will automatically become irrevocable upon the death of the settlor.

Fixed trusts v Discretionary trusts

7.17 A fixed trust is so-called because the terms of the trust define the share of the trust property that the beneficiary is entitled to receive or enjoy. In such cases the trustee has *no discretion* as to how the trust property is to be allocated between the beneficiaries.

7.18 A 'bare trust', common in a commercial context, is the simplest form of fixed trust. The trustee holds the trust property on trust for a sole beneficiary, without any limitations or conditions attaching. The beneficiary must be an adult with full mental capacity. In such cases, the trustee handles the trust property, as permitted by law, as the beneficiary dictates. The beneficiary may end the trust at any time by demanding that the trustee transfers to him or her the legal title (see *Saunders v Vautier*[4]). Upon this taking effect, the beneficiary would become the outright owner and the trust would cease to exist.

4 *Saunders v Vautier* 41 ER 482, [1841] Cr & Ph 240.

Illustrations: examples of different types of 'fixed' trust

Example A: a fixed interest trust with vested property owned beneficially for lifetime and in remainder

Laura owns a block of residential flats, which are commercially-let. These are held on trust. Julia is to receive 100% of the benefit of the income for the duration of her (Julia's) lifetime, and on her death the trust property will pass in its entirety to Nico in remainder.

Example B: a fixed interest trust with contingent beneficial interests in possession and in remainder

Cian holds a property on trust for Philip if he returns to live in the UK before the age of 45, but if Philip reaches that age without meeting that contingency, then for Cian's father, Michael.

Example C: a fixed interest trust with vested property beneficially owned absolutely, a so-called 'bare trust'

Iain holds some valuable pieces of artwork on trust for Rory. Rory was a child when the trust was created, but he is now aged 35 and he has full mental capacity.

7.19 A fixed trust must be distinguished from a discretionary trust. The latter form is very frequently encountered in matrimonial proceedings as it is a vehicle conventionally used for managing financial assets for the benefit of multiple family members, including future generations. With discretionary trusts, the trustee is placed under a duty to exercise his discretion as to which beneficiaries from an identified class are to receive, and in what proportions, the income, capital or other enjoyment of the trust property.

7.20 The beneficiaries must fall within a defined class, which may include those who have not yet come into existence. The class may be construed narrowly (eg, 'the settlor's parents') or broadly (eg, 'any undergraduate student of this university'). In some cases, the trustees have a power to add or remove beneficiaries from the class.

7.21 No individual beneficiary named in a discretionary trust instrument has an equitable interest in the trust property until such time as the trustees exercise their discretion in his or her favour. Until then the beneficiary has only a hope that the trustees will choose him or her to benefit[5].

7.24 The extent of the trustees' discretion will be determined by the trust instruments. Again this may be prescribed narrowly (eg, 'each beneficiary

5 See **Chapter 9** of this book for the approach taken by matrimonial courts to cases where one party is a beneficiary of a discretionary trust. The fact that being so named as a beneficiary does not convey a proprietorial interest to that beneficiary does not preclude the court from taking the trust assets into account as a 'financial resource' that may be available to the party at present or in the foreseeable future.

shall receive a minimum award of 5% of the trust property, with the trustees to exercise their discretion as to the distribution of the remainder') or broadly (eg, 'the trustees to exercise their discretion as to whether to advance any capital or income from the trust property to any of the beneficiaries, and if so, when and in what proportions'). However, even where the trustees are seemingly afforded a wide discretion, they are likely to be guided (as with all areas of trustee discretion) by the terms of the letter of wishes from the settlor.

7.25 In any event, at *all times*, the trustees remain under an obligation to execute their fiduciary duties to manage the trust property for the benefit of the beneficiaries, and this applies to the exercise of their discretion. If there is any concern that a trustee's exercise of discretion, eg, in making a decision not to confer any benefit from trust property to a named beneficiary, might be in breach of this duty, the court of the jurisdiction whose law governs the trust may intervene in the exercise of its supervisory function over the trust. Most such applications are brought by beneficiaries. In many cases however they are brought by the trustees themselves, seeking the court's guidance as to the exercise of their functions. In England and Wales, such applications are made to the Chancery Division of the High Court.

Illustrations: examples of different types of 'discretionary trust'

Example A: a discretionary trust with a limited class of beneficiaries

Connie's will directs that a trust fund of £40,000 be set up to provide for the educational expenses of her three children, Stephen, Anthony and John, at the absolute discretion of the trustee, her brother Roger. At the time of Connie's death, Stephen has graduated from university and is in full-time employment. Anthony is training to be a doctor and has five years left of study. His fees are £9,000 per annum and his living expenses at university are £10,000 per annum. John has decided not to go to university and is engaged in temporary work but he has enrolled on a part-time Spanish language course as he intends to look for permanent work in Mexico, where his partner lives. Roger decides to distribute the fund of £40,000 in two outright payments: of £35,000 to Anthony and £5,000 to John. He makes no payment to Stephen. There is nothing to suggest this is an improper exercise of Roger's discretion.

Example B: a discretionary trust with a defined but unlimited class of beneficiaries

At the time of Sergei and Tracey's marriage, Tracey's mother Jane settles the sum of USD $1 million into a trust fund, for the benefit of Sergei, Tracey, or any children or future descendants they may have. The trustees are empowered to use their discretion to distribute income and/ or capital from the trust resources from time to time as they see fit.

The trustees make no advancement at all for the first ten years of Sergei and Tracey's marriage, at which point they purchase a property for $500,000 (also said to be held subject to the terms of trust) in which the couple and their only child, Dimitri, begin to live. Dimitri's school fees of £33,000 per annum are later paid out of the trust for a period of five years. Sergei and Tracey request the trustees to make a further distribution to pay for a car, but the trustees refuse, choosing to preserve the remaining funds for future generations. There is nothing to suggest this is an improper exercise of their discretion.

Express trusts: brief overview

7.26 Trusts may be created expressly, or they may be implied. The first observation to make, and it is crucial, is that in either case the trust can only be established by operation of law, specifically the law of the country which governs the trust[6].

7.27 Under English law, where a trust is said to be express, the relevant formalities *must all* have been complied with. Where a trust is said to be implied (whether resulting or constructive), very narrow factual circumstances must be established. Matrimonial practitioners must be alive to the warning of Munby J in *A v A and St Georges Trustees*[7] [Emphasis added]:

> '…even in the Family Division, a spouse who seeks to extend her claim for ancillary relief to assets which appear to be in the hands of someone other than her husband must identify, and **by reference to established principle**, some **proper basis for doing so**. The court cannot grant relief merely because the husband's arrangements appear to be artificial or even 'dodgy'… the typical case in the Family Division may differ from the typical case in (say) the Chancery Division. But what it is important to appreciate (and too often, I fear, is not appreciated at least in this Division) is that **the relevant legal principles which have to be applied are precisely the same in this Division as in the other two Divisions.**'

7.28 This book does not cover in detail the requirements and/or formalities required to create a valid express trust under English law, which is a complex and legally detailed issue worthy of its own volume[8]. Set out below is a concise summary of the key features that are required.

7.29 A settlor may create an express trust under English law during the course of his or her lifetime in one of two ways:

By declaring himself a trustee of property	or	By transferring property to trustees on trust

in either case, such property thereafter is held for the benefit of another.

6 The 1985 Hague Convention imposes fairly modest requirements as to formalities for the creation of trusts, but the domestic law of its signatories impose requirements and formalities that must be honoured in the specific jurisdiction governing the trust.

7 [2007] EWHC 99 (Fam), [2007] 2 FLR 467.

8 Practitioners are referred to the comprehensive guidance given in *Lewin on Trusts*, (19th edition, Sweet & Maxwell, 2017), which does justice to this complex issue.

7.30 Settlors may validly create express trusts in their wills, but they do not come into existence (and consequently have no legal effect) until the testator dies.

7.31 To create a valid express trust, the settlor must:

Make a valid declaration of trust.	+	Ensure that the property is properly vested in the trustee(s).

7.32 The declaration of trust, in order to be valid, must observe the following essential requirements[9]:

The three certainties of intention, subject matter and objects	+	The beneficiary principle	+	The rule against perpetuities	+	Formalities for express declaration of trusts

7.33 A review of these individual constructs is beyond the scope of this book. Where disputes as to the validity of an express trust arise in practice, reference should be made to authorities focussing on the issues engaged. Where the trust is governed by the law of another country, specialist advice will usually be required in that jurisdiction. As will be seen, the gravity of challenging the validity of a trust within a matrimonial case can be significant, indeed in some cases it will be determinative of outcome[10]. In cases where this arises, it will sometimes need to be decided as a preliminary issue so the court can identify and compute the assets capable of division prior to performing its distributive function.

Implied trusts (1): Resulting trusts

7.34 As indicated above, not all trusts are created expressly. Some trusts may be implied from a manner of dealing with the property and/or assertions of intent. In matrimonial cases this is likely to arise in two scenarios, where the court is being asked to find that either:

Assets legally owned by a third party are actually beneficially owned by a party to the marriage.	or	Assets legally owned by a party to the marriage are actually beneficially owned by a third party.

9 The formalities differ depending on, *inter alia*, (i) the type of trust, and (ii) the type of trust property. For example, specific statutory formalities are prescribed for testamentary trusts created by will (Wills Act 1837, s 9), trusts of land (Law of Property Act 1925, s 53(1)(b)), and dispositions of existing equitable interests (Law of Property Act 1925, s 53(1)(c)). These are isolated examples.
10 Considered in greater detail at Section B of this Chapter, below.

7.35 A third scenario might be the spouse who claims the *other spouse* legally holds assets beneficially for *him or her*, eg, if the family home is held in the wife's sole name but the husband claims he can establish that a beneficial share belongs to him by reference to principles of resulting or constructive trust. However, such arguments are rarely pursued in matrimonial courts for the practical reason that the distributive powers of the family courts between spouses are so wide-reaching that the husband in this example is unlikely to improve his position under the MCA 1973 by first succeeding in a property claim.

7.36 In any of these illustrations, the absence of a formal trust instrument will not preclude the existence of a beneficial interest if the court finds that as a matter of fact, applying principles of implied trusts, assets legally held by one party are beneficially owned by another.

7.37 There are two types of implied trust: 'resulting' and 'constructive' trusts[11]. Both concepts, derived from equity, have been the subject of extensive judicial guidance over many years. The basic principles only are set out here.

7.38 In *Westdeutsche*[12], Lord Browne-Wilkinson identified two sets of circumstances that give rise to a presumption of resulting trust:

(i) where A makes a voluntary payment to B or pays (wholly or in part) for the purchase of property which is vested either in B alone or in the joint names of A and B, there is a presumption that A did not intend to make a gift to B: the money or property is held on trust for A (if he is the sole provider of the money) or in the case of a joint purchase by A and B in shares proportionate to their contributions[13];

(ii) where A transfers property to B on express trust, but the trust declared does not exhaust the whole beneficial interest. For example, if the settlor created a trust for X if she obtains the age of 25 but X died prior to attaining the age of 25 and there was no provision for a residual beneficiary. In such circumstances, X's interest having never vested, the trustees would hold the trust property on resulting trust for the settlor.

7.39 Both types of resulting trust are traditionally regarded as examples of trusts giving effect to the common intention of the parties[14]. A resulting trust is *not imposed* by law *against the intentions of the trustee* (unlike, potentially, a constructive trust) but instead gives effect to his or her presumed intention.

11 Proprietary estoppel falls outwith the scope of this book as although it is a remedy in equity, it is not a form of trust. The principle should not be overlooked in cases where implied trusts are in issue, as it may provide adjacent or parallel arguments.

12 *Westdeutsche Landesbank Girozentrale v Islington LBC* [1996] AC 669, [1996] 2 WLR 802, HL, per Lord Browne-Wilkinson at 708.

13 See also *Birch v Blagrave* (1755) 1 Amb. 264; *Childers v Childers* (1857) 1 De G. & J. 482; *In Re Vinogradoff; Allen v Jackson* [1935] W.N. 68; *In Re Muller; Cassin v Mutual Cash Order Co Ltd* [1953] N.Z.L.R. 879. Note that in these circumstances 'B' would not be a trustee, nor accountable as such, until such time as he became *aware* of the circumstances that gave rise to the resulting trust. Per Lord Browne-Wilkinson at 705 in *Westdeutsche*.

14 Per Lord Browne-Wilkinson at 708 in *Westdeutsche*.

7.40 In the first illustration cited by Lord Browne-Wilkinson, the creation of a resulting trust is merely a presumption, which would be rebutted either by the counter-presumptions of advancement or by direct evidence of A's intention to make an outright transfer.

7.41 Equally, in the second case, Lord Browne-Wilkinson observed that the establishment of a resulting trust would be rebutted if there was direct evidence to suggest that the settlor had abandoned his or her beneficial interest in the trust property; in such circumstances, there would be no resulting trust and instead the property would vest in the Crown as bona vacantia[15].

7.42 Applying the same rationale of intention, it is now established that resulting trusts will not readily be implied in the context of domestic property ownership between cohabiting couples[16]. It matters not which party in a relationship paid a deposit or the mortgage instalments over the years. In the absence of any express declaration of trust in the case of a domestic property the relevant doctrine of implied trust is that of *constructive trust* (below), which makes the starting point for beneficial ownership the legal title, unless positive evidence of a common intention to depart from the legal ownership gives rise to ownership in other shares. The doctrine of *resulting trust* is not appropriate to the context of cohabiting partners due to the practical realities of financial mingling in romantic relationships. As Lord Walker and Baroness Hale stated in their joint leading judgment in *Jones v Kernott* at paras 24–25 [Emphasis added]:

> 'In the context of the acquisition of a family home, **the presumption of a resulting trust made a great deal more sense when social and economic conditions were different** and when it was tempered by the presumption of advancement…Instead, the tool which equity has chosen to develop law is the "common intention" constructive trust. Abandoning the presumption of advancement while retaining **the presumption of resulting trust would place an even greater emphasis upon who paid for what, an emphasis which most commentators now agree to have been too narrow**: hence the general welcome given to the 'more promising vehicle' of the constructive trust…'
>
> 'The time has come to make it clear, in line with *Stack v Dowden* [2007] 2 AC 432 (see also *Abbott v Abbott* [2008] 1 FLR 1451), that **in the case of the purchase of a house or flat in joint names for joint occupation by a married or unmarried couple, where both are responsible for any mortgage, there is no presumption of a resulting trust arising**

15 See *Westdeutsche*, at 708, here expressly disagreeing with Megarry J in *In Vandervell's Trusts (No 2)* [1967] 2 AC 291, who considered that the resulting trust would be 'automatic' and not rebuttable by evidence of contrary intention. That view has been overruled by *Westdeutsche*.

16 See two Supreme Court cases concerning the property rights of unmarried cohabitants: *Stack v Dowden* [2007] UKHL 17, [2007] 2 AC 432; and *Jones v Kernott* [2011] UKSC 53, [2012] 1 AC 776, [2011] 3 WLR 1121. Note that in both cases it was suggested (obiter) that the doctrine of resulting trust may still be appropriate if the cohabitants were also business partners: *Stack v Dowden* [para 32]; *Jones v Kernott* [para 31].

from their having contributed to the deposit (or indeed the rest of the purchase) in unequal shares. The presumption is that the parties intended a joint tenancy both in law and in equity. But that presumption can of course be rebutted by evidence of a contrary intention, which may more readily be shown where the parties did not share their financial resources.'

7.43 However, the doctrine of 'resulting trust' is still of relevance in family cases, particularly in cases where a party to a marriage has transferred assets to a third party (which may be a company), and in the context of later financial proceedings relies on the company's legal ownership of the property as being determinative of the fact that it is no longer available to the transferor. It is common in such cases for the other party to allege that the third party or company holds the property on resulting trust for the transferring spouse.

7.44 Establishing a resulting trust in a matrimonial context will be highly fact specific, but if either of the following can be proved on the facts, a rebuttable presumption will be created:

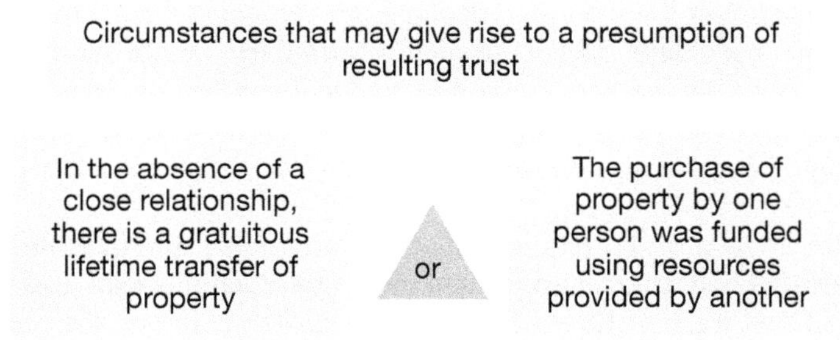

7.45 The issue of resulting trusts in this context came before the Supreme Court in *Prest v Petrodel Resources*[17]. In that case, the court concluded that the husband was the beneficial owner (by virtue of resulting trusts) of various properties situated in the UK that were legally owned by separate commercial companies. The Supreme Court emphasised that the family court should not be deterred, when the evidence supports it, from making findings that a company holds property on behalf of the controller by virtue of an implied trust relationship.

7.46 It is important to qualify the statement in the preceding paragraph, as has been emphasised elsewhere[18], by acknowledging that control or direction over a company by a spouse does not automatically give rise to a finding that he or she beneficially owns its assets. However, where the evidence supports such a finding, a resulting trust may be implied.

17 *Prest v Petrodel Resources* [2013] UKSC 34, [2013] 2 AC 415, SC considered in greater detail at paras **7.61** to **7.75** below.

18 See for example Munby J at paras 120–127 in *Ben Hashem v Ali Shayif* [2008] EWHC 2380 (Fam), [2009] 1 FLR 115.

7.47 As Lord Sumption remarked in *Prest* at para 52:

> 'Whether assets legally vested in a company are beneficially owned by its controller is a highly fact-specific issue. It is not possible to give general guidance going beyond the ordinary principles and presumptions of equity, especially those relating to gifts and resulting trusts. But I venture to suggest, however tentatively, that in the case of the matrimonial home, the facts are quite likely to justify the inference that the property was held on trust for a spouse who owned and controlled the company. In many, perhaps most cases, the occupation of the company's property as the matrimonial home of its controller will not be easily justified in the company's interest, especially if it is gratuitous. The intention will normally be that the spouse in control of the company intends to retain a degree of control over the matrimonial home which is not consistent with the company's beneficial ownership. Of course, structures can be devised which give a different impression, and some of them will be entirely genuine. But where, say, the terms of acquisition and occupation of the matrimonial home are arranged between the husband in his personal capacity and the husband in his capacity as the sole effective agent of the company (or someone else acting at his direction), judges exercising family jurisdiction are entitled to be sceptical about whether the terms of occupation are really what they are said to be, or are simply a sham to conceal the reality of the husband's beneficial ownership.'

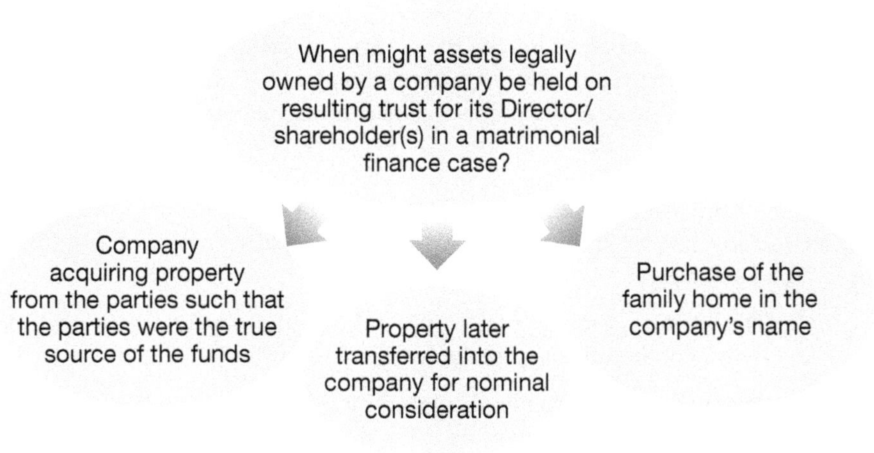

7.48 The factors shown in the graphic above were all present in *Prest*, which led to the findings of resulting trust being made in that case.

Implied trusts (2): Constructive trusts

7.49 A constructive trust arises by operation of law rather than by a deliberate act of the settlor. In *Paragon Finance v DB Thakerer & Co*[19], Millett LJ held:

> '[A] constructive trust arises by operation of law whenever the circumstances are such that it would be unconscionable for the owner of property (usually but not necessarily the legal estate) to assert his beneficial interest in the property'.

7.50 The term 'constructive trust' has been used to describe a diverse range of situations including (i) the remedy against a trustee who has made an unauthorised profit, (ii) the remedy against third parties who are found guilty of recipient liability and (iii) trusts of family homes. There is no single unifying concept beyond that they arise in certain circumstances when it would be unconscionable for the legal owner of property to deny the claimant an equitable interest. Such claims are often pleaded in parallel to claims for proprietary estoppel.

7.51 In the family courts, principles of constructive trusts arise with most frequency in applications to determine the respective beneficial shares of unmarried cohabiting couples in residential property. It is now well-established that in the absence of any express declaration of beneficial interest, the court will apply principles of 'constructive trust' to identify the beneficial ownership. The 'starting point' of a constructive trust is that equity follows the law, (ie, in the case of a property in joint names, that the beneficial interest is shared; and in the case of a property in sole name, that the beneficial interest lies only with the legal owner). That however may be displaced if positive evidence of a 'common intention' to own the property other than in accordance with the legal title is found[20].

7.52 As Lord Walker and Baroness Hale stated in their leading judgment in *Jones v Kernott*[21], at 51, if the court is required 'to construe' a trust, it will follow these broad principles:

> '(1) The starting point is that equity follows the law and they are joint tenants both in law and in equity.
>
> (2) That presumption can be displaced by showing (a) that the parties had a different common intention at the time when they acquired the home, or (b) that they later formed the common intention that their respective shares would change.
>
> (3) Their common intention is to be deduced objectively from their conduct:

19 [1999] 1 All ER 400, CA at 409.

20 See *Stack v Dowden* [2007] UKHL 17, [2007] 2 AC 432, HL; and *Jones v Kernott* [2011] UKSC 53, [2012] 1 AC 776, SC.

21 [2011] UKSC 53, [2012] 1 AC 776, SC.

'the relevant intention of each party is the intention which was reasonably understood by the other party to be manifested by that party's words and conduct notwithstanding that he did not consciously formulate that intention in his own mind or even acted with some different intention which he did not communicate to the other party': Lord Diplock in *Gissing v Gissing* [1971] AC 886, 906.

Examples of the sort of evidence which might be relevant to drawing such inferences are given in *Stack v Dowden* [2007] 2 AC 432, para 69.

(4) In those cases where it is clear either (a) that the parties did not intend joint tenancy at the outset, or (b) had changed their original intention, but it is not possible to ascertain by direct evidence or by inference what their actual intention was as to the shares in which they would own the property, 'the answer is that each is entitled to that share which the court considers fair having regard to the whole course of dealing between them in relation to the property': Chadwick LJ in *Oxley v Hiscock* [2005] Fam 211, para 69. In our judgment, 'the whole course of dealing ... in relation to the property' should be given a broad meaning, enabling a similar range of factors to be taken into account as may be relevant to ascertaining the parties' actual intentions.

(5) Each case will turn on its own facts. Financial contributions are relevant but there are many other factors which may enable the court to decide what shares were either intended (as in case (3)) or fair (as in case (4)).'

7.53 Thus in defining the terms of a constructive trust, the court will in the first instance strive to give effect to the intentions of the parties, so far as they can be ascertained. Only in default of positive evidence of intention, the court will impose what it deems to be 'fair' in all the circumstances.

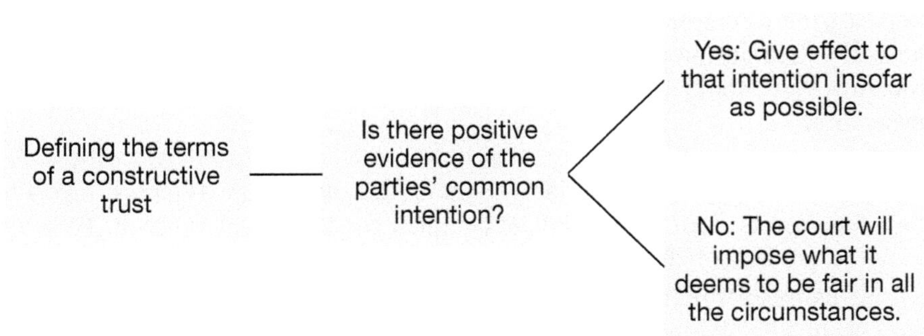

B. HIDDEN OWNERSHIP: THE SEARCH FOR REALITIES IN MATRIMONIAL CASES

The 'realities' of ownership in the context of trust and/or company assets

7.54 When determining a financial remedies application following divorce, the court must take into account all 'financial resources' that are likely to be available to either or both of the parties at present or in the foreseeable future[22]. When tasked with identifying all relevant resources, the family courts may be required to look beyond the black letter of legal title and ostensible declaration of beneficial interest to consider 'realities', which may imply equitable interests that have not been disclosed by one of the parties.

7.55 An assessment of 'realities' is, inevitably, going to be highly fact-specific. The court will not hesitate to reject the presentation of a party if the evidence does not support it, but it cannot impute ownership or access to funds belonging to third parties merely because it would be arithmetically convenient to expand the sums capable of division.

7.56 In *Thomas*[23], in which the disputed assets were not held in trust, but owned by a company owned in turn by the husband and members of his family, the Court of Appeal explained the rationale behind the court's forensic investigation into the 'realities' of beneficial ownership [Emphasis added]:

> 'The discretionary powers conferred on the court by [the MCA 1973] to redistribute the assets of spouses are almost limitless. That represents an acknowledgement by Parliament that **if justice is to be achieved between spouses at divorce the court must be equipped, in a society where the forms of wealth-holding are diverse and often sophisticated, to penetrate outer forms and get to the heart of ownership**.'

7.57 In *J v V*[24], Coleridge J firmly rejected a husband's attempts to distance himself from a complex business structure that held assets used by the husband, including the matrimonial home and a yacht. The judge issued a clear warning to parties who would seek to conceal the reality of a resource behind a mask of ownership:

> [17] '...Applicants justifiably believe that advantage is being taken to hide assets from view amongst complex corporate undergrowth. To begin the process of disclosure, as here, by, without more, denying legal and beneficial ownership of all-important assets in the case by virtue of such arrangements is, quite simply, foolish and unhelpful.'
>
> ...

22 MCA 1973, s 25(2)(a).

23 *Thomas v Thomas* [1995] 2 FLR 668, [1996] 2 FCR 544, CA.

24 *J v V (Disclosure: Offshore Corporations)* [2003] EWHC 3110 (Fam), [2004] 1 FLR 1042.

[130] 'Secondly, clients whose cases fall into this category do need to be reminded by their advisers that these sophisticated offshore structures are very familiar nowadays to the judiciary who have to try them. They neither impress, intimidate nor fool anyone. The courts have lived with them for years. If clients 'duck and weave' over months or years to avoid coming clean they cannot expect much sympathy when it comes to the question of paying the costs of the enquiry which inevitably follows.'

7.58 In *A v A*[25], Munby J identified the tension between (i) the need to establish the reality of ownership, and (ii) the court's inability to make findings other than within the strict confines of legal principle. In support of the first proposition, he cited his own judgment in the earlier case of *Re W (Ex Parte Orders)*[26] at para 18 [Emphasis added]:

'As I said myself in *Re W (Ex Parte Orders)* at 938:

'...the court will not allow itself to be bamboozled by husbands who put their property in the names of close relations in circumstances where, taking a realistic and fair view, it is apparent that the recipient is a bare trustee and where the answer to the real question – Whose property is it? – is that it remains the husband's property.'

And I went on to refer to:

'...the robustness with which the Family Division ought to deal in appropriate cases with husbands who seek to obfuscate or to hide or mask the reality behind shams, artificial devices and similar contrivances. Nor do I doubt for a moment the propriety and utility of **treating as one and the same a husband and some corporate or trust structure which it is apparent is simply the alter ego or creature of the husband.**'

7.59 He then went on to articulate the other side of this tension at para 19:

'But this does not mean ... that the court can simply ride roughshod over established principle, least of all where there are, or appear to be, third party interests involved. As I went on to comment in *Re W* at p 938:

"On the other hand, and as *Nicholas v Nicholas* [1984] FLR 285... demonstrates, the court does not – in my judgment cannot properly – adopt this robust approach where, for example, property is held by a company in which, although the husband has a minority shareholding, the minority shareholdings are what Cumming-Bruce LJ at 287G called "real interests" held by individuals who, as Dillon LJ put it at 292G, are not nominees but business associates of the husband."'

25 *A v A and St Georges Trustees* [2007] EWHC 99 (Fam), [2007] 2 FLR 467.
26 *Re W (Ex Parte Orders)* [2000] 2 FLR 927.

7.60 In *TL v ML*[27], the court accepted a husband's evidence that the family home, which was legally owned by his brother, was not a 'financial resource' available to the husband for the purposes of MCA 1973 s 25(2)(a), despite the financial support that had been given to the husband by his family over the years. Mr Nicholas Mostyn QC determined that it would be inappropriate in such circumstances to make any award to the wife which exceeded the personal assets and income of the husband. He awarded the wife c.2/3 of the husband's available resources, having determined on a *Thomas v Thomas* basis that the husband's own resources were likely to be replenished to some extent by his parents in future[28], but held that it would place improper pressure on them to do so were the court to exceed this amount.

Companies as 'alter egos': the guidance in *Prest*

7.61 In many matrimonial cases, a significant percentage of the parties' wealth will be tied up in a company founded or run by one of the parties. That party may be the sole or majority shareholder, as well as, if they are a director or hold other management roles within the company, having effective control over its functioning. In such cases, it is not uncommon for the other party to argue that a family court looking at financial 'realities' should conclude that the company is little more than the alter ego of the party with control of/a stake in it. It may be said that the company is subject to that party's unrestricted control and through it he or she holds 'company' assets which in reality are available to the husband/wife.

7.62 This argument is often colloquially referred to as 'piercing the corporate veil', it being suggested that the spouse is hiding his or her assets behind the 'veil' of corporate ownership.

7.63 Arguments of this species must be advanced with caution. The family courts have very limited powers to make orders in relation to assets that are legally and/or beneficially owned by a company. It is a fundamental principle of English law that a company is a separate persona from its shareholders. Shareholders, qua shareholders, have no interest, legal or beneficial, in the assets of a company[29]. This applies equally to a one-man company as to a large multi-national corporation[30]. The company is its own legal person and any assets it holds are owned by the *company* not its shareholders. Family judges do not enjoy a free-standing jurisdiction to raid the assets of a company in the interests of 'fairness' to spouses.

27 *TL v ML (Ancillary Relief: Claim against assets of extended family)* [2005] EWHC 2860 (Fam), [2006] 1 FLR 1263, [2006] 1 FCR 465.

28 See para 109 of the judgment.

29 *Salomon v A Salomon & Co Ltd* [1897] AC 22. See also Munby J at para 101 in *Ben Hashem v Ali Shayif* [2008] EWHC 2380 (Fam), [2009] 1 FLR 115.

30 See para 8 of the Supreme Court's judgment in *Prest* per Lord Sumption; see also Munby J at para 103 in *Ben Hashem v Ali Shayif*, above.

7.64 Further, if a court cannot make a direct order against company property, it is not permitted to achieve the same result through the back door, ie, by making an order against the spouse who controls the company requiring him or her 'to cause' the transfer of company property. Even if it had such powers, it would be unprincipled for the family court to elevate the party's financial obligations to the other party, qua spouse, above his or her duties to the company, qua director. Requiring a large distribution to be paid out of company assets to the director's spouse to settle matrimonial claims may require the director to act in opposition to his or her fiduciary duties to the company.

7.65 The complex area of dealing with company assets and the 'alter ego' doctrine, was subject to detailed consideration in *Prest v Petrodel Resources*[31].

Leading case: *Prest v Petrodel Resources*

<u>Facts and findings at first instance:</u>

- H was the sole owner of offshore oil companies ('the Petrodel Group').
- W alleged that H used the Petrodel Group to hold legal title to UK properties that were in fact beneficially owned by him. H denied this.
- H breached orders for disclosure. The companies (joined as parties) failed to file a defence or comply with orders for disclosure.
- Moylan J found H to be worth c. £37.5 million and held 'all the assets held within the companies are effectively the husband's property'[32]. Since H had the practical ability to procure the transfer of the properties, he was 'entitled' to the properties within the meaning of MCA 1973, s 24(1)(a).
- The corporate veil could be pierced and H was ordered to transfer Petrodel properties worth £17.5m.

<u>Appeals:</u>

- The Court of Appeal allowed the companies' appeal: the corporate veil could not be pierced.
- W's further appeal was allowed by the Supreme Court, which upheld the decision that the corporate veil could not be pierced but reinstated the order for different reasons.

<u>Key principles to be derived from the Supreme Court's judgments:</u>

- When it is alleged that a company is the alter ego of a party, the court must ascertain whether the 'concealment principle' or the 'evasion principle' apply[33]:

31 *Prest v Petrodel Resources* [2013] UKSC 34, [2013] 2 AC 415.

32 Moylan J's findings quoted at para 39 of the judgment of Thorpe LJ in the Court of Appeal, above.

33 Per Lord Sumption, at para 28.

- The 'concealment principle': where a party has interposed a company to conceal the identity of the 'real actors', the court can make orders against the party without piercing the corporate veil. Here, the court does not 'pierce' the veil but 'looks behind it' to see the 'reality' of ownership.
- The 'evasion principle': where a legal right against the person in control of a company exists independently of the company's involvement, but that person has interposed the company so that the separate legal personality of the company will defeat or frustrate the enforcement of the right against him or her personally, the court may disregard the corporate veil. Where this applies, the corporate veil can be 'pierced'.

– Where there is no justification for piercing the corporate veil there is no power in the MCA 1973 to authorise the transfer by one party to the marriage to the other assets that beneficially belong to another person or company. English property law is applied uniformly and has no special meaning in a family court.

7.66 In *Prest*, at para 34 Lord Sumption identified certain key principles [Emphasis added]:

> '… **the corporate veil may be pierced only to prevent the abuse of corporate legal personality**. It may be an abuse of the separate legal personality of a company to use it to evade the law or to frustrate its enforcement. It is not an abuse to cause a legal liability to be incurred by the company in the first place. It is not an abuse to rely on the fact (if it is a fact) that a liability is not the controller's because it is the company's. On the contrary, that is what incorporation is all about.'

7.67 Thus the established commercial principles about the separation of legal personality were preserved, with only a narrow aperture being permitted, restricted to cases of fraud. He went on at para 35 [Emphasis added]:

> '.. there is a limited principle of English law which applies when a person is under an existing legal obligation or liability or subject to an existing legal restriction which **he deliberately evades** or whose enforcement he **deliberately frustrates** by interposing a company under his control. The court **may then pierce the corporate veil for the purpose, and only for the purpose, of depriving the company or its controller of the advantage** that they would otherwise have obtained by the company's separate legal personality.'

7.68 The Supreme Court declined to pierce the corporate veil of the Petrodel Group as the evasion principle was not engaged. Lord Sumption held at para 36 [Emphasis added]:

'...The husband has acted improperly in many ways. In the first place, he has misapplied the assets of his companies for his own benefit, but in doing that he was neither concealing nor evading any legal obligation owed to his wife. Nor, more generally, was he concealing or evading the law relating to the distribution of assets of a marriage on its dissolution. It cannot follow that the court should disregard the legal personality of the companies with the same insouciance as he did....**Whatever the husband's reasons for organising things in that way, there is no evidence that he was seeking to avoid any obligation** which is relevant in these proceedings. The judge found that his purpose was 'wealth protection and the avoidance of tax': para 218. It follows that the p**iercing of the corporate veil cannot be justified in this case** by reference to any general principle of law.'

7.69 Moylan J had determined that MCA 1973, s 24(1)(a) conferred power on the court to order a transfer of any property found to be 'effectively owned' by the husband, such that he was able to control their disposal or transfer at will. The Supreme Court disagreed, holding that the section applied only to property in which a party held 'a proprietary right, legal or equitable.[34]'

7.70 Thus, while the court's findings that a party 'effectively owns or controls' property, will inform its assessment of the party's 'resources' for the purposes of MCA 1973, s 25(2)(a)[35], the court *must* proceed to make findings of *ownership* before it may make orders under MCA 1973, s 24[36].

7.71 In this respect the court implicitly endorsed the approach of Munby J in the earlier case of *Ben Hashem v Al Shayif*[37], where, in response to allegations by a wife that assets owned by her husband's company were in fact beneficially owned by him, or that in default the company was his 'alter ego', Munby J commented at para 82 [Emphasis added]:

'...the logical starting point, in my judgment, is to consider first the assertion that [the company holds its assets] upon constructive trusts for the benefit of the husband alone – **for if this claim is made good then none of the other claims arises** – and then in turn to consider the assertion that the children's shareholdings in the company are all subject to resulting trusts in favour of the husband. **Only if both those claims fail** does the assertion that the company is simply the husband's alter ego...and that it is therefore appropriate **to pierce or lift the corporate veil, arise for consideration**.'

7.72 The following graphic illustrates when the court may be entitled to make orders under the MCA 1973 against assets held by a company:

34 See paras 37–39, per Lord Sumption.

35 See more generally **Chapter 9** of this book on the treatment of 'resources' when there is no proprietary interest.

36 See para 40, per Lord Sumption.

37 *Ben Hashem v Ali Shayif* [2008] EWHC 2380 (Fam), [2009] 1 FLR 115.

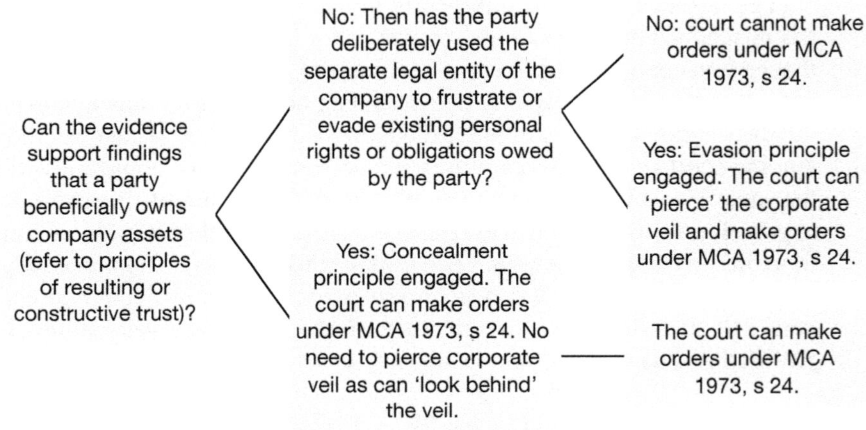

7.73 The Supreme Court in *Prest* found that the husband beneficially owned all of the properties held by the Petrodel Group. The particular circumstances in which the properties came to be vested in the companies gave rise to resulting trusts, such that the companies were merely holding the properties as bare trustees for the husband. Since the 'concealment principle' was engaged, the court could make orders under the MCA 1973, s 24(1)(a) against the husband to transfer the properties to the wife; because the court was not invading 'company' assets but merely transferring the assets beneficially owned by one spouse, to the other.

7.74 The Supreme Court was influenced by the husband's persistent non-disclosure, and gave some guidance on the proper role of inference in reaching findings where evidence was incomplete due to the non-cooperation of one of the parties. The family court, which has an inquisitorial function in financial remedy cases, is entitled to draw evidentially supportable inferences. Judges should not be slow to make findings that the beneficial ownership of company assets lies with a party to the marriage where, as here, the evidence justifies it[38].

7.75 *Prest* was followed in *M v M*[39] where assets were held in a complex web of offshore structures created by the husband. There were English properties worth £14m and Russian assets of £93m. The husband failed to engage in proceedings but the companies did offer a defence, namely that (a) they were the true owners of the relevant properties, and (b) this was part of bona fide tax planning. King J rejected this defence and found that, at all material times, the husband was the beneficial owner, with trusts having been created under constructive and resulting trust principles. She ordered the husband to transfer the English properties to the wife; and pay a further lump sum of £38m against the Russian portfolio.

38 See para 45, per Lord Sumption.
39 *M v M* [2013] EWHC 2534 (Fam), [2014] 1 FLR 439, [2015] 1 FCR 12.

C. 'SHAM' TRUSTS

What is a 'sham'?

7.76 Faced with a trust that (on the surface) appears to have been validly constituted, all formalities having been duly complied with and any property correctly vested, the court will only disregard it in circumstances where it is shown to be a 'sham'. At its heart, a document is a 'sham' if it professes to be one thing, while it is in fact something completely different[40]. In the case of a document purporting to establish a trust, the court will not readily find a sham (as to do so would potentially prejudice beneficiaries by jeopardising the very existence of the trust) but a 'sham' may be found if at the time it was created the settlor and trustee had a *joint intention* to create legal rights and obligations other than those set out in the trust documents.

7.77 The now widely accepted definition of what constitutes a 'sham' comes from the dicta of Diplock LJ in *Snook v London and West Riding Investments Ltd*[41], in which the Court of Appeal identified the key elements which must be proven in order to establish a sham transaction. On the meaning of the word his Lordship said (at 802C–F) [Emphasis added]:

> '…it means **acts done or documents executed by** the parties to the "sham" **which are intended by them** to give to third parties or to the court **the appearance** of creating between the parties legal rights and obligations **different from the actual rights and obligations (if any) which the parties intend to create**. But one thing, I think, is clear … that for acts or documents to be a "sham", with whatever legal consequences follow from this, all the parties thereto **must have a common intention that the acts or documents are not to create the legal rights and obligations which they give the appearance of creating.** No unexpressed intentions of a "shammer" affect the rights of a party whom he deceived.'

7.78 Crucially, it is not the 'trust' that is said to be a sham, but the document(s) purporting to create it. In essence, a trust deed is a 'sham' if:

The settlor lacked the intention to create a valid trust in the terms expressed in the trust deed; and,	+	At the time of the purported inception of the trust, the trustee (a) knew of and (b) cooperated or at the very least acquiesced in the creation of this falsehood.

7.79 The word 'sham' is not a term of general abuse. It is a construct with a very specific legal meaning, comprising of elements that must (each) be

40 Adopting (in paraphrase) the words of Lord Wilberforce in *WT Ramsey Ltd v Inland Revenue Commissioners, Eilbeck (Inspector or Taxes) and Rawling* [1982] AC 300 at 323.

41 *Snook v London and West Riding Investments Ltd* [1967] 2 QB 786, [1967] 2 WLR 1020, [1967] 1 All ER 518. This was cited with approval by the House of Lords in *WT Ramsey*, above, per Lord Fraser at 337.

proven in order to establish the whole. Where sham is alleged, pleadings must be focused and principled. Analysis must also be given to the legal and practical consequences of *succeeding* in the argument. It may be that a party endeavouring to show that certain trust assets are available by obtaining a finding of 'sham' only succeeds in pushing those same assets beyond reach[42]. Further, careful thought must be given to whether 'sham' is consistent with other arguments being advanced by a party to matrimonial proceedings[43].

7.80 While a finding of sham will invalidate the document found to be the 'sham', the consequences as to where, with whom and how the legal and beneficial titles are arranged following that finding will depend wholly on the facts. It may be that a trust of sorts was created (and survives), but of a different nature from that indicated by the trust deed. For example, consider these factual scenarios:

Illustrations: examples of 'sham' in practice

Example A: The settlor/purported trustee never lost beneficial ownership ⇒ beneficial ownership remains with settlor

Anna and Michael own their house in joint names. On their 40th wedding anniversary they execute a deed of trust in respect of the property, naming their children as 100% beneficiaries. They retain the legal title but state on the face of the deed that they shall hold the property on trust for the children in equal shares. In fact they have no intention of divesting themselves of beneficial ownership; they intend to continue to live in the property and have no intention to pay rent or other fees as a consequence of their occupation. Their sole objective in executing the deed of trust is to avoid inheritance tax being paid by their estates in the event of their death.

In this case, the deed of trust may be found to be a sham since it did not create the legal relationships and interests stated on its face. Anna and Michael did not intend to divest themselves of their beneficial interest in the property. They remain both the legal and beneficial owners.

Example B: Legal ownership did not pass to trustee, a 'transactional' sham ⇒ the trust was never created; settlor retains legal and beneficial title

Cathy is a Director and 100% shareholder of a recruitment company she founded in 2003. She is married to Stephen. In 2013 she executed a deed of trust stating that the shares were to be held by her sister, Margaret, in a discretionary trust for a class of beneficiaries made up of members of Cathy's family, including (at Margaret's discretion) Cathy, Stephen, their children, and others that Margaret may add or remove from time to time. The

42 For one example, the wife in *A v A & St George Trustees Ltd* [2007] EWHC 99 (Fam), [2007] 2 FLR 467 alleged that trusts settled by her husband's father and brother were a sham. The effect of her argument (had it succeeded) that the trust was a sham would have been that the trust property still belonged legally and beneficially to the settlors (the husband's father's estate, and his brother) and *not* to her husband.

43 See para **9.45** in **Chapter 9** for guidance on ensuring clarity of attack, particularly when alternative arguments may be available drawing upon the line of authorities from *Thomas*.

shares were never transferred to Margaret, and remained in Cathy's name. Neither Margaret nor Cathy took any steps to vest the property in Cathy, both intending that Cathy would remain in control of the company and its shares, and continue to receive 100% of the dividend income.

When Cathy and Stephen divorce in 2018, Stephen argues, successfully, that the trust is a 'sham', since the trust property never vested in the trustee, Margaret, and Cathy never intended for Margaret to take control of the shares. Cathy never ceased to be both legal and beneficial owner.

Example C: Legal title passed but not beneficial ownership ⇒ a trust exists but a 'bare trust' benefitting the settlor, regardless of the terms of the trust deed

Daniel and Romi were married in 1992. Their home is a house bought in Daniel's sole name in 1998. In 2000 Daniel transferred the legal title of the property to his brother, Mark, and executed a deed providing for Mark to hold the property on trust for himself (Mark), his wife, Alison, and their child Sophie. At that time Mark and Alison, who are US citizens, were emigrating to UK and it assisted their visa application to hold assets in this country. Daniel and Romi continued to live in the property and they did not intend to pay (nor did they) any occupation rent to Mark and Alison.

The deed of trust may be found to be a sham since neither the settlor (Daniel) nor the trustee (Mark) intended the beneficial ownership to pass to the beneficiaries named in the trust deed. Nothing invalidates the transfer of legal title to Mark, so the property remains vested in him, subject to a resulting trust in favour of Daniel. Mark holds the property on bare trust for Daniel, and at any time Daniel could bring the trust to an end and insist upon the transfer of legal title back to him (Daniel).

Key principles: *Snook* and *Hitch v Stone*

7.81 A summary of the key principles applying to sham transactions was set out by Arden LJ in *Hitch v Stone*[44] at paras 62–69 [Emphasis added]:

> 'An inquiry as to whether an act or document is a sham requires **careful analysis of the facts** and the following points emerge from the authorities.
>
> First, in the case of a document, the court is **not restricted to examining the four corners of the document**. It may examine external evidence. This will include the parties' explanations and circumstantial evidence, such as evidence of the **subsequent conduct** of the parties.
>
> Second, ...**the test of intention is subjective**. The parties must have intended to create different rights and obligations from those appearing from (say) the relevant document, and in addition they must have intended to give a false impression of those rights and obligations to third parties.

44 *Hitch v Stone* [2001] EWCA Civ 63, [2001] STC 214, CA.

Third, the fact that the act or document is uncommercial, or even artificial, does not mean that it is a sham. A **distinction is to be drawn between the situation where parties make an agreement which is unfavourable** to one of them, or artificial, and a situation where they **intend some other arrangement to bind them**. In the former situation, they intend the agreement to take effect according to its tenor. In the latter situation, the agreement is not to bind their relationship.

Fourth, the fact that parties **subsequently depart** from an agreement does not necessarily mean that they never intended the agreement to be effective and binding. The proper conclusion to draw may be that they **agreed to vary** their agreement and that they have become bound by the agreement as varied...

Fifth, the intention must be a **common intention**: see *Snook's* case, above.'

7.82 A further principle to be added to this list relates to the *timing* of the relevant intention of the settlor and trustee. In *A v A*[45], Munby J held that the trustee and settlor had to form the requisite intention *at the time the trust was being created,* for it to be held a sham. A trust that was not a sham at its genesis could not become a sham later, even if the trustee and settlor subsequently formed the requisite intention to deceive. Once the trust is established, actions taken against the trust documents are a breach of trust, and subject to the remedies against the trustee for acting in opposition to his duties; they do not invalidate the trust itself. Munby J stated [Emphasis added]:

'... a trust which is not initially a sham cannot subsequently become a sham. ... Once a trust has been properly constituted ... the property cannot lose its character as trust property save in accordance with the terms of the trust itself.'

'A trustee who has bona fide accepted office as such cannot divest himself of his fiduciary obligations by his own improper acts. If, therefore, a trustee who has entered into his responsibilities, and without having any intention of being a party to a sham, subsequently purports, perhaps in agreement with the settlor, to treat the trust as a sham, **the effect is not to create a sham where previously there was a valid trust**. The only effect, **even if the agreement is actually carried into execution**, is to expose the trustee to a claim for breach of trust, and it may well be, to expose the settlor to a claim for knowing assistance in that breach of trust. Nor can it make any difference, **where the trust has already been properly constituted**, that a trustee may have entered into office – may indeed have been appointed a trustee in place of an honest trustee – **for the very purpose and with the intention of treating the trust for the future as a sham**. If, having been appointed trustee, he has the trust property under his control, he cannot be heard to dispute either the fact that it is trust property or the existence of his own fiduciary duty.'

45 *A v A and St Georges Trustees* [2007] EWHC 99 (Fam), [2007] 2 FLR 467, paras 42–43.

7.83 The principles set out by Munby J may be summarised as follows:

Can a trust that was previously not a sham subsequently become a sham? —— **NO**. See Munby J at [42]–[43] in *A v A*, above

BUT:

Can a trust that started as a sham subsequently cease to be a sham? —— **YES**. See Munby J at [49], below

7.84 While these two statements may initially seem to be converse, the second point is a logical extension of the first in practice. At para 49 of *A v A*, Munby J explained:

> 'The corollary of all this can be stated very simply. Whatever the settlor or anyone else may have intended, and whatever may have happened since it was first created, a trust will not be a sham – in my judgment cannot as a matter of law be a sham – if *either*:
>
> (i) the original trustee(s), *or*
>
> (ii) the current trustee(s)
>
> were not, because they lacked the relevant knowledge and intention, party to the sham at the time of their appointment, in the first case, the trust will never have been a sham. In the second case, the trust, even if it was previously a sham, will have become a genuine – valid and enforceable – trust as from the date of the appointment of the current trustee(s).'

7.85 Thus a trust will cease to be a sham if a new trustee is appointed without the requisite knowledge or intention to establish the sham.

Snapshot: establishing a 'sham':

- For a trust to be a sham both the settlor and the trustee must have intended that the true position should be otherwise than as set out in the trust deed which they both executed[46].
- A party who is reckless as to the effect of the transaction to which he is a party is to be taken as having the necessary intention for a sham[47].

46 *Re the Esteem Settlement (aka Abacus (C.I.)) Ltd Grupo Torras SA and Culmer v Al-Sabah* [2004] WTLR 1, [2003] JLR 92 at para 53; *Shalson v Russo* [2003] WTLR 1165 (Ch), [2005] Ch 281, [2005] 2 WLR 1213 at para 38; *A v A and St Georges Trustees* [2007] EWHC 99 (Fam), [2007] 2 FLR 467 at para 40.

47 See *Re the Esteem Settlement*, above at paras 58–59; *Minwalla v Minwalla* [2004] EWHC 2823 (Fam), [2005] 1 FLR 771, [2006] WTLR 311; *A v A and St Georges Trustees*, above at para 52.

But 'going along with' the settlor is not enough if he or she did not have sufficient knowledge or involvement to establish legal recklessness[48].

- The time for ascertaining the intention of the settlor and trustees is at the time of the creation of the settlement, or, if assets are subsequently added, at the later time when the assets were added[49].
- In order to establish that a trust is a sham it is not enough to allege in general terms that the settlor has de facto control of the trust assets: what needs to be done is to focus in each case on a particular asset and ask if it has become a trust asset[50].
- It is common for trustees to accede to requests of a settlor without abdicating their fiduciary duties and responsibilities and so it is not surprising or worthy of criticism when trustees act in that way[51].
- Whether or not a trustee has a reckless intention to create a sham trust is a matter of fact. The burden of proof lies on the person alleging sham.

Sham in a matrimonial finance case

7.86 The principles in *Snook v London and West Riding Investments Ltd* and *Hitch v Stone* have been applied in subsequent family cases, such as *Minwalla*, *A v A*, and *Re M & L Trusts*[52].

7.87 The first observation to be made is that the family courts have not developed an independent subset of jurisprudence on the establishment of sham, and consequently all of the (non-family) authorities cited above are of direct application to any financial case following divorce or dissolution. Munby J was at pains to emphasise this point in *A v A*[53] [Emphasis added]:

> 'In this sense, and to this limited extent, the typical case in the Family Division my differ from the typical case in (say) the Chancery Division. But what is important to appreciate (and too often, I fear, is not appreciated at least in this division) is that the relevant legal principles which have to be applied are precisely the same in this division as in the other two divisions. There is not one law of "sham" in the Chancery Division and another law of "sham" in the Family Division. There is **only one law of "sham" to be applied equally in all three Divisions** of the High Court, just as there is

48 See *Re the Esteem Settlement*, above, at 24C–25C.

49 *A v A and St Georges Trustees*, above at para 42.

50 See *Shalton v Russo*, above at 1238F–H.

51 See *Re the Esteem Settlement*, above at 61C–H.

52 *Minwalla v Minwalla* [2004] EWHC 2823 (Fam), [2005] 1 FLR 771, [2006] WTLR 311; *A v A and St Georges Trustees* [2007] EWHC 99 (Fam), [2007] 2 FLR 467 at para 21; *Re M & L Trusts (aka Nearco Trust Co (Jersey) v AM* [2003] WTLR 491.

53 This point mirrors what was said in the quotation cited at para **7.27**, where the same point was emphatically made by Munby J in relation to the identification of beneficial ownership.

but one set of principles, again equally applicable in all three divisions, determining whether or not it is appropriate to "pierce the corporate veil".'

7.88 Insofar as there is a distinctive feature of cases involving 'sham' in a family court (as opposed to other divisions) it is chiefly the co-existence of other principles and remedies, unique to matrimonial cases, that affect how cases must be pleaded and advanced.

7.89 For this reason, it is always worth identifying all available remedies at the earliest opportunity. For example, where a spouse has transferred assets to a third party, purportedly to be held on trust, one legitimate avenue of attack may be to allege that the trust is a 'sham', but it may also be available (and potentially much more straightforward) for the other party to avail him or herself of the court's powers under MCA 1973, s 37 to set aside the transaction. In order to do so, the applicant must be able to demonstrate that the transferor intended to frustrate the applicant's claim, or to put beyond the court's powers, assets that until then beneficially belonged to the transferor. Depending on the case, it may be more or less straightforward to obtain such findings than to prove a sham. Ultimately it will be a subject of litigation advice how best to present the claimant's case if both routes are evidentially and procedurally available.

7.90 Equally, a case that a trust deed is a 'sham' may run directly contrary to another available argument that trust assets are a resource available to a party under the principles derived from *Thomas v Thomas*[54]. This was the potentially hazardous position adopted by the wife in *A v A*. Again, careful consideration must be given to the other remedies and arguments available before the course is taken.

7.91 A final word of warning to practitioners: since the burden of proving a 'sham' falls to the person alleging it[55] (with possible costs ramifications), particular care ought to be taken to restrict the use of the allegation to circumstances in which reasonable confidence is held that it can be proven. Once asserted, it may give rise to a full factual investigation. A failure to prove an allegation of such gravity is likely to result in an adverse order for costs.

54 [1996] 2 FCR 544, [1995] 2 FLR 668, CA.

55 This is a well-established principle, but confirmed again by Munby J in *A v A and St Georges Trustees*, above at para 80.

CHAPTER 8

Nuptial Settlements

Content at a Glance:

A. INTRODUCTION

8.1 This chapter provides an overview of the court's power to vary an ante-nuptial or post-nuptial settlement.

8.2 The jurisdiction to vary such settlements has existed since the Matrimonial Causes Act 1859. It has been used relatively rarely in reported cases. However, it has come increasingly to the fore in recent years, given the greater incidence of, and focus upon, the holding of assets in corporate and trust structures and other more exotic mechanisms.

8.3 Whilst the power was originally bestowed on the courts to allow them to vary true 'marriage settlements', since 1973 these settlements rarely if ever exist and the width of the section has been adapted to take in an ever-greater range of more common asset-holding schemes.

8.4 The current iteration is in s 24(1) of the Matrimonial Causes Act 1973 ('MCA 1973') which provides:

> *24. Property adjustment orders in connection with divorce proceedings, etc.*
>
> (1) On granting a decree of divorce, a decree of nullity of marriage or a decree of judicial separation or at any time thereafter (whether, in the case of a decree of divorce or of nullity of marriage, before or after the decree is made absolute), the court may make any one or more of the following orders, that is to say— …
>
> (c) an order varying for the benefit of the parties to the marriage and of the children of the family or either or any of them any ante-nuptial or post-nuptial settlement (including such a settlement made by will or codicil) made on the parties to the marriage, other than one in the form of a pension arrangement (within the meaning of section 25D below).

8.5 The potential importance of the provision cannot be overstated. The legislation allows the court to access funds that are far greater than those disclosed as 'normal' matrimonial assets.

8.6 In cases where either party to a marriage is a beneficiary of a family trust or assets are held for one or more of their benefit in some other way, the following questions are to be asked:

- Is there a settlement within the (wide) meaning of the section?
- Is the settlement 'nuptial' in character?
- What are the assets of the settlement?
- Should the court vary the settlement in favour of a party to the marriage?

8.7 The answer to the first two questions has to be 'yes' before unlocking the next two questions:

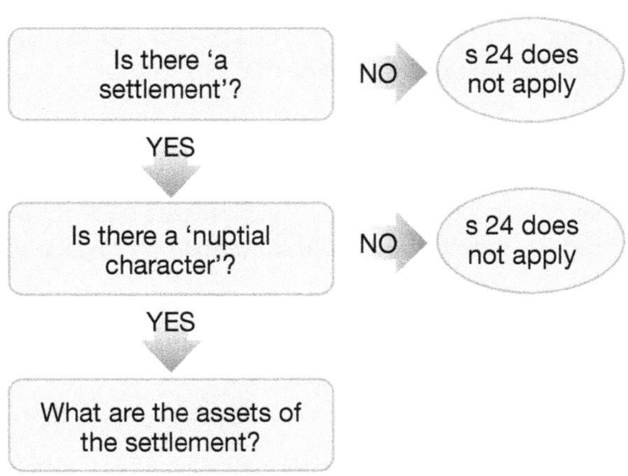

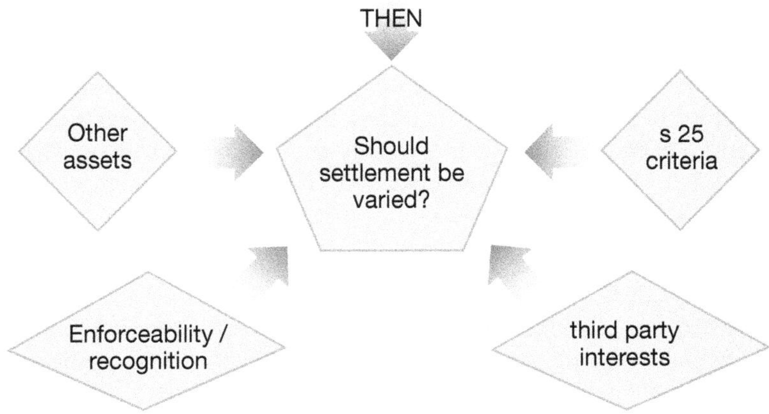

8.8 There is no statutory definition of 'nuptial settlement' nor of its two constituent elements. Further, the distinction within the legislation between 'ante-' and 'post-' nuptial settlements is now largely unnecessary[1]. The same two elements apply to both, though they are more easily identified in post-nuptial settlements.

8.9 There is an element of overlap in the way in which the authorities have addressed these issues, but the approach to defining a 'settlement' is the clearer and less controversial, and each will be considered therefore separately.

B. WHAT IS THE MEANING OF SETTLEMENT?

8.10 Although 'settlement' is used in current and historical matrimonial legislation, it is not used as a legal term of art as it would be in the Chancery Division.

8.11 It is instead given a practical definition. In this context, a settlement can be considered to be simply the act of giving outright or creating some ancillary benefit between individuals. Therefore, there is no requirement that there be a fixed trust of a classic nature. As was held in *Princep v Princep*[2] (citing with approval Wallington J in *Gunner*[3]):

> 'a transaction may be a settlement within the meaning of [the then equivalent of s.24(1)(c)][4], although it falls far short of being a settlement such as Chancery judges and practitioners in the Chancery Courts would require before they could hold that there was a settlement.'

1 Per Lord Nicholls in *Brooks v Brooks* described these as '*archaic expressions*' and went on to say '*These expressions are apt to embrace all settlements in respect of the particular marriage whether made before or after the marriage.*'
2 [1929] P 225.
3 [1949] P 77.
4 Supreme Court of Judicature (Consolidation) Act 1925, s 192.

8.12 This therefore will draw in many instruments and arrangements that would not, at first blush, obviously be considered 'settlements'.

8.13 When considering whether something is a settlement the core consideration to have in mind is that first expressed in *Blood v Blood*[5]:

> 'Those words are extremely wide, and I am anxious that they should not, by any construction the Court may put upon them, be narrowed in any way. To narrow them would be undesirable for this reason: the various circumstances which come before the Court, and for which this section is brought into operation, are so diverse that it is to my mind extremely important that, so far as possible, the Court should have power to deal with all the cases that come before it, and, in dealing with them, to meet the justice of the case. I, therefore, do not desire to see any narrow interpretation placed upon the words of the section.'

8.14 Accordingly, a very wide range of instruments and arrangements have across case law, been caught. What follows is not an exhaustive list of instances where a settlement has been found, but illustrations of the width of 'settlement'.

Case	Reference	Type of arrangement
Worsley v Worsley	(1869) L.R. 1 P. & D. 648	A Deed of Separation
Dormer (otherwise Ward) v Ward	[1901] P 20	A husband's covenant to pay his wife £200pa during their joint lives
Bosworthick v Bosworthick	[1927] P 64	A bond yielding an annuity
Brown v Brown	[1959] P 86	Rental/lease money from a property owned in joint tenancy
Cook v Cook	[1962] P 181	A resulting trust after contributions to purchase price of FMH
Brooks v Brooks	[1996] AC 375	A pension
Charalambous v Charalambous	[2004] EWCA Civ 1030	A significant trust power
N v N and F Trust	[2006] 1 FLR 856	An arrangement where a company owned by a trust, of which H was a beneficiary, purchased a property to be the matrimonial home of H and his intended and was then used by them as such, despite the fact that (after about three years) H and W were granted an assured short-hold tenancy
D v D and I Settlement	[2011] 2 FLR 29	A trust which had no beneficiaries (as the trust held assets which prior to being settled had been beneficially owned by the husband)

5 [1902] P 78 per Gorrell Barnes J at 82.

Case	Reference	Type of arrangement
BJ v MJ	[2012] 1 FLR 667	A trust despite the parties being specifically excluded as beneficiaries of it (it was. linked to another trust (which was unquestionably a post- nuptial settlement)

8.15 In many of the above cases, a 'settlement' was found due to the real nature of the arrangements in practice. Thus, for example, a court will look behind appearances to discern the true nature, in reality, of the arrangement and whether it confers, or is capable of conferring benefit on a party to the marriage. A prime example of this is *D v D and I Settlement*[6] in which Baron J made an overarching finding that:

> '…as a matter of reality, I am clear that this trust has always operated for the benefit of the husband and through him the wife. He is the de facto settlor, there are no beneficiaries and the letters of wishes are only self-serving documents which were, prima facie, brought into being so as to convince this court that the husband had no interest in the I Trust. I am also clear that the wife has directly benefited from trust assets because she was able to live in the farmhouse for a period and during the marriage she received housekeeping and benefits which derived from farm income.'

8.16 What will not qualify, however connected to a marriage, is a disposition or arrangement which does not make 'continuing provision'. The following are examples of types of provision which have been held not to amount to settlements:

(1) An outright gift to a mistress in the hope that she will marry the donor once he is divorced from his current wife, and even (she having done so) the outright appointment to her by trustees of a settlement of even more money – *Hindley*[7].

(2) A deed, even though specifically entitled 'Settlement on Marriage', insofar as it provided for W to make (which she had done) an absolute gift to H of £15,000 in securities – *Prescott v Fellowes*[8].

8.17 Given the above, there is a live issue as to whether a company, simpliciter, can amount to a 'settlement'. Most recently Mostyn J in *DR v GR and Others*[9] has considered that it can:

> 'Indeed it is clear to me that a family company which under an arrangement makes some form of continuing provision for both or either of the parties to a marriage is capable of itself of amounting to a variable nuptial settlement whether or not the company is owned by a trust of which the spouses are formal beneficiaries.'

6 [2011] 2 FLR 29.
7 [1957] 1 WLR 898.
8 [1958] P 260.
9 [2013] 2 FLR 1534 at para 16.

8.18 It must however be borne in mind that this view is considered to be somewhat controversial. It certainly enlarges the scope of application of s 24(1)(c) wider than any prior authority had established. It is a first instance decision, not tested on appeal and was decided before the Supreme Court decision in *Prest v Petrodel Resources Limited*[10], which emphasised the long-established principle that a company is a separate legal personality. The point was raised, but not argued, in the Supreme Court and in that decision Lord Sumption stated at para 53 that:

> 'The wife sought special leave to argue that the companies constituted a nuptial settlement within the meaning of section 24(1)(c) of the Act. The court ruled in the course of the hearing that leave would be refused. The point was not argued below and does not appear to be seriously arguable here.'

8.19 This issue therefore remains open, and debatable, and should necessarily be treated with a degree of caution unless and until it is considered in greater detail by other cases.

8.20 As ever, each case is fact specific. Little by way of commentary can improve on the words of Lord Nicholls in the leading modern case of *Brooks v Brooks*[11]:

> '...The section is concerned with a settlement "made on the parties to the marriage". So, broadly stated, the disposition must be one which makes some form of continuing provision for both or either of the parties to a marriage with or without provision for their children.[12]'

> '....Beyond this the authorities have consistently given a wide meaning to settlement in this context and they have spelt out no precise limitations. This seems right because this approach accords with the purpose of the statutory provision. Financial provision that is appropriate so long as the parties are married will often cease to be appropriate when the marriage ends. In order to promote the best interests of the parties and their children in a fundamentally changed situation, it is desirable that the court should have power to alter the terms of the settlement. The purpose of the section is to give the court this power. This object does not dictate that settlement should be given a narrow meaning. On the contrary the purpose of the section would be impeded, rather than advanced by confining its scope[13].'

10 [2013] UKSC 24, [2013] 2 AC 415, SC.
11 [1996] AC 375, HL.
12 Above at 391.
13 Above at 392.

C. THE 'NUPTIAL' ELEMENT

8.21 If a particular arrangement is a settlement, it needs also to be 'nuptial' in character for s 24(1)(c) relief to be available.

8.22 Just as there is no definition of 'settlement' in statute, there is no statutory explanation of what 'nuptial' means. Neither is there a single, all encompassing definition provided by case law.

8.23 This is certainly the most fact sensitive aspect of the section, and arguably one of the last truly untested areas of financial remedies.

8.24 Much of the case law on the topic is ancient, and/or first instance and/or not wholly clear in its conclusions. There is no real consistency of approach, and the court tends to take a 'one knows it when one sees it' approach.

8.25 The timing of the creation of a settlement is not necessarily the test. Whilst it may be more difficult to identify a nuptial character where the settlement was made before the marriage when there was no 'husband' or 'wife', the statute itself envisages that some settlements may be nuptial. Equally, it cannot be the case that every settlement made after a marriage is automatically 'nuptial'. Rather the court will look at a constellation of factors.

8.26 In *Melvill v Melvill*[14] Greer LJ said:

> 'As I understand [counsel's] argument it was this, that any settlement is a post-nuptial settlement, if it is a settlement during marriage by one of the parties, which gives some interest to either of the spouses or their offspring. That is a proposition which appeals to me as a fair and reasonable representation of what the section means.'

8.27 This is likely to be too wide a definition to withstand scrutiny. That can be seen from:

(1) Generally from *Brooks*, wherein Lord Nicholls held (in the context of a pension scheme) that even a settlement set up after a marriage that is used exclusively for the benefit of a party to the marriage will not without more be sufficiently 'nuptial', notwithstanding that those assets will be used for the benefit of both parties to the marriage:

> 'It would be difficult to conclude that a scheme under which benefits were payable exclusively to the scheme member was a marriage settlement, even though in a broad sense the benefits in such a case could be described as family assets. **Something more is needed**.' (at 394C) [Emphasis added]

14 [1930] P 159, CA.

(2) Specifically, in relation to the offspring of the spouses from *Dharamshi v Dharamshi*[15] wherein Thorpe LJ held a settlement made solely to benefit the children/grandchildren of a marriage is not a nuptial settlement. There must be additional circumstances of the settlement which connect it to the husband or wife themselves. If the husband and/or wife are simply trustees, this will unlikely be sufficient.

8.28 What is clear is that the basic notion is that the settlement must be capable of providing some form of continuing provision to one or both spouse. This is not (per *Brooks)* of itself enough.

8.29 Identifying in each case 'the something more' referred to in *Brooks* is fact specific. In *Brooks* itself, it was only the fact that under the particular terms of the pension scheme the husband had power under the trust to direct that assets should be payable to the wife and the trustee had power to apply assets for the wife's benefit after the husband's death that made it a nuptial settlement[16].

8.30 In *Prinsep v Prinsep*[17], Hill J identified some factors of import (at 232) when putting the question of nuptiality thus:

> 'Is it upon the husband **in the character of husband or in the wife in the character of wife**, or upon both in the character of husband and wife? If it is, it is a settlement on the parties within the meaning of the section... **it should provide for the financial benefit** of one or other or both of the spouses **as spouses** and **with reference to their married state.**' [Emphasis added]

8.31 Similarly so, *Joss v Joss*[18] in which it was held that a settlement made 'because of marriage' actually means a settlement whereby the settlor takes *a particular* marriage into account when settling property. As Henn Collins J said: [Emphasis added]

> 'what is really meant [by 'because of' a marriage']...is that **the particular marriage must be a fact of which a settlor takes account in framing the settlement.** If the particular marriage is recited or referred to, it is patently a factor. Hence, a settlement made before marriage, but not in relation to or contemplation of the particular marriage, is not within the section, but a settlement is within it if from its recitals or substance it is apparent that

15 [2001] 1 FLR 736, CA.

16 See *Brooks at* 394B–C, referring back to the rules dealt with at 393E–F. Caution must be had in relying only on the quotation in *Brooks* at 391 (set out at in the first part of the quote at para **8.20** above). Arguably that passage is not the ratio. Per Thorpe LJ in *C v C* (see below) at paras 48-49 *'That [passage in Brooks] is, of course, an unimpeachable generalisation that was perfectly sufficient for the needs of the case then before the House. It is, in my judgment, unrealistic to suggest that it is conclusive of a point that was not before the House and one that is not covered by any existing authority'*.

17 [1929] P 225.

18 [1943] P 18.

it is related to a particular marriage. Similarly, the case of a settlement made after marriage. If the marriage is recited or expressly referred to it is patently a factor, but if it is not recited or referred to it may still be a factor, and, since the marriage is an existing fact which the settlor must have had in mind, the absence of recital makes little difference. This, I think, is what Greer LJ [in *Melvill v Melvill* [1930] P 159] meant by the passage in his judgment in which he drew the distinction between a pre-nuptial and a post-nuptial settlement.' [at 20]

'It is the substance and not the form which must be regarded, and to construe the settlement I must put myself in the position of the settlor, and take as, in effect, recited the relevant facts, including his then existing marriage and the existing issue of that marriage...Although not recited they must, in my judgment, be taken into account in determining the effect of the settlement...' [at 20–21]

8.32 Further support for the focus on whether the settlement made provision on a party in their capacity as a spouse in a particular marriage, can be taken from *Loraine v Loraine & Murphy*[19]. There it was held that the power to vary a nuptial settlement:

'... is a power enabling the Court in terms to vary and alter settlements and settlements only, made either before or after the marriage of the husband and wife whose marriage is in question.'

In that specific case, the wife's father's will trust, under which the wife was entitled for her separate use to the income of a fund (subject to a life interest in favour of her mother) was held by the Court of Appeal not to be nuptial (per Cozens-Hardy MR at 227). It simply did not relate to the particular marriage in question or the wife as wife. Rather it related to the wife's status as daughter of the settlor.

8.33 It is important for practitioners to hold in mind that more modern case law than *Prinsep, Joss* or *Lorraine* has posited a much lower bar for finding nuptiality. In *DR v GR & Ors (Financial Remedy: Variation of Overseas Trust)*[20] Mostyn J considered that the mere flow of benefit to a spouse during a marriage was sufficient, without any greater requirement for specificity to the particular marriage in the initial settlement being necessary.

8.34 The court, in determining whether the necessary nuptial element is present, is not confined to the four corners of any governing document or rules of the settlement but can (and will) look at the surrounding circumstances of why and how the arrangement constituting the settlement came about – per *Brooks* (at 393–394):

19 [1912] P 222, 228.
20 [2013] 2 FLR 1534.

> 'In considering the purpose of the husband when entering into the scheme, the scheme must be looked at in the round and in the context of the circumstances then subsisting. Viewed in this light, the husband is to be taken to have entered into this scheme with the intention of providing for the retirement of himself and his wife by the highly tax efficient means afforded by this scheme.'

8.35 The range of factors in the constellation to be considered cannot exhaustively be stated. There are as many potential points (either way) as there are factual scenarios that could occur in a party's financial life. However, some key matters to be considered can be set out thus:

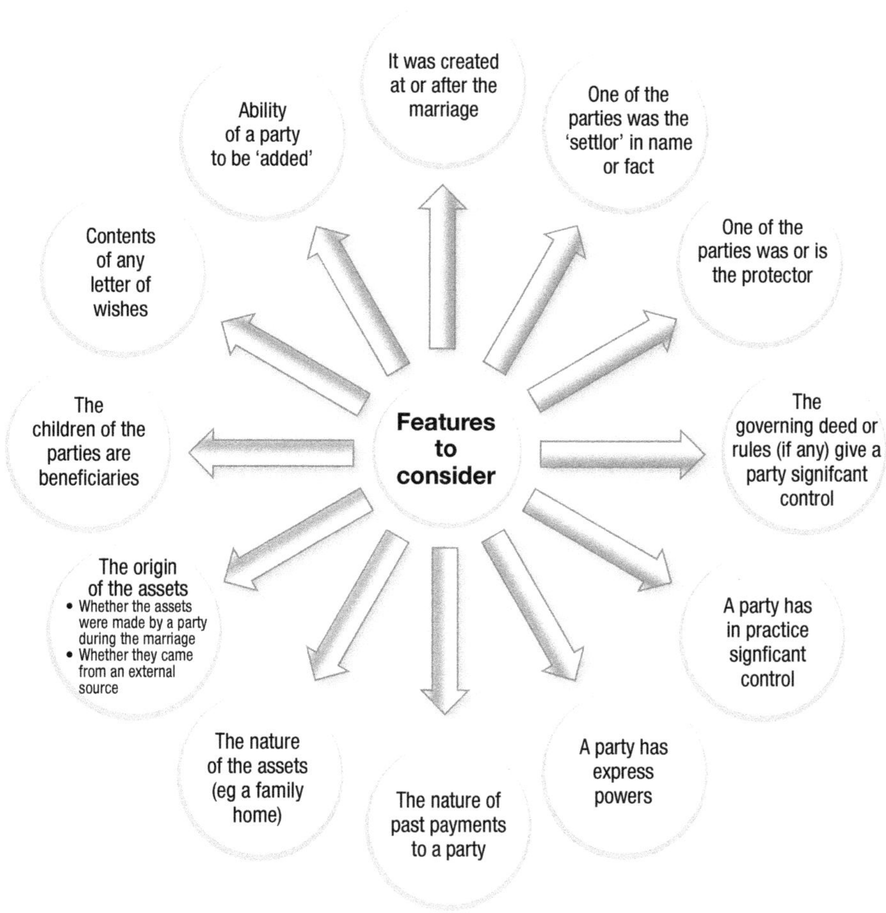

8.36 The presence or absence of any one or more of the above features is not of itself determinative of the issue.

8.37 The case of *C v C (Variation of Post-Nuptial Settlement)*[21], provides a good example of the range of issues which practitioners may need to consider. It

21 [2004] 2 FLR 1.

was heard at first instance by Wilson J and then by the Court of Appeal (reported as *C v C (Ancillary Relief: Nuptial Settlement)*[22] and concerned a formal trust of which the parties had been beneficiaries, but from which they were both subsequently excluded. An issue arose as to whether the settlement had been 'denuptialised' (ie deprived of its nuptial features so as to render it at the time of the hearing not susceptible to variation).

8.38 Wilson J considered the following features relevant[23]:

- Under the deed of settlement, the parties remained its joint protector and had to remain so during their joint lives.
- Under that deed the husband, acting alone, continued to have power to replace the trustees (and indeed had exercised it since his exclusion).
- At any stage the trustees could, with the consent of the protector, add the husband or the wife back into the class of beneficiaries.
- The trustees had power to lend money to the husband or the wife, even without interest, independent of his or her status as a beneficiary (and had done so significantly historically).
- The trustees had power to invest in companies or lend money thereto for the indirect benefit of the husband or wife, also independent of his or her status as a beneficiary (and had done so to a company in order that the husband could operate a business through it).
- There was no evidence that the power to make a payment to or for a beneficiary had ever been exercised.
- The identity of those in the class of beneficiaries from time to time did not appear to have been relevant to the operation of the trust.

8.39 The Court of Appeal agreed and identified other factors (at para 45):

- The children remained in the beneficial class.
- The removal of the husband and wife was apparently motivated by the desire to preserve the assets against claims that might be brought by the spouses' creditors.
- Any decision of the trustees to distribute or accumulate required the consent of the protector (the husband and wife remained joint protector).

8.40 The Court of Appeal thus upheld Wilson J on whether the settlement had ceased to be nuptial by the removal of the parties as beneficiaries. The issue

22 [2005] Fam 250. The cases are also reported under the names of *Charalambous v Charalambous*.
23 At paras 26-27.

for both courts was one of substance, not mere form. The status or not of the parties to the marriage as actual beneficiaries was *a* factor, but not *the* factor. This highlights to the practitioner the importance of:

- Careful examination of the precise terms of and powers within the governing deeds, rules or terms of the settlement in question; and
- Ascertaining the historic factual basis upon which the settlement has operated and the role it played (or plays) in the reality of the parties' financial lives.

Both these issues are important ones that can, and should, in the appropriate case be explored with a searching questionnaire. The latter issue will in many cases necessitate questions going to what many tribunals might otherwise consider to be ancient history and inclined to disallow. It is for this reason that a more detailed than customary statement of issues and case summary may be required to set the appropriate context.

D. CAN A NUPTIAL SETTLEMENT SUBSEQUENTLY LOSE ITS NON-NUPTIAL CHARACTER?

8.41 Wilson J in *C v C* had held[24] (in addition to the above) that *even if* the settlement *had* (which it had not) its nuptial element removed, the fact that it was *once* nuptial meant that for all time thereafter it was variable under s 24(1)(c). The Court of Appeal disagreed and held (obiter dicta) that it is possible for settlement to lose its nuptial character.

8.42 When considering whether or not a 'de-nuptialisation' has occurred, the practitioner needs to bear in mind that context is all, and the words of Thorpe LJ in the appeal in *C v C* that:

> '... whether the removal of the spouses from the beneficial class does or does not erase the nuptial element must, in my judgment, depend on the facts and circumstances of the individual case.'

E. CAN A NON-NUPTIAL SETTLEMENT SUBSEQUENTLY ACQUIRE A NUPTIAL CHARACTER?

8.43 As with s 24(1)(c) generally, this seemingly simple question cannot receive a simple answer.

24 At paras 23–24: '*[23]...My first task must be to look at the words of s 24(1)(c). They confer jurisdiction to vary an "ante-nuptial or post-nuptial settlement ... made on the parties to the marriage". The word "made" looks to the past and there is no express requirement that the features which made the settlement nuptial should subsist....'.... '[24] I hold that, provided that it exists at the date of the order, the court has jurisdiction to vary a settlement which, when made, was ante-nuptial or post-nuptial, notwithstanding that prior to the date of the order the features which made it nuptial have been removed from it*'.

8.44 The two most recent decisions on the point are both first instance and directly contradict each other.

8.45 In *Quan v Bray*[25] Sir Paul Coleridge observed that in principle it is possible for a non-nuptial settlement to become 'nuptialised':

> '[60] In my judgment on the authorities, a settlement which is non-nuptial at its creation could itself later become 'nuptialised' if there was, in fact, a flow of benefit to the parties during the marriage from the trust. Alternatively a later disposition from the trust can itself constitute a post nuptial settlement without the main or superior trust necessarily becoming nuptial.'

8.46 He further stated at para 69(c) that:

> '…if all that is established is a vague, unspecified intention at some time in the future, depending on the circumstances then prevailing, to benefit the parties possibly by way of amending the trust deed or in other ways, that is not enough to turn a non-nuptial settlement into a post-nuptial settlement. That cannot amount to an existing disposition.'

8.47 To the contrary, Sir Peter Singer in *Joy v Joy- Morancho & Ors (No 3)*[26] considered but declined to follow the *Quan* decision stating that it does not reflect the law (at para 106). He went on (para 109):

> 'Were it to be otherwise every truly dynastic settlement, bereft of nuptial character at the outset but providing benefits for an individual who subsequently becomes either a husband or a wife, would arguably become variable under section 24(1)(c) as soon as that individual, once married, received any benefits. I am satisfied that that is not the law, notwithstanding the breadth of attribution historically afforded to settlements treated as nuptial.'

8.48 This provides something of a counter-point to Mostyn J's width of definition of 'nuptial' in *DR v GR,* referred to above.

F. WHAT PROPERTY IS TO BE REGARDED AS BEING WITHIN THE SETTLEMENT?

8.49 Particular attention must be paid to what is actually comprised in the relevant settlement – even if it is a case involving a formal trust. Again, matters are entirely fact dependent.

25 [2015] 2 FLR 546.
26 [2015] EWHC 2507 (Fam), [2016] 1 FLR 815.

8.50 In *Brooks*, only that part of the pension 'settled' by H – not surplus funds which, by the terms of the pension, were to become the property of his employer company – were held to be comprised in the nuptial settlement and therefore available to be varied.

8.51 In *N v N and F Trust*[27] Coleridge J held that the purchase by a non-nuptial trust of a family home for the parties gave rise to a nuptial settlement in respect of the licence to occupy the property. It is important to note that the settlement did not extend to the ownership of the home, or the capital value it represented. The court had only limited powers to vary the terms of the licence and could not make orders providing for the applicant to have an interest in the property.

8.52 In *Ben Hashem v Al Shayif*[28] Munby J followed Coleridge J's approach in *N v N and F Trust*. The settlement in question was a licence to occupy a property granted to the parties by a company. Munby J emphasised that while the settlement comprised that licence it did not extent to the property itself. A more recent decision to similar effect is *NR v AB*[29].

8.53 This was not an approach followed by Mostyn J in *AB v CB*[30], where a trust that was not nuptial 'on its face' was settled by the husband's father to hold a property (according to a contemporaneous letter) '*to make provision for a home there for our younger son CB and his wife.*' Mostyn J held that the settlement was obviously nuptial and that:

> '51 The more difficult question is whether the arrangement only brings within the scope of the Court's powers the right to occupy. I am satisfied, however, that this would not be the right conclusion to draw in this case. Had clause 5.2 not been present I might have reached a different decision, it would then have been more borderline. However, the existence of clause 5.2, which gives the trustees the specific power to advance all of the property to the husband during his lifetime, in my view makes clear to me that this settlement as a whole, and all of the property which it captures, is to be regarded as a variable nuptial settlement.'

8.54 The reader will appreciate that the matter turned on the precise wording of a particular clause of the trust instrument.

8.55 In *BJ v MJ*[31] Mostyn J held that a trust (on the face of it non-nuptial in character) was to be regarded as part of an overall scheme and therefore to be considered in conjunction with a separate nuptial trust. The two together

27 [2006] 1 FLR 856.
28 [2009] 1 FLR 115.
29 [2016] EWHC 277 (Fam).
30 [2015] 2 FLR 25 (approved on appeal at [2015] EWCA Civ 47, but the nuptiality finding was not challenged).
31 [2012] 1 FLR 667.

formed part of the same nuptial settlement (one was 'integral' to the other) and therefore the court's powers extended to all of the property held by each of them.

8.56 On the facts this conclusion may be far from surprising, given the entire structure was one set up to shelter a husband's wealth from Capital Gains Tax, such wealth deriving from an IPO of a business that he built up during the marriage. The court went on to identify the trust property as entirely matrimonial, falling for equal division.

G. THE EXTENT OF THE POWER TO VARY AND RIGHTS OF OTHER BENEFICIARIES

8.57 As expressed in *Ben Hashem v Al Shayif*[32] the court's discretion under s 24(1)(c) is both unfettered and, in theory, unlimited. The power can range from (for example) wholly excluding a beneficiary spouse from the settlement to transferring some or all assets to a non-beneficiary spouse, free from all encumbrance by the terms or nature of the settlement in question.

8.58 In *E v E (Financial Provision)*[33] and *C v C (Variation of Post-Nuptial Settlement: Company Shares)*[34] property held on trust was transferred free from any trusts to the wife (in *E v E* this was a cash sum of £50,000 and in *C v C* this was shares in a Cayman company).

8.59 Having established that that the court has jurisdiction to vary a settlement under s 24(1)(c), it is not uncommon to have to consider the rights of third parties. In cases of formal 'trusts', this will mean the other beneficiaries or potential beneficiaries. In cases involving settlements in the widest sense this may include not only third parties who do or could themselves benefit from the arrangement, but also potential creditors of the arrangements (this issue will most typically arise if a corporate entity forms part of the settlement).

8.60 As with all the financial remedy powers, the court's decision is arrived at as an exercise of discretion. Munby J in *Ben Hashem* summarised the relevant principles to be considered[35] and these have since been considered again in *BJ v MJ*[36], the position now being thus:

32 [2009] 1 FLR 115, Munby J.
33 [1990] 2 FLR 233, Ewbank J.
34 [2005] Fam 250, CA.
35 At 290.
36 [2012] 1 FLR 667, Mostyn J.

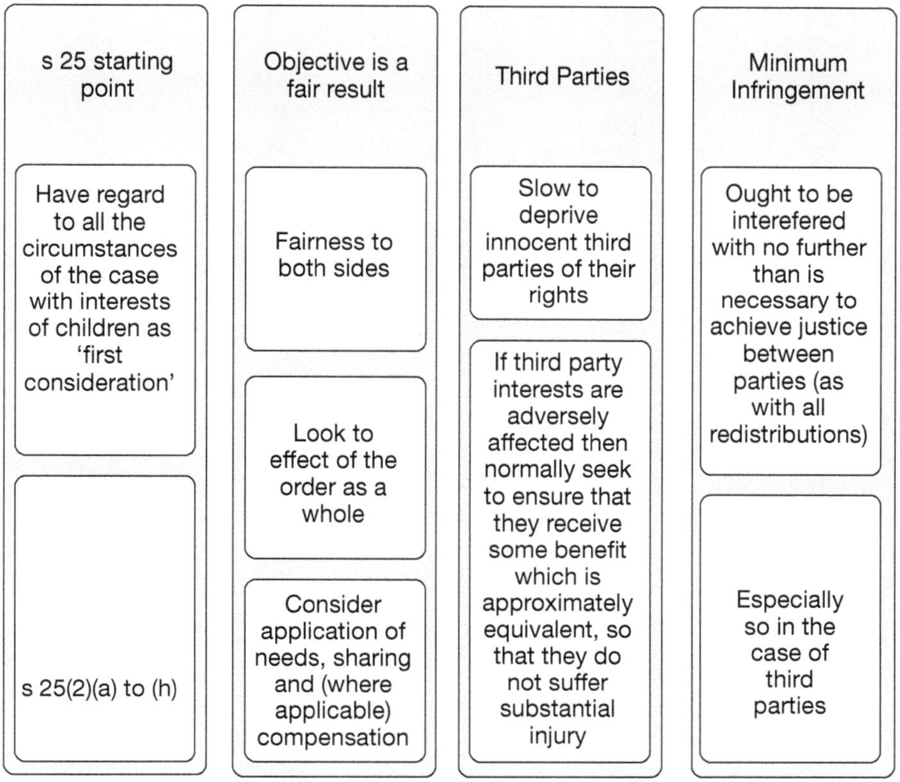

8.61 The fact that an asset is held within a settlement, as opposed to by one of the parties outright, is a relevant factor which the court determines the extent to which the settlement should be varied.

8.62 Thus, in circumstances where it might be open to the court to vary a post-nuptial settlement so as to transfer a matrimonial home unencumbered to a wife, it may nonetheless direct some less intrusive form of variation, such as:

- to transfer the property to the wife for life and thereafter to the other beneficiaries;
- to confirm the right to remain in occupation indefinitely without any form of transfer; or
- to direct that the applicant has a right to remain in occupation until (say) other orders made have been complied with[37].

8.63 The extent to which outright provision rather than a more encumbered form of benefit may be made for a party, is one that against turns on the facts of the particular case. Mostyn J in *BJ v MJ* drew particular attention to a tension in determining the degree of variation:

37 As above.

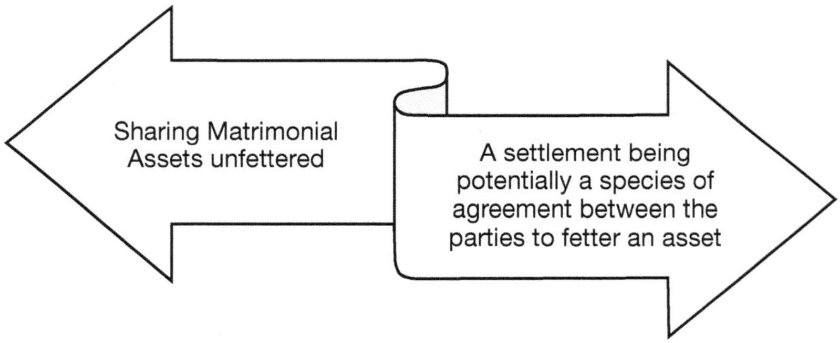

8.64 Where on the scale the variation falls will depend on all the circumstances of the case, and it is suggested a particularly key consideration will be the original source of the assets in the settlement. The more 'matrimonial' their nature (eg, made by one or both parties during the marriage as a result of their work or skill), the more likely it is that an outright order will be made. Conversely the more external to the marriage an asset (eg, inheritance, gift, pre-acquisition) the more likely it is that the variation may not provide absolute ownership to the claiming spouse.

H. TELESCOPING ORDERS

8.65 It is very often the case that assets held within a trust structure are not owned by the trustee directly. Instead, the trustee owns shares in a company which may own shares in another company which, in turn, owns an underlying asset that is the target of the claim. Indeed, the chain is often longer, and even more complex. However, in *Hope v Krejci*[38], the fact that the trustees did not own the underlying assets (which were owned by a company), did not prevent Mostyn J from extracting and transferring to the wife those assets.

8.66 This approach became known as 'telescoping', ie, looking down the structure from its nuptial head to the constituent elements below and imbuing them with the same variable character as the originating settlement.

8.67 There has been expressed considerable doubt by practitioners and commentators as to whether reaching down into a sub-company and dealing with its assets, as telescoping requires, can survive the subsequent decision of the Supreme Court in *Prest v Petrodel Resources*[39]. That case underlined the importance of treating companies as the separate legal personalities that they are.

38 [2013] 1 FLR 182.
39 [2013] UKSC 34, [2013] AC 415, SC.

8.68 In *DR v GR*[40] Mostyn J acknowledged that the Court of Appeal decision in *Prest* appeared to be inconsistent with the notion of telescoping orders. Nevertheless, he distinguished the decision and repeated the view he had expressed in *Hope v Krejci* that the court had the power to make such orders. His judgment merits reading in full, although it should be borne in mind that the majority of practitioners consider it to be controversial and incompatible with the Supreme Court decision in *Prest*[41].

I. ENFORCEMENT CONCERNS

8.69 Finally, the practitioner has to be aware of a further potential hurdle to be cleared, even if a settlement is identified and its nuptial character clear, or found to exist by a court, or conceded: whether the order sought is capable of enforcement.

8.70 A court would be unlikely to make a variation order where both the trust and its assets are overseas unless it is satisfied that the order would be implemented by the court exercising effective control over the settlement (*BJ v MJ*[42], *Goff v Goff*[43], *Hamlin v Hamlin*[44] and *Quan v Bray*[45]).

8.71 **Chapters 3** and **11** of this edition considers these points in greater detail. Suffice it to say that it may be necessary for the practitioner to be alive at the earliest stage to role of the foreign court in actually obtaining the fruit of the order sought, if made.

8.72 Given the proliferation in offshore jurisdiction of so called local 'firewall' legislation, designed to protect trusts and entities governed by or based in those jurisdictions, the automatic or easy implementation or enforcement of decisions of an English court varying a foreign settlement is by no means to be assumed.

8.73 There can be no substitute for ensuring at the earliest possible stage that specialist foreign law expert advice is taken, before embarking on an attempt to vary a nuptial settlement not based in England and Wales.

8.74 The ability to enforce or implement an order overseas may need to be proved in proceedings on evidence before a substantive order is made. Such evidence would be, most usually, by way of expert report from a suitably locally qualified lawyer.

40 *DR v GR (Financial Remedy: Variation of Overseas Trust)* [2013] EWHC 1196, [2013] 2 FLR 1534.
41 [2013] UKSC 34, [2013] AC 415, SC.
42 [2011] EWHC 2708 (Fam), [2012] 1 FLR 667.
43 [1934] P 107.
44 [1986] Fam 11.
45 [2014] EWHC 3340 (Fam), [2015] 3 FCR 436, Sir Paul Coleridge.

CHAPTER 9

Trusts as Resources: *Thomas v Thomas*

Content at a Glance:

A. Introduction: Trust assets as 'resources'
- Taking account of 'resources'
- When will a court find that a trust asset is a resource?
- The leading case of *Thomas*: the key legal principles

B. Looking for 'realities' post-*Thomas*
- Assets owned by discretionary trusts and settlements
- When does judicious encouragement become improper pressure?
- Quantification before distribution
- Exceeding the total assets or income owned outright by a party

C. Practical Guidance in *Thomas* cases
- Involvement of trustees in proceedings as parties/witnesses
- Alternative cases: the importance of clarity in the attack

A. INTRODUCTION: TRUST ASSETS AS 'RESOURCES'

Taking account of 'resources'

9.1 The court hearing a financial remedy claim is required to take into account *all* financial resources available to the parties (those existing both at present and in the foreseeable future), including those of a non-proprietary nature. Its concern is not limited to assets that are legally or beneficially owned by either or both of the parties, or nuptial settlements, which are capable of variation by the court[1].

9.2 The family courts have always looked beyond the surface of legal ownership when assessing resources. As Lord Merrivale observed at p 327 in *N v N*[2], in matrimonial cases the courts have [Emphasis added]:

> 'showed a degree of **practical wisdom**...They were not misled by appearances...**they looked at realities**.'

1 The powers of the court to vary or otherwise interfere with nuptial settlements are considered in **Chapter 8** of this book.

2 *N v N* [1928] 44 TLR 324.

9.3 This principle is now preserved in statute. When hearing a financial remedies claim the court is required to have regard, amongst other matters, to:

> '…[the] property and other financial resources which each of the parties to the marriage has or is likely to have in the foreseeable future…'[3]

9.4 Thus, if a trust or other third party provides, or in the foreseeable future is likely to provide, financial support to one or either of the parties, the court is *obliged* to take the fact into account.

9.5 There is no limitation upon the 'nature' of the third party or 'type' of resource to which s 25(2)(a) applies. A finding of 'ownership' is not required. Provided the court is satisfied that a resource is likely to be *made available* to the party to proceedings, it is a relevant 'financial resource'. The cases referred to in this chapter include examples where the 'resource' comprises:

- an asset legally owned by a third party, including a trust or company (eg *Charman*[4]);
- an income provided by a company (eg *Thomas*[5]*; J v V*[6]; *SK v WL*[7]);
- security provided by a company for personal borrowing (eg *Thomas*);
- the value of a hotel purchased by a previous generation (*O'D*[8]);
- a UK-based or foreign trust (eg *Howard*[9]; *Charman*[10]; *Browne v Browne*[11]; *B v B*[12]; *Whaley*[13]);
- Loans or other distributions from a discretionary trust to a beneficiary (or his or her spouse) to provide for housing, payment of debts or other needs (eg *RK v RK*[14]; *G v G*[15]) or

3 MCA 1973, s 25(2)(a). See also **Chapter 2** of this book for an overview of the statutory principles in matrimonial finance cases.
4 *Charman v Charman (No 4)* [2007] EWCA Civ 503, [2007] 2 FCR 217, CA.
5 *Thomas v Thomas* [1995] 2 FLR 668, [1996] 2 FCR 544, CA.
6 *J v V (Disclosure: Offshore Corporations)* [2003] EWHC 3110 (Fam), [2004] 1 FLR 1042, Coleridge J.
7 *SK v WL (Ancillary Relief: Post-Separation Accrual)* [2010] EWHC 3768 (Fam), [2011] 1 FLR 1471, Moylan J.
8 *O'D v O'D* [1976] Fam 83, CA.
9 *Howard v Howard* [1945] P1, [1945] 1 All ER 91, CA.
10 *Charman v Charman (No 4)* [2007] EWCA Civ 503, [2007] 1 FLR 1246, [2007] 2 FCR 217, CA.
11 *Browne v Browne* [1989] 1 FLR 291, [1989] FCR 275, CA.
12 *B v B* [1982] 3 FLR 298.
13 *Whaley v Whaley* [2011] EWCA Civ 617, [2012] 1 FLR 735, [2011] 2 FCR 323, CA.
14 *RK v RK (Financial Resources: Trust Assets)* [2011] EWHC 3910 (Fam), [2013] 1 FLR 329, [2012] 3 FCR 44, Moylan J.
15 *G v G (Financial Remedies: Short Marriage: Trust Assets)* [2012] EWHC 167 (Fam), [2012] 2 FLR 48, Charles J.

– a voluntary payment made by a relative or other third party (*X v X (Y and Z Intervening)*[16]; *SR v CR*[17]; *AM v SS*[18]).

9.6 The practical differences that arise with each of these different types of resource are considered below, but the underlying legal principles remain the same.

Checklist: What types of additional 'resource' may be relevant under section 25(2)(a)

Company assets, where one party substantially owns or controls the company (eg *SK v WL*)	Company assets, where the company is partly or wholly legally owned by third parties (eg *J v V, Thomas, O'D*)	Future income or other distributions from a trust, including to a spouse/ parent of a beneficiary upon exit from a marriage (eg *Charman, Browne v Browne, RK v RK*)
Assets held subject to a trust of which one party is a discretionary beneficiary, including those based off-shore (eg *Charman, Browne v Browne*)	Present or future income from a trust or company structure (eg *Thomas, O'D*)	Future distributions from a 'dynastic' family trust (eg *Whaley*)
Voluntary gift(s) offered by a party's family members (eg *X v X (Y and Z intervening), SR v CR, AM v SS*)	Security for personal borrowing against company assets (eg *Thomas*)	Loans from a discretionary trust to a beneficiary, to provide for housing or other needs (eg *G v G*)

When will a court find that a trust asset is a resource?

9.7 Notwithstanding the family court's broad discretion, its powers can only be exercised *in the light of* the parties' circumstances; it cannot make orders to compel a third party to *change* their circumstances.

16 *X v X (Y and Z Intervening)* [2002] 1 FLR 508, [2002] Fam Law 98, Munby J.

17 *R v R (Ancillary Relief: Family Trusts) (aka SR v CR (Ancillary Relief: Family Trusts))* [2008] EWHC 2329 (Fam), [2009] 2 FCR 69, Singer J.

18 *AM v SS* [2014] EWHC 865 (Fam), Coleridge J.

9.8 In *Howard*[19] the Court of Appeal determined that it would be inappropriate to make an order forcing trustees to make additional provision to a discretionary beneficiary for the sole purpose of enabling that beneficiary to discharge the order in favour of the payee. This 1945 case remains good law on this point of principle, despite it having been decided before the modern statutory regime.

Case illustration: *Howard v Howard*[20]

Facts and order at first instance:

- H (bankrupt and unable to work) had previously been the recipient of more than £500 per annum from a family trust of which he, any wife or child of his, were discretionary beneficiaries. The trustees ceased to make direct payment to him but provided maintenance for his son and medical expenses.
- H's total income from non-trust resources was (lately) only £150 per annum.
- The judge at first instance ordered the husband to make periodical payments to his former wife of £100 per annum.

On appeal:

- The order was overturned and replaced with an order for periodical payments of one shilling per week.
- The judge was wrong to make an order in excess of what H could reasonably afford from his own income, designed to induce the trustees to pay him when they otherwise would not have done.

Key principles from the appeal Judgment [Emphasis added]:

> 'In my opinion there is no jurisdiction in the Divorce Court to make an order which will leave the husband in a state of starvation (to use rather picturesque language) with a view to putting pressure on trustees to exercise their discretion in a way which they would not have exercised it but for that pressure…[21]'

9.9 The Court of Appeal was satisfied in *Howard* that the trustees' expressed intention not to make any further financial provision to the husband was not only genuine, but a proper exercise of their discretion. It would be a different situation if the trustees had been found to be *likely* to make such provision [Emphasis added]:

19 *Howard v Howard* [1945] P1, [1945] 1 All ER 91, CA.
20 *Howard v Howard* [1945] P1, [1945] 1 All ER 91, CA.
21 *Howard v Howard* [1945] P1 at p 4.

> 'I must not be misunderstood. It is, of course, legitimate ... to treat a **voluntary allowance** as something which the court can, **in proper circumstances, infer will be likely to continue and make an order on that basis.**'[22]

9.10 Whether or not such provision will be made is, therefore, a question of fact. The court is not entitled to influence the trustees' proper use of their discretion; but it is required to ask what they are *likely* to do.

9.11 The principles set out in *Howard* are now reflected the wording of MCA 1973, s 25(2)(a), and have been applied by the courts in more recent cases.

Case illustration: *B v B*[23]

Facts and order at first instance:

- W was ordered to pay £50,000 to H, taking into account the value of two settlements of which she was a beneficiary.
- The trustee gave evidence (rejected by the court) that he did not intend to consent to the distribution of any more funds from the settlement to the wife.

On appeal:

- W argued that the order put pressure on the trustees to exercise their discretion in such a way that they would not ordinarily have exercised it but for the order.
- The Court of Appeal distinguished *Howard* on the facts and commented:

> 'One might expect that the trustees would wait to see the outcome of the proceedings before exercising their discretion under the settlement...We did not think that the judge was putting or attempting to put pressure on the trustees; on the contrary it could be said that the trustees were attempting to put pressure on the court. She [the judge] was dealing in practical terms with the realities of the case and refusing to be misled by appearance.'

22 At p 4-5.
23 *B v B* [1982] 3 FLR 298.

Case illustration: *Browne v Browne*[24]

Facts and order at first instance:

- W was the sole beneficiary of at least £430,000 of trust assets. The trustees objected to paying any sums to W that would eventually be paid to H.
- W was ordered to pay £175,000 (only c.£115,000 could be paid from non-trust resources).

On appeal:

- Appeal dismissed. The judge was entitled to find that W had effective control of the trusts, and that the trustees would follow her direction.
- At p 293 Butler-Sloss LJ commented:

> 'it is of some relevance to note that, prior to the divorce ... every application by the wife for funds for herself and for her husband ... was met and the sums asked for were advanced at the request of the wife. Although perhaps the phrase 'effective control' might more appropriately be expressed as 'immediate access to the funds', in my judgment the judge was entirely justified in coming to the conclusion as at 6 February that every request had been granted and that she was in a position to ask for money and to have it paid, and there was nothing to show that the trustees would not do so.'

9.12 The extent of 'other financial resources' available for the purpose of MCA 1973, s 25(2)(a) is ultimately a question of fact. The essential question for the court is not:

> 'What might be made available if certain orders could be made to induce it?' But:

> 'What income, property or other financial resource *does* either party *presently* have, or *is likely to have* in the foreseeable future?'

Note: See paras 9.17 and 9.30 for 'When does judicious encouragement become improper pressure?'

24 *Browne v Browne* [1989] 1 FLR 291, [1989] FCR 275, CA.

The leading case of *Thomas*: the key legal principles

9.13 In the leading case of *Thomas*[25] the Court of Appeal gave further guidance that is applicable to cases involving allegations that 'additional' financial resources are available to parties apart from their strictly defined legal or beneficial interests.

9.14 It is worth noting that *Thomas* did not concern a trust but a successful family company. The husband was a minority shareholder, but the court found that the husband and his brother *jointly* had effective control over all aspects of company policy. Their policy was to reinvest profits and pay themselves relatively modest salaries and generous pension contributions.

9.15 The husband had discharged debts by charging the family home which had equity of less than £30,000. He asserted that he was unable to provide any alternative means of security for his loans and that he could not increase his income to meet school fees. The court at first instance rejected both aspects of his case and the decision was upheld by the Court of Appeal. Waite LJ observed at p 670-1:

> '...where a spouse enjoys access to wealth but no absolute entitlement to it (as in the case, for example, of a beneficiary under a discretionary trust or someone who is dependent on the generosity of a relative), the court will not act in direct invasion of the rights of, or usurp the discretion exercisable by, a third party. Nor will it put upon a third party undue pressure to act in a way which will enhance the means of the maintaining spouse. This does not, however, mean that the court acts in total disregard of the potential availability of wealth from sources owned or administered by others. There will be occasions when it becomes permissible for a judge deliberately to frame his orders in a form which affords judicious encouragement to third parties to provide the maintaining spouse with the means to comply with the court's view of the justice of the case. There are bound to be instances where the boundary between improper pressure and judicious encouragement proves to be a fine one, and it will require attention to the particular circumstances of each case to see whether it has been crossed.'

9.16 Waite LJ held that the husband's 'substantial means' were such that the burden had been on *him* to satisfy the court that those resources were not liquid and available to him for the purposes of any matrimonial order:

> 'The order that [the husband] was suggesting was paltry when measured against his total resources and expectations, assessed in the broad terms which the Act requires. On such a husband a heavy onus lay to satisfy the court that all means of access to liquid funds to support suitable outright provision for his wife had been thoroughly explored and found

25 *Thomas v Thomas* [1995] 2 FLR 668, [1996] 2 FCR 544, CA.

to be impossible. If he failed to demonstrate that, he ran the risk of having the inference drawn against him that ways and means could be found of funding suitable provision for the wife's capital needs.'[26]

9.17 Glidewell LJ summarised the key principles as follows[27]:

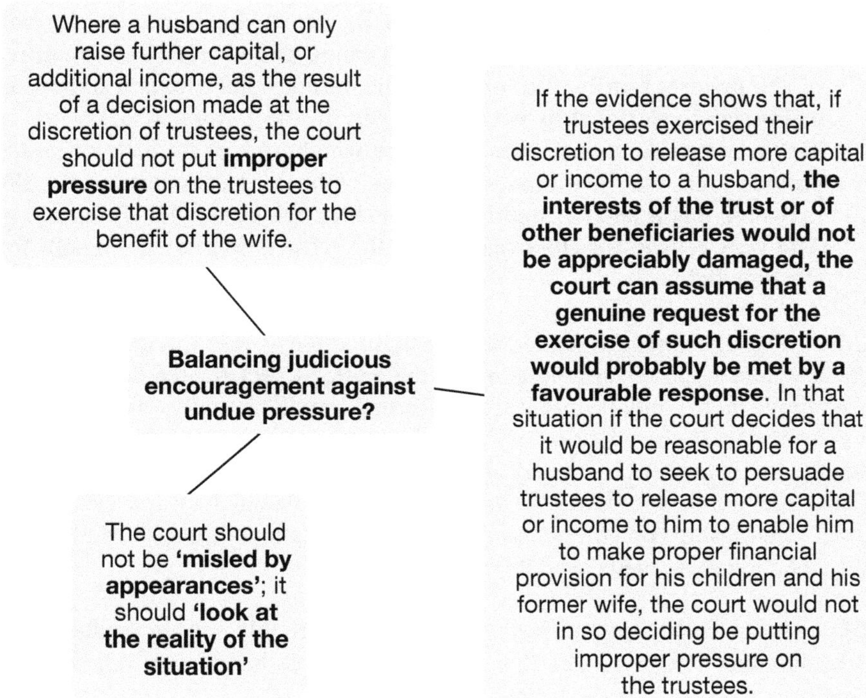

B. LOOKING FOR 'REALITIES' POST-*THOMAS*

Assets owned by discretionary trusts and settlements

9.18 Where a case involves allegations that a party had been masking his or her true ownership of an asset either through a company structure or third party, the court will apply principles of trust and property law to make findings about the actual ownership of the asset. At the conclusion of the evidence, the court may conclude that equitable ownership may be other than that suggested by the legal title or formal trust document. The principles governing the search for 'realities' in such cases is considered elsewhere in this book at **Chapter 7**.

9.19 Where assets are held in a *trust* of which one party is a beneficiary (whether sole or in a class of beneficiaries) it is not necessarily the structure which can conceal the resource, but the uncertainty of trustee discretion. Largely the same principles apply, as in all cases the court must look to the 'reality'.

26 At p 676 of the judgment of the Court of Appeal.
27 At p 678, as above.

However, it has been suggested that the courts should more readily expect, or even seek to encourage, future financial support from a trust administered formally by a *trustee* than a *non-trust resource*, such as a member of the payer's family who might be expected to be generous. In *TL v ML*[28] the court held at para [86] [Emphasis added]:

> 'I think that a **clear distinction is to be drawn between, on the one hand, the position where the person being encouraged is a member of the payer's family and, on the other hand, where he is a trustee in a fiduciary relationship with the payer**. In the former case, the payee has no more than a mere spes of bounty which may, at the election of the provider, reasonably or unreasonably, be withheld. **In the latter case, the provider has a legal obligation to consider the beneficiary's interests. The very reason for the existence of the trust is to provide benefit for the beneficiary**.'

9.20 The underlying rationale for this distinction is that the existence of a fiduciary duty imposes an obligation on the trustee to act for the benefit of the beneficiary; such a duty is absent from informal familial largesse. And while the purpose of a trust, the intention of the settlor, or the existence of other (actual or potential future) beneficiaries may all constrain the trustees' exercise of discretion against authorising the release of trust funds to the beneficiary, the fact of that formal relationship can still be used to support an argument that funds are more likely than not to be made available.

9.21 In *Re The Esteem Settlement*[29] the Royal Court of Jersey highlighted some of the fundamental principles that govern the trustee-beneficiary relationship. These principles include the following:

28 *TL v ML (Ancillary Relief: Claim against assets of extended family)* [2005] EWHC 2860 (Fam), [2006] 1 FLR 1263, [2006] 1 FCR 465, Mostyn QC.

29 *Re the Esteem Settlement (aka Abacus (C.I.) Ltd Grupo Torras SA and Culmer v Al-Sabah* [2003] JLR 188 at paras 163 onwards of the judgment. See also *Letterstedt* (1884) 9 App Cas 371 at 38.

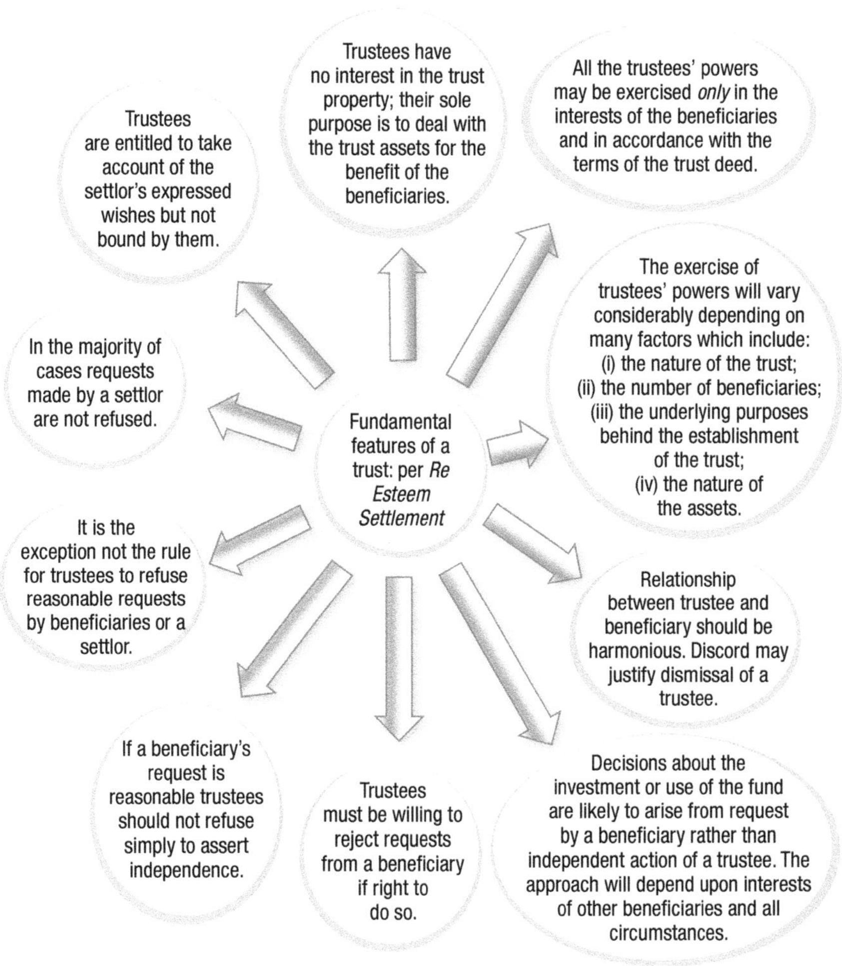

9.22 *Re Esteem Settlement* was relied upon in *TL v ML*[30] at [para 88] to support the proposition that a finding of additional resource will more readily be made where a party is a beneficiary of a trust than in cases involving other forms of resource:

> 'If the court makes a reasonable request of trustees to make funds available to meet an ancillary relief award, then it can assume that ordinarily the trustees will accede to such a request. The same cannot be assumed of a request of a mere donor, for it is his prerogative to be unreasonable, if that is his inclination.'

9.23 In determining whether assets held in trust can be considered a resource of a spouse, the court must consider all the circumstances. Particular attention will ordinarily be given to the following factors:

30 As above.

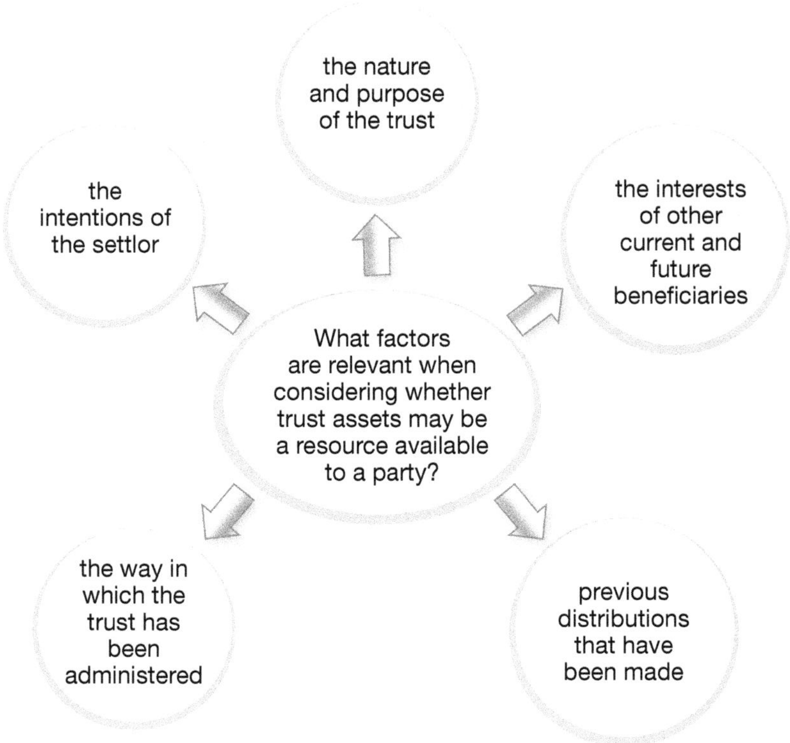

9.24 The finding that trustees had exercised their discretion to terminate financial support for the husband in favour of providing further support to another beneficiary, his child, was part of the justification for allowing the appeal in *Howard*[31]. Equally, the court may conclude that funds are less likely to be advanced to a living beneficiary in the case of a 'dynastic' trust, settled in order to preserve funds for future generations of a family, than in the case of a trust that was set up to hold the assets of a particular person on the expectation those funds would nonetheless be released upon request.

9.25 In *Charman*[32] the court held that the assets of a trust created by the husband upon an expression of wish that during his lifetime he should be the primary beneficiary were a resource available to him. The following features of the trust were significant:

31 As above.
32 *Charman v Charman (No 4)* [2007] EWCA Civ 503, [2007] 2 FCR 217, CA.

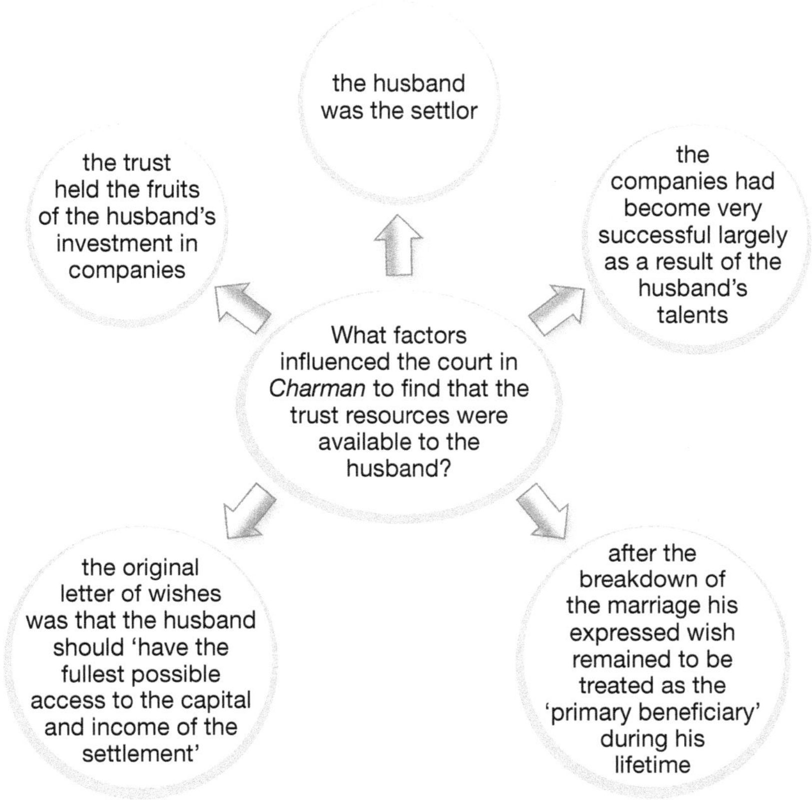

9.26 In *Charman* the court emphasised the importance of undertaking a thorough investigation to identify *all* assets directly and indirectly available to the parties, particularly those that had accrued during the marriage, highlighting that:

> '...it is essential for the court to bring to [its enquiry] a judicious mixture of worldly realism and of respect for the legal effects of trusts, the legal duties of trustees and, in the case of off-shore trusts, the jurisdiction of off-shore courts.'[33]

9.27 The critical question in *Charman* was '*Would the trustees be likely to advance all of the capital of the trust to the husband on his request?*' The same or similar questions have been posed in other comparable cases at first instance[34]. In *A v A*[35], for example, Munby J asked:

33 See para 57 of the judgment of the Court of Appeal.

34 See, for example, *A v A* [2007] EWHC 99 (Fam), [2007] 2 FLR 467, Munby J at para 92 of the judgment; *RK v RK (Financial Resources: Trust Assets)* [2011] EWHC 3910 (Fam), [2012] 3 FCR 44, Moylan J at para 60 of the judgment; *Whaley v Whaley* [2011] EWCA Civ 617, [2011] 2 FCR 323, CA at para 113 of the judgment; *BJ v MJ (Financial Order: Overseas Trust)* [2011] EWHC 2708 (Fam), [2012] 1 FLR 667, Mostyn J at para 15 of the judgment.

35 *A v A and St Georges Trustees* [2007] EWHC 99 (Fam), [2007] 2 FLR 467, Munby J.

'Can the wife demonstrate that, if asked, the trustees would be 'likely', immediately or in the foreseeable future, to exercise their powers in favour of or in some other way for the benefit of the husband?'[36].

9.28 This is now considered to be the key question in cases where the resource issue arises. In *Whaley*[37] Black LJ held at para 40:

'At times, it seemed that [the husband] was submitting that what the law required was something close to a certainty that the trustees would come up with the funds so that unless a judge finds that the trustees *will* provide, the trust is irrelevant. … Such an approach would not be consistent with [s.25 of the MCA 1973] which refers to the property and other financial resources which each of the parties to the marriage 'is likely to have in the foreseeable future' and is not in line with the authorities which contemplate a finding (which will obviously be made on the balance of probability) that the trustees are likely to comply with what is requested of them.'

9.29 The court's discretion is better retained by asking the single question, '*Would the trustees be likely to advance all of the capital of the trust to the husband on his request?*', having regard to all facts, than by an overly rigid classification of 'types' of trust, or the development of specific presumptions or principles to each. Indeed, the Court of Appeal issued a warning about over-use of stratified terminology in *Whaley*:

'[the husband] referred to the Farah trust as a 'dynastic trust'. I use that term in this judgment only because he did and certainly not intending to give the impression that I endorse it as some sort of technical term, still less some sort of ancillary relief concept with its own body of attendant principles. Individual trusts vary considerably and global labels for them may be unhelpful as they risk deflecting attention from the particular terms of the trust under consideration.'[38]

36 At para 92 of the judgment.
37 *Whaley v Whaley* [2011] EWCA Civ 617, [2011] 2 FCR 323, CA.
38 See para 48 of the judgment of Black LJ in the Court of Appeal.

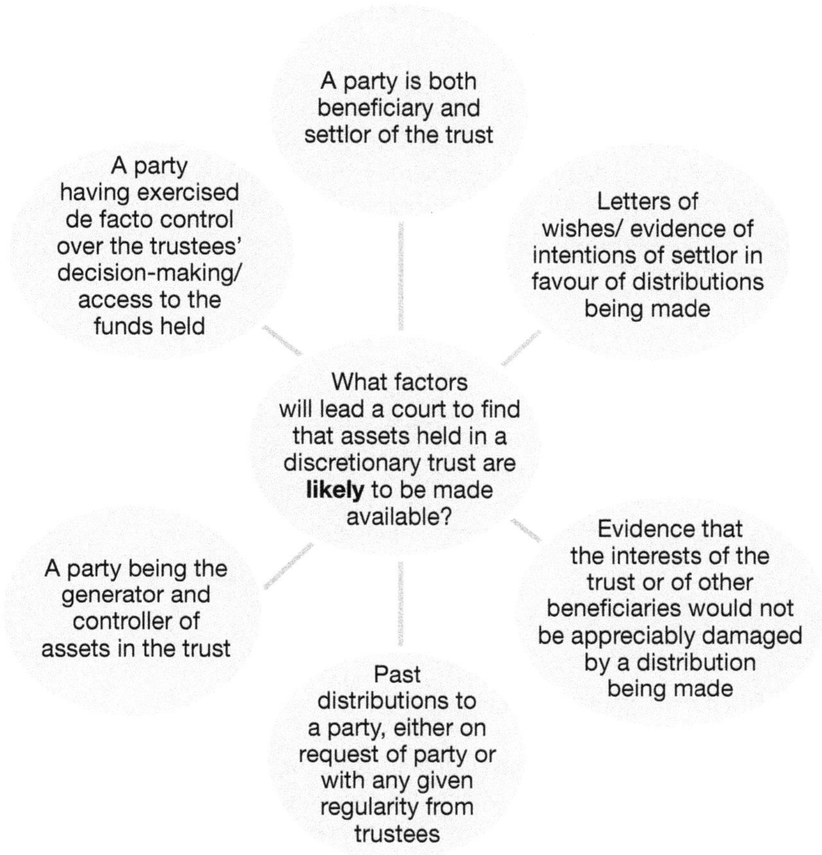
A party is both beneficiary and settlor of the trust
A party having exercised de facto control over the trustees' decision-making/ access to the funds held
Letters of wishes/ evidence of intentions of settlor in favour of distributions being made
What factors will lead a court to find that assets held in a discretionary trust are **likely** to be made available?
A party being the generator and controller of assets in the trust
Evidence that the interests of the trust or of other beneficiaries would not be appreciably damaged by a distribution being made
Past distributions to a party, either on request of party or with any given regularity from trustees

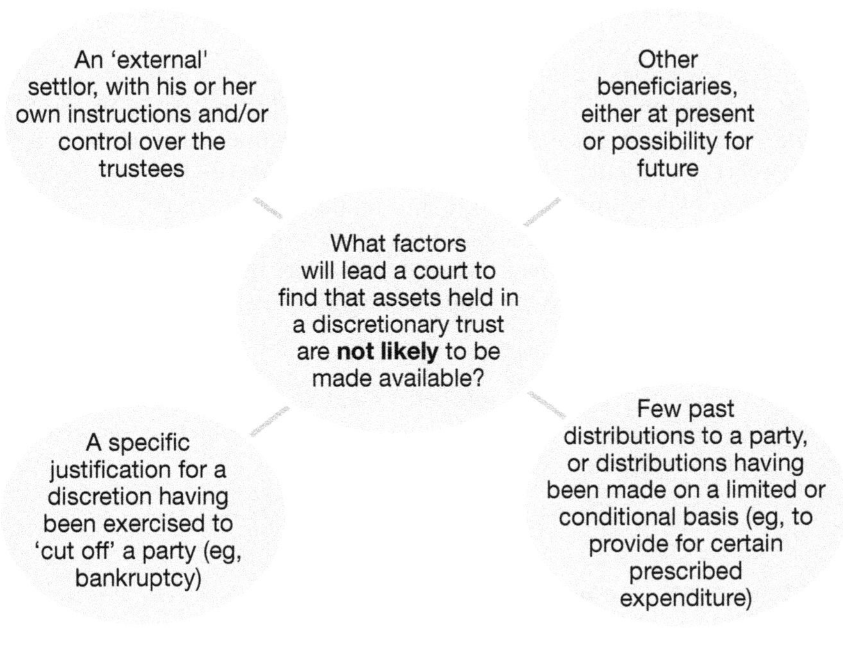
An 'external' settlor, with his or her own instructions and/or control over the trustees
Other beneficiaries, either at present or possibility for future
What factors will lead a court to find that assets held in a discretionary trust are **not likely** to be made available?
A specific justification for a discretion having been exercised to 'cut off' a party (eg, bankruptcy)
Few past distributions to a party, or distributions having been made on a limited or conditional basis (eg, to provide for certain prescribed expenditure)

When does judicious encouragement become improper pressure?

9.30 It would be wrong in principle to make an order intended to influence trustee discretion by exposing one party to hardship. However, the court *can* make an order in the hope and expectation that it might encourage funds to be provided to a party to discharge the same. There is a tension between these seemingly conflicting propositions, and the distinction between the two is not always clear in practice.

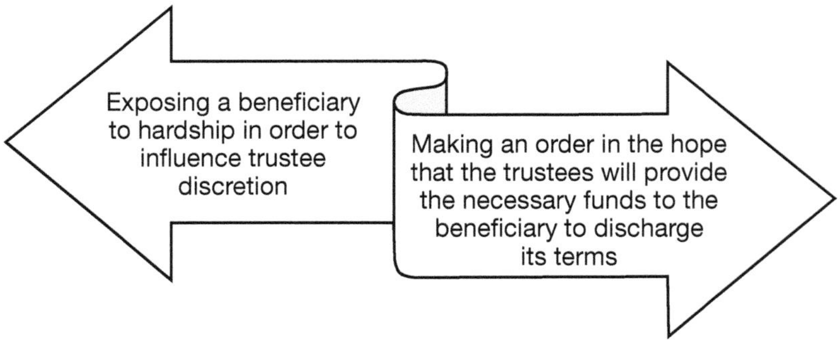

9.31 In *Thomas* Waite LJ observed:

> '…the judges who administer this jurisdiction have traditionally accepted the Shakespearean principle that 'it is excellent to have a giant's strength but tyrannous to use it like a giant'. **The precise boundaries of that judicial self-restraint have never been rigidly defined – nor could they be, if the jurisdiction is to retain its flexibility.**'[39] [Emphasis added]

9.32 The law recognises that orders are not made in a vacuum, and are likely to influence the actions of those whom they affect. It is artificial to exclude the fact of an order being made from an analysis of what a trustee is *likely* to do. And the court is entitled to consider the *effect* of an order on the *probability* of a trustee acting. Plainly much is held to turn on the wording of the statute asking what a party 'is *likely* to have in *the foreseeable future*' and if the party who is a discretionary beneficiary is made subject to an order that influences what he is likely to receive in the future, this falls within the bounds of acceptable judicial encouragement.

9.33 In *Whaley*[40], Lewison J referred to and summarised the comments of Glidewell LJ in *Thomas*, in which the circumstances in which an order will *not* amount to 'undue pressure', were characterised[41].

39 See above at p 670 of the judgment in the Court of Appeal.

40 *Whaley v Whaley* [2011] EWCA Civ 617, [2011] 2 FCR 323, CA.

41 Per Lewison J in *Whaley* at para 114 and Glidewell LJ in *Thomas* at p 678 (bullet point (c)).

An order **will not** amount to 'undue pressure

IF

the interests of other beneficiaries would not be appreciably damaged by the release of funds to facilitate compliance

AND

the court considers it reasonable for a spouse to seek to persuade trustees to release capital to enable him to make financial provision for the other spouse

9.34 Applying these principles, 'judicious encouragement' has been deployed over the years to induce considerable financial support to parties from discretionary trust assets.

Case illustration: *SR v CR*[42]

Facts and first instance decision:

- Non-trust assets of £7.25–£7.88 million.
- H (not W) was a beneficiary of trusts with assets > $170 million. H had received distributions from the trusts and payments from his father (the settlor) to fund the parties' lifestyle at a rate of c.£1 million pa.
- H's business had failed, and he had not yet obtained further employment.
- H's father had directed the trustees not to advance any further financial support to H. The trustees had never previously made a distribution against the settlor's wishes, but conceded that if H was in abject need they would likely make 'exceedingly modest' provision for him.
- Singer J awarded 80% of the non-trust assets to W concluding that the order would induce the trustee to replenish H's resources.

Key principles from the Judgment:

- Unlike *Charman* the settlor was a third party whose instructions would influence the trustees' discretion. This was taken into account, but rejected as being determinative. The court ultimately found H's father's instructions to the trustees would be other than as he said to the court.
- This demonstrates the difficulty in assessing the hypothetical future realities before they come to pass [Emphasis added]:

  'The tension between the court and (in this case) the trustees can only be resolved ex post facto, and so **a key component of the court's role is to determine on whatever evidence is available how the trustees are likely to exercise their discretion** in the situation postulated by the award which the court has it in mind

42 *R v R (Ancillary Relief: Family Trusts) (aka SR v CR (Ancillary Relief: Family Trusts))* [2008] EWHC 2329 (Fam), [2009] 2 FCR 69, Singer J.

to make. **That balance involves an exercise both in fact finding and prediction, and therefore necessarily a large element of uncertainty**.

...

The balance is made more delicate if, as here, the trust funds in question derive entirely from an external settlor...to whose wishes the trustees will very properly pay regard, although they are not bound by them. **The trustees have as primary obligation to exercise what is their own discretion in favour of the whole class of beneficiaries, weighing the impact of what is proposed for one against its effect on the interests of the others**.'

– Singer J rejected the father's stated position and was prepared to use his order as a means of judicious encouragement to the trustees (and/or the settlor) to act. He commented that [Emphasis added]:

> 'a protective attitude may lead to **an artificial presentation of the underlying reality**, to which I must attempt to penetrate.
>
> There is...clear evidence of deliberate misrepresentation sufficient to persuade me that I cannot accept the proposition that H's pot will not be replenished, even if not so munificently as in the past.'

Case illustration: *RK v RK*[43]

Facts:

– H was a beneficiary of a trust whose assets were largely illiquid. The liquid assets in trust were worth c. £540,000.

– There were other beneficiaries, whose interests also needed to be taken into account.

– H had debts to the trust of c.£300,000. W had personal debts of £245,000.

– The trustees had historically loaned H funds to clear his debts, but were now saying that they were intending to take a firmer stance in future.

– The trustees agreed to provide a housing fund of £400,000 to W on the basis of a life interest, but not to discharge her debts.

Approach of the court at trial:

– The court ordered payment of a lump sum of £475,000 comprised of a life interest in £425,000 as a housing fund and £50,000 for debts.

43 *RK v RK (Financial Resources: Trust Assets)* [2011] EWHC 3910 (Fam), [2012] 3 FCR 44, Moylan J.

Key principles from the Judgment:

- Moylan J accepted the stance of the trustees was reasonable, in particular their reluctance to use virtually all of the trust's liquid capital for the benefit of the parties, when there were other beneficiaries.
- Since the largest element of W's award would revert to the trust upon her death, he concluded that the trust could afford to be more generous. Though the trustees had said they would not advance capital for debts he said:

> 'I have to decide what sum the trustees are likely to provide to the wife and/or to the husband to enable him to discharge any order for a lump sum that I might make.
>
> When the trustees consider this issue, they will no doubt reflect on the fact that the wife came into this marriage with significant resources and leaves it with significant debts. They will also reflect on the fact that she is the mother of three of the next generation of beneficiaries of the trusts. I would also expect them to appreciate that this was a case in which the wife required legal representation at a level similar to that which was provided to the husband. His legal costs by the date of the first appointment were £36,000.
>
> Looking at the landscape, as I would expect the trustees to look at it, I consider it likely that the trustees will agree to provide the wife direct and/or provide the husband with resources to enable him to pay a lump sum of £50,000.'

9.35 What if trustees do not in fact provide the funds the court found them likely to provide? The court cannot compel them to do so; it can only *encourage* them to act. If the trustee ignores the encouragement, there is little that can be done[44].

Quantification before distribution

9.36 The court is required to identify and quantify the assets before making a decision about distribution[45]. Logically, in cases where it is asserted that a trust is a resource the court must ask the following questions, in sequence:

44 See again para 95 of the judgment in *A v A*.

45 This applies whether or not there are trust/company assets to take into account. See *Livesey v Jenkins* [1985] AC 424, HL at p 437 per Lord Brandon of Oakbrook. See also **Chapter 2** of this book for an overview of matrimonial finance principles, and in particular para **2.4** where the 'tri-partite' process of (i) identification of resources, (ii) computation of value, and (iii) distribution is set out.

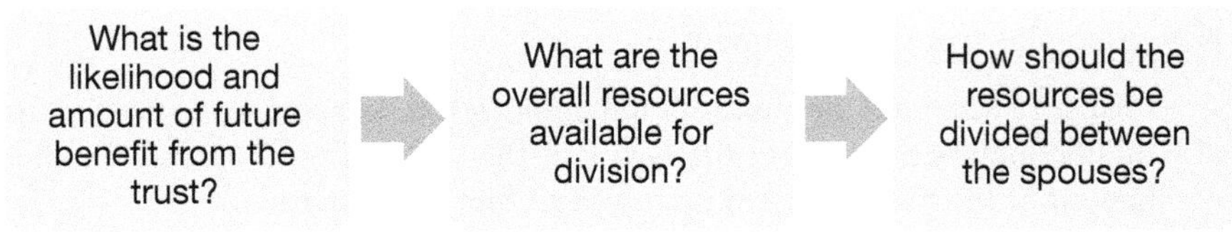

9.37 This sequential approach was adopted by Mostyn J in *BJ v MJ*[46] and by Charles J in by Charles J in *G v G*[47].

9.38 However, if the court is required to consider a trustee's likely response *in the light of* its order it may not be possible to identify whether a trust comprises 'a resource' in isolation from the court's proposed order. Thus, in some cases judges have first *provisionally* identified the award they proposed to make before asking whether it is likely that sufficient funds will be released to justify the making of the award. This approach was adopted in *SR v CR*[48] where Singer J said [Emphasis added]:

> '…a key component of the court's role is to determine on whatever evidence is available **how the trustees are likely to exercise their discretion in the situation postulated by the award which the court has it in mind to make.**'[49]

9.39 It can thus be seen that the courts have not adopted a uniform approach to the question of sequence. However, the distinction is one of emphasis and nuance in the exercise of discretion, rather than one of fundamental principle.

46 *BJ v MJ (Financial Order: Overseas Trust)* [2011] EWHC 2708 (Fam), [2012] 1 FLR 667, Mostyn J.

47 *G v G (Financial Remedies: Short Marriage: Trust Assets)* [2012] EWHC 167 (Fam), [2012] 2 FLR 48, Charles J.

48 *R v R (Ancillary Relief: Family Trusts) (aka SR v CR (Ancillary Relief: Family Trusts))* [2008] EWHC 2329 (Fam), [2009] 2 FCR 69.

49 See para 33 of the judgment in *R v R (Ancillary Relief: Family Trusts) (aka SR v CR (Ancillary Relief: Family Trusts))* [2008] EWHC 2329 (Fam), [2009] 2 FCR 69, Singer J.

Traditional 'tripartite' approach: quantification always comes before distribution	'Holistic' approach: quantification partly informed by an assessment of the trustees' likely reaction to order
– The court asks the following questions (without deviation from sequence): (1) What is the likelihood and amount of future benefit from the trust? (2) What are the overall resources available for division (taking into account the answer to Q1)? (3) How should those resources be divided between the spouses? – Examples of this approach being applied in practice: *BJ v MJ*[50] and *G v G*[51]	– The court asks the following questions, in the round: (1) What order does the court have in mind to make (based on the section 25 factors[52])? (2) How are the trustees likely to exercise their discretion in the event of the court making such an order? (3) What are the overall resources available for division (taking into account the likely exercise of trustee discretion under Q2)? (4) How should the resources be divided between the spouses? – Example of this approach being applied in practice: *SR v CR*[53]

Exceeding the total assets or income owned outright by a party

9.40 If a party is likely to benefit from a third party's largesse, to an extent that it would be fair to pay their spouse a sum which *exceeds* the total value of their non-trust assets, there is no reason in principle why such an order should not be made. However, in practice it is rare for an award to exceed a party's 'hard' assets, especially in a case where the third party in question is a relative as opposed to a trust with fiduciary obligations to its beneficiary[54]. Such orders requiring a trustee to 'backfill'[55] the funds of the paying spouse may risk straying beyond the bounds of appropriate judicial encouragement into improper pressure by requiring the trustees to make provision to a non-beneficiary spouse in order to avoid bankruptcy or being in contempt of court.

9.41 It is more common for the court to award the majority of the non-trust assets to the receiving party and to leave the paying party more or less dependent

50 *BJ v MJ (Financial Order: Overseas Trust)* [2011] EWHC 2708 (Fam), [2012] 1 FLR 667, Mostyn J.

51 *G v G (Financial Remedies: Short Marriage: Trust Assets)* [2012] EWHC 167 (Fam), [2012] 2 FLR 48, Charles J.

52 See **Chapter 2** of this book for the applicable principles to the court's exercise of discretion under MCA 1973, s 25.

53 *R v R (Ancillary Relief: Family Trusts) (aka SR v CR (Ancillary Relief: Family Trusts))* [2008] EWHC 2329 (Fam), [2009] 2 FCR 69, Singer J.

54 See para 101 in *TL v ML (Ancillary Relief: Claim against assets of extended family)* [2005] EWHC 2860 (Fam), [2006] 1 FLR 1263, [2006] 1 FCR 465, Mostyn QC; para 39 in *AM v SS* [2014] EWHC 865 (Fam), Coleridge J.

55 The term 'backfill' is used in this context by Coleridge J at para 39 in *AM v SS* [2014] EWHC 865 (Fam).

on his trust resources. By taking this approach, the court encourages trustees to replenish the funds of its beneficiary rather than making funds directly available to meet an award to a third party (spouse) of the beneficiary. This distinction was highlighted in *TL v ML*[56].

Snapshot: Matrimonial awards expressed as a % of non-trust assets where there were additional 'resources' held in trust	
Case	**% of non-trust assets awarded to the recipient party**
B v B	44% (£50k)
Browne	152% (£175k)
Charman	87% (£48m)
BJ v MJ	50% (£2.96m)
SR v CR	80% (£6.25m)
Whaley	94% (£3m)

9.42 The above cases all concerned assets held in a trust. The court in *TL v ML* raised in discussion with counsel the question of whether a family court had *ever* (before or after *Thomas*) made an award that exceeded 100% of the paying party's assets and which therefore could only be met from provision from a third party other than a trustee. Only two cases were cited in argument in which this was said to have happened, and both were distinguished by the court on their facts: *M v M (Maintenance Pending Suit)*[57], which was an MPS case, and *X v X (Y and Z Intervening)*[58], in which the outcome was influenced by the existence of a separation agreement. The court expressed the view that neither authority gave much guidance on the issue of the proper exercise of judicial encouragement in a more conventional *Thomas* case.

C. PRACTICAL GUIDANCE IN *THOMAS* CASES

Involvement of trustees in proceedings as parties/witnesses

9.43 Trustees are frequently reluctant to play any role in divorce proceedings concerning a beneficiary, or potential future beneficiary, of their trust, particularly where the trust or its assets are based in other jurisdictions.

9.44 There are a number of factors that may properly weigh against the involvement of trustees in proceedings, which are considered generally at length in **Chapter 4** of this book. With these factors in mind, trustees must consider carefully whether co-operation with the matrimonial court will be in the interests of the trust. In *Thomas* cases, where a court is being asked to make findings as to whether a trust asset is a party's resource, the court is highly likely to be assisted

56 At para 101.
57 *M v M (Maintenance Pending Suit)* [2002] EWHC 317 (Fam), [2002] 2 FLR 123.
58 *X v X (Y and Z Intervening)* [2002] 1 FLR 508, [2002] Fam Law 98, Munby J.

by the active involvement of trustees in the proceedings[59]. Further, the absence of evidence from the trustees may actively harm the party seeking to minimise the significance of trust assets as the court may draw inferences from the trustees' non-participation[60]. It may also create presentational difficulties for a party claiming independence from a trust to be the sole source of evidence in respect of the trustees' likely position.

Alternative cases: the importance of clarity in the attack

9.45 It is not uncommon for a party challenging his or her spouse's presentation of a trust to do so on alternative bases[61] such as:

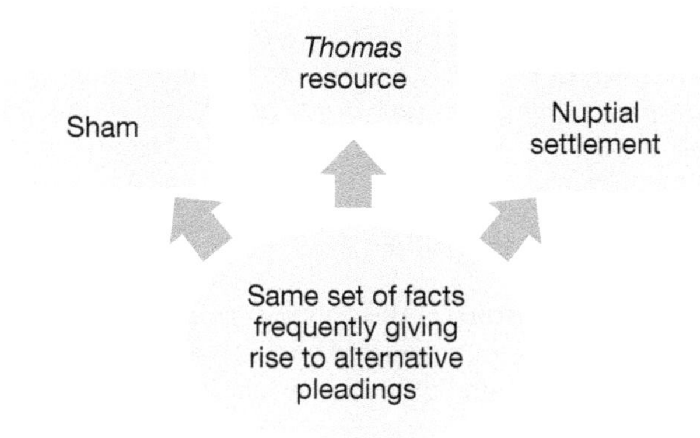

Case illustration: *A v A*[62]

Facts:

- The parties had interests in three companies including 46% of the shares in HDC set up prior to the marriage by H's father. Two trusts (of which H and members of his family were beneficiaries) held 54%.
- W argued that the two trusts were a 'sham' and H should be treated as owning not 23% of the shares but 77%.

59 See para 41 of *A v A and St Georges Trustees* [2007] EWHC 99 (Fam), [2007] 2 FLR 467, Munby J.

60 See para 47 at p 495 of the judgment of Lord Sumption in *Prest v Petrodel Resources Ltd and others* [2013] UKSC 34, [2013] 2 AC 415, SC.

61 For example, see *Quan v Bray* [2014] EWHC 3340 (Fam), [2015] 3 FCR 436, Sir Paul Coleridge; and *A v A and St Georges Trustees* [2007] EWHC 99 (Fam), [2007] 2 FLR 467, Munby J. In respect of sham: see in particular *A v A*; in respect of nuptial settlement: see in particular *Quan v Bray*. Note the report of *Quan v Bray* cited here is of the first instance decision (since the point under discussion is how the parties chose to present their cases at trial) but the case was subsequently subject to an appeal, reported at *Quan v Bray and others* [2017] EWCA Civ 405, [2017] 3 FCR 648, CA.

62 *A v A and St Georges Trustees* [2007] EWHC 99 (Fam), [2007] 2 FLR 467, Munby J.

- W also argued in the alternative that the trust's assets were a *Thomas* resource as H had control of the trusts and treated the company shares as his own.

Approach of the court:

- The court observed the prima facie inconsistency of running alternative cases of (i) sham, and (ii) *Thomas*, and emphasised the need for clearly defined pleadings[63].
- W's 'sham' case was rejected. It was held that a trust could not be a sham, regardless of the intentions of the settlor, if the original or subsequently appointed trustees had not been a party to it at the time of their appointment.
- The resource question was that formulated in *Charman*, ie, '*If asked, would the trustees be 'likely', either immediately or in the foreseeable future, to exercise their powers in favour of, or for the benefit of, the husband?*'
- The trustees were not likely to make trust assets available to H, and therefore they did not constitute a 'resource'. The court had particular regard to:
  - there being no history of distributions from the trust to H,
  - H was only one of a number of beneficiaries, and
  - the trust did not hold liquid cash resources, but company shares.

Case illustration: *Quan v Bray*[64]

Facts:

- During the marriage the parties together set up a conservation project to save the Chinese tiger species from extinction through a charitable trust vehicle. H had supported the project with a loan and a donation from his own funds. W was removed as a Director of the charity when the parties separated.
- The trust had assets of c.£25m; the parties had next to nothing in their names.
- W's case changed during the proceedings. Initially she accepted that the trust was set up for purely charitable purposes but averred that it had later been used as a resource by the parties.
- She later argued that it was a nuptial settlement, set up at least in part to provide a financial benefit to the parties personally (including saving

63 See paras 16, 17, and 27 of the judgment.

64 *Quan v Bray* [2014] EWHC 3340 (Fam), [2015] 3 FCR 436, Sir Paul Coleridge for the first instance case, and *Quan v Bray and others* [2017] EWCA Civ 405, [2017] 3 FCR 648, CA for the report of the appeal.

tax) and/or that it had acquired a nuptial character as it had funded the parties' lifestyle.

Approach of the court:

- The judge found the evidence did not support W's case and the trust was not held to be a nuptial settlement or a resource.
- W's subsequent appeal was dismissed[65].

9.46 The issues of principle arising in cases of 'sham' are considered in **Chapter 7**, but practitioners should be generally wary that running alternative cases can give rise to evidential and presentational difficulties. Allegations that a trust is both a '*sham*' and '*Thomas*' resource are likely to be prima facie inconsistent, a point noted by Munby J in *A v A*[66]. Before pleading alternative contrasting cases, practitioners should consider whether their client's presentation will be stronger evidentially if they focus upon a single allegation. It is important at an early stage to assess the evidence and be clear about the case being advanced.

65 *Quan v Bray and others* [2017] EWCA Civ 405, [2017] 3 FCR 648, CA.

66 See paras 16, 17 and 27 of *A v A and St Georges Trustees* [2007] EWHC 99 (Fam), [2007] 2 FLR 467, Munby J.

CHAPTER 10

Avoidance of Dispositions

Content at a Glance:

A. INTRODUCTION

10.1 The court has a number of powers at its disposal in order to prevent attempts to defeat or reduce claims for financial relief.

10.2 Trust structures, particularly those off-shore, are often looked upon with suspicion and are (erroneously) presumed to be operated with mischief in mind. Per Coleridge J[1]:

> 'Nothing is more calculated to set the bells ringing in a specialist family lawyer's mind than to be faced by such wealth contained within such a structure. It is designed and intended to be impenetrable and when it supports a lavish standard of living it is invariably like a red rag to a bull. …'

10.3 Despite this, there are few reported decisions concerning the avoidance of dispositions in the context of trusts, although this is gradually changing. Family practitioners are increasingly asked to advise about such situations.

10.4 This chapter focuses on the following potential remedies for preventing or setting aside transfers to or from a trust[2]:

- Section 37 of the Matrimonial Causes Act 1973 ('MCA 1973');
- Section 37 of the Senior Courts Act 1981 ('SCA 1981') and the inherent jurisdiction;
- Section 423 of the Insolvency Act 1986 ('IA 1986').

10.5 The chapter also provides a brief overview of the remedies available against trustees.

B. SECTION 37 OF THE MATRIMONIAL CAUSES ACT 1973

- A specific matrimonial tool
- Operates to set aside or prevent dispositions
- Reliant on intention which, in certain circumstances, may be presumed

Overview

10.6 The court has the power to prevent and avoid dispositions designed to defeat an applicant's claims for financial relief by virtue of the MCA 1973, s 37(2). This is a bespoke statutory tool for matrimonial finance cases and will usually be the first application to consider.

1 *J v V (Disclosure: Offshore Corporations)* [2003] EWHC 3110 (Fam), [2004] 1 FLR 1042 at 1047.

2 It should be noted that there are other potential remedies available that are beyond the scope of this work. For instance, the Civil Jurisdiction and Judgments Act 1982, s 25 empowers the High Court to grant interim relief in support of proceedings either commenced or to be commenced in a foreign jurisdiction.

10.7 Section 37 provides two kinds of remedy:

- A pre-emptive injunction preventing any future disposal, dealing or transfer, including out of the jurisdiction, of any property; ie a freezing injunction[3].

Section 37(2)(a) A pre-emptive freezing application	=	Is the respondent about to make any disposition or to transfer out of the jurisdiction or otherwise deal with any property?	+	Does the respondent have the intention of defeating the claim for financial relief? This may be a rebuttable presumption.	+	To prevent a disposition, the court may make such an order as it thinks fit for restraining the respondent and/or protecting the claim.

- The setting aside of a reviewable disposition made before[4] or after[5] financial relief.

Section 37(2)(b) and (c) A set-aside application	=	Has the respondent made a reviewable disposition? This may be before or after financial relief.	+	Does the respondent have the intention of defeating the claim for financial relief? This may be a rebuttable presumption.	+	The court will set aside the disposition.

Financial relief

10.8 Financial relief is defined for the purposes of s 37 as an application under any of the following provisions of the MCA 1973:

- Section 22 (Maintenance Pending Suit).
- Section 23 (Periodical Payment and Lump Sum Orders).
- Section 24 (Property Adjustment Orders).
- Section 24B (Pension Sharing Orders).
- Section 27 (Financial Provision Orders in cases of failure to maintain).

3 MCA 1973, s 37(2)(a).
4 MCA 1973, s 37(2)(b).
5 MCA 1973, s 37(2)(c).

- Section 31 (Applications for variation save for section 31(6)).
- Section 35 (Alteration of a Maintenance Agreement).

The requisite intention

10.9 In each situation, the court must be satisfied on the balance of probabilities that the respondent acted with the requisite intention, namely an intention to defeat the claim for financial relief.

10.10 'Defeating the claim' means preventing or reducing the claim or frustrating or impeding the enforcement of any order which might be or has been made[6].

10.11 There is a rebuttable presumption of intention where the court is satisfied that the disposition has or would have the consequence of defeating the applicant's claim and either[7]:

- The disposition took place less than three years before the date of the application; or
- The disposition is about to take place.

In *AAZ v BBZ sub nom. Akhmedov v Ahkmedova* [2016] EWHC 3234 (Fam); [2018] 1 FLR 153, W sought an order under MCA 1973, s 37 and IA 1986, s 423 setting aside a deed of trust dated 17th March 2015 under which the husband purported to assign to a Bermudan 'Cipher' trust virtually his entire wealth. The disposition was made four days prior to H signing his witness statement in the ongoing financial remedy proceedings and the presumption applied. H produced no evidence to rebut the presumption and the disposition was accordingly set aside.

10.12 Outside the three-year period, actual intention must be shown:

- The court is concerned with the respondent's intention in a subjective sense. This requires an investigation of the respondent's state of mind[8].
- The court is entitled to rely on inferences to ascertain a respondent's true intentions and the court may infer intention from the natural consequences of the respondent's actions[9].
- The intention to defeat the claim need not be the sole or dominant intention[10].

6 MCA 1973, s 37(1).
7 MCA 1973, s 37(5).
8 *Kemmis v Kemmis (Welland Intervening)* [1988] 1 WLR 1307 per Lloyd LJ at 1326.
9 *Kemmis v Kemmis (Welland Intervening)* [1988] 1 WLR 1308 per Lloyd LJ at 1326.
10 *Kemmis v Kemmis (Welland Intervening)* [1988] 1 WLR 1308 per Nourse LJ at 1331; *Kremen v Agrest & Fishman* [2010] EWHC 2571; [2011] 2 FLR 478.

– Timing can be highly relevant. If the disposition predates the divorce and/or marital difficulties by some years, this would weigh against such an intention.

– Purpose is also highly relevant. If it can be shown that the disposition was made for an apparently legitimate, innocent or benevolent purpose, the court may decline to set it aside such as in the case of *Mubarak v Mubarik*[11].

In *Mubarak*, H and W settled a trust in Jersey into which had been transferred their respective shares in the family company in 1997. In 2005, in attempting to enforce a financial remedy order, W applied to set aside the transfer under section 37. Holman J held that the requisite intention had not been proven:

'The fact is that [H] plainly did have legitimate and appropriate intentions, namely orderly succession and, very critically, avoidance of tax, which are capable of fully and wholly explaining and justifying the setting up of the trust and the transfer of the shares. All the available documentary evidence supports those intentions and gives no hint of any other.'

Meaning of disposition and reviewable disposition

10.13 'Disposition' includes any conveyance, assurance or gift of property of any description, whether made by an instrument or otherwise, in which either or both of the parties has or had a beneficial interest (either in possession or reversion)[12]. It will therefore include transfers to offshore trusts[13] but will not include:

– a provision contained in a will or codicil[14]; or

– an instrument of exclusion from a discretionary trust[15]. This is because such an instrument does not purport to dispose of property but of a beneficiary's right to be considered. It remains an open question as to whether removing a party as a beneficiary would amount to a 'dealing'.

10.14 Setting aside a disposition requires the disposition to be reviewable. A disposition is not reviewable if it was made for valuable consideration to a person acting in good faith and without notice of any intention on the part of the respondent to defeat the applicant's claim[16]. The following points are worth noting:

– A sale at an undervalue, although possibly satisfying the 'valuable consideration' test, may communicate an improper motive on the respondent's

11 [2007] EWHC 220 (Fam), [2007] 2 FLR 364.

12 MCA 1973, s 37(6).

13 See for instance *AAZ v BBZ* and *AC v DC (Financial Remedy: Effect of s.37 Avoidance Order) (No.1)* [2012] EWHC 2032 (Fam), [2013] 2 FLR 1483: the latter being a case which involved the transfer of assets to a Manx employee benefit trust.

14 MCA 1973, s 37(6).

15 *Mubarak v Mubarik* [2007] EWHC 220 (Fam), [2007] 2 FLR 364.

16 MCA 1973, s 37(4).

part to the transferee so that the latter will not take in good faith (a fact-specific concept)[17].

- Though a sale may be at full value, the transaction may be set aside if the transferee had actual or constructive notice[18].
- Though the legal burden of proof remains on the applicant to prove the negative (ie, that the transferee had no notice of the respondent's intentions) the evidential burden shifts to the transferee due to the obvious difficulties of having to prove a negative or lack of knowledge[19].

10.15 A reviewable disposition must have been made by the '*other party to the proceedings*'. However, dispositions made by the respondent's servants, agents, nominees or trustees may be considered to have been made by him personally where they are indistinguishable from him (ie, his alter ego)[20].

In *Ansari v Ansari* [2008] EWCA Civ 1456, [2010] Fam 1, [2009] 1 FLR 1121, the Court of Appeal considered the situation where the original transferee subsequently made an onward transfer of the property.

The Court expressed the view, without formally deciding the point, that if all the parties conspired together to defeat the wife's claim then the power under section 37 was broad enough to permit subsequent transactions to be set aside. To hold otherwise would create an easy way of defeating a legitimate claim.

Preventing a disposition

10.16 The court may make such an order as it thinks fit for restraining the respondent and/or protecting the claim, should the court be satisfied that the respondent:

Has the intention of defeating the claim for financial relief.	+	Is about to make a disposition, transfer or dealing.

10.17 As for the exercise of its discretion:

17 As to the meaning of 'good faith' see *Kemmis* and *Midland Bank Trust Co Ltd v Green* [1981] AC 513.

18 See eg, *Everclear v Agrest* [2011] EWCA Civ 232, [2011] 2 FLR 506 where the husband transferred a bearer share to a friend who then sold it for valuable consideration to another friend. Notice was established on the facts such that the first instance decision of *Kremen v Agrest (No 2)* [2010] EWHC 3091 (Fam), [2011] 2 FLR 490 was upheld.

19 *Kremen v Agrest & Fishman* [2010] EWHC 2571 (Fam), [2011] 2 FLR 478.

20 *Kemmis v Kemmis (Welland intervening)* [1988] 1 WLR 1307.

- In some cases it will be appropriate to freeze the asset[21] whilst in others it may be sufficient for the respondent to pay money into court or to give notice of any proposed dealing[22].
- An application preventing a disposal should not extend beyond those assets necessary to safeguard an applicant's claim for financial relief. The court will not freeze a party's entire asset-base[23].
- An order, unless the court orders otherwise, must contain an undertaking by the applicant to the court to pay any damages which the respondent sustains which the court considers the applicant should pay[24].

Setting aside a disposition

10.18 The court may make an order setting aside the disposition, if the court is satisfied that the respondent:

Has the intention of defeating the claim for financial relief.	+	Has made a reviewable disposition before or after a financial remedy order.

10.19 An order setting aside a transaction has the effect of restoring the status quo:

- It is suggested that, for tax purposes, the effect is as if the transaction had never taken place[25].
- The Order may provide for the applicant to recover the reasonable costs of undoing the effect of the respondent's disposition[26].

Procedure

10.20 Applications under s 37 may be made to a District Judge and above depending on complexity, the size of the assets and any international elements[27].

21 Including foreign assets though the court will refuse to do so where it would be ineffectual: *Hamlin v Hamlin* [1986] Fam 11, [1986] 1 FLR 61.
22 *Spencer-Churchill v Faggionato Fine Arts* [2012] EWHC 2318 (Ch).
23 *Ghoth v Ghoth* [1992] 2 All ER 920, [1992] 2 FLR 300.
24 FPR PD 20A, para 5.1(a).
25 *AC v DC (Financial Remedy: Effect of s.37 Avoidance Order) (No.1)* [2012] EWHC 2032 (Fam), [2013] 2 FLR 1483.
26 *Ali v Ansar-Ali* [2016] EWCA Civ 781; [2017] 1 FCR 1.
27 FPR r 9.6 read with r 2.5(2).

10.21 The Part 18 application procedure applies[28] and in respect of setting aside applications the application is made in Form A[29] whereas restraining order applications are made on Form D50G.

10.22 Applications may be made without notice but[30]:

– The applicant must show that the matter is one of extreme urgency or that giving notice of any kind would defeat the purpose of the order sought. In any other case at least short, informal notice should be given.

– The evidence given to the court must be detailed and precise. There is a heavy duty on those presenting an application without notice to ensure that the court is directed to all the relevant facts, both favourable and unfavourable.

C. SECTION 37 OF THE SENIOR COURTS ACT 1981 AND THE INHERENT JURISDICTION

- Remedies not specific to financial remedy claims
- Operate to prevent dispositions

Overview

10.23 In the rare situation that the provisions of the MCA 1973, s 37(2)(a) are insufficient, practitioners should be aware that the court is empowered to grant a 'freezing injunction' under the SCA 1981, s 37 and the High Court has an inherent jurisdiction in family proceedings to make freezing orders in support of financial remedy applications[31].

10.24 SCA 1981, s 37 provides:

> '(1) The High Court may by order (whether interlocutory or final) grant an injunction…in all cases in which it appears to the court to be just and convenient to do so.
>
> (2) Any such order may be made either unconditionally or on such terms and conditions as the court thinks just.
>
> (3) The power of the High Court under subsection (1) to grant an interlocutory injunction restraining a party to any proceedings from removing from the jurisdiction of the High Court, or otherwise dealing with, assets located within that jurisdiction shall be exercisable in cases where that party is, as well as in cases where he is not, domiciled resident or present within that jurisdiction.'

28 FPR Pt 18.

29 FPR PD 5A, para 3.1.

30 *UL v BK* [2013] EWHC 1735 (Fam), [2014] Fam 35.

31 Though a spate of recent first instance decisions suggest the inherent jurisdiction does not extend the court's powers beyond those stipulated by the MCA 1973 and/or SCA 1981.

10.25 Though the statutory provision refers to the High Court, SCA 1981, s 37(6) confirms that the remedy applies to the Family Court as it applies to the High Court. The Family Procedure Rules 2010 ('FPR') r 20.2(1) further provides that the Family Court may grant an order (referred to as a 'freezing injunction') restraining a party:

- from removing assets from the jurisdiction; or
- from dealing with any assets whether located within the jurisdiction or not.

Ambit

10.26 SCA 1981, s 37 is a remedy available at general law and is not a specific matrimonial tool. Its use, in all circumstances, is confined to orders which are ancillary to, or supportive of, a separate, substantive, legal or equitable right (eg, a financial remedy claim)[32].

10.27 The remedy acts *in personam* and can thus be made in respect of assets outside the jurisdiction (albeit there is a high threshold)[33].

10.28 An order may be made at any stage of the proceedings, including post-judgment and as part of enforcement proceedings[34].

10.29 An order may also be made without notice though the same conditions apply as set out above in relation to MCA 1973, s 37. Moreover, the Order should do no more than necessary to protect the claim and, where possible, should only freeze a portion of the available funds representing broadly the likely quantum of the claim. The order should also allow the party against whom it is obtained to have his living expenses met, to meet day-to-day business expenditure and to meet ordinary debts (including legal costs)[35].

Requirements

10.30 Relief may be granted where the court is satisfied that[36]:

The applicant has a good arguable case against the respondent.

+

There is a real risk of prejudice by reason of the disposal by the respondent of his assets, unless he is restrained from doing so.

+

It would be just and convenient in all the circumstances of the case to grant the relief sought.

32 See for instance *Goyal v Goyal* [2016] EWCA Civ 792, [2016] 4 WLR 140, [2017] 2 FLR 223.

33 *Babanaft International Co SA v Bassatne* [1990] Ch 13, [1989] 2 WLR 232.

34 Though not as a free-standing enforcement procedure in its own right: *B v B* [1998] 1 WLR 329, [1997] 2 FLR 148.

35 *Law Society v Shanks* [1988] 1 FLR 504.

36 *Ninemia Maritime Corp v Trave Schiffahrts GmbH & Co KG (The Niedersachsen)* [1983] 1 WLR 1412.

10.31 Other than in exceptional cases, the first requirement will be met by the existence of an easily demonstrable financial remedy claim. The second limb, however, requires solid evidence of a risk of dissipation[37]. Moreover, *prima facie* proof of a risk of dissipation requires, at least in general and broad terms, proof of *an intention* to dissipate[38]. In this way, it has been stated that there is little real difference between MCA 1973 and SCA 1981 save that the existence of the statutory presumption may make an application under the MCA 1973 easier[39].

The inherent jurisdiction

10.32 There are a number of reported authorities recognising the High Court's inherent jurisdiction in family proceedings to make freezing orders, ie, without reference to the MCA 1973, s 37 or SCA 1981, s 37. However, judges in more recent authorities have suggested it is unlikely that the High Court has any further powers beyond those prescribed by statute[40]. Thus the inherent jurisdiction cannot be called upon to fill any perceived gaps in the legislation or a particular case. It is suggested that, if the power does exist, it serves little practical purpose in modern financial remedy proceedings.

D. SECTION 423 OF THE INSOLVENCY ACT 1986

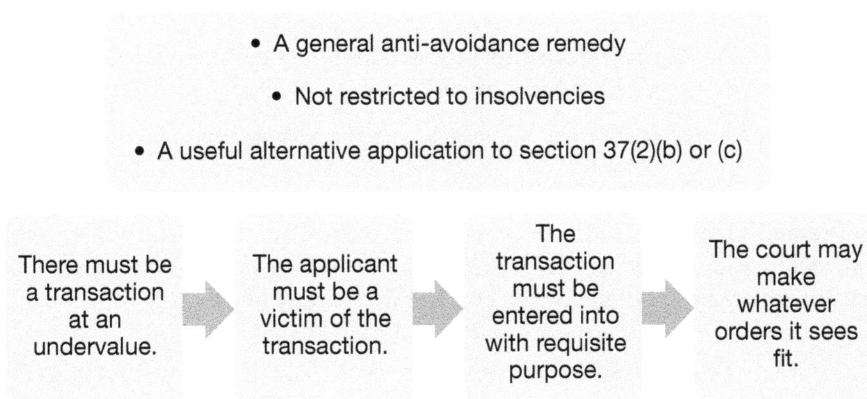

Overview

10.33 An application under IA 1986, s 423 is a potential alternative to MCA 1973, s 37(2)(b) or (c). The former is an anti-avoidance remedy under the general law and is not restricted to cases of insolvency whereas the latter

37 See for instance *Araghchinchi v Aragchinchi* [1997] 2 FLR 142, CA.

38 *UL v BK* [2013] EWHC 1735 (Fam), [2014] Fam 35.

39 *UL v BK* [2013] EWHC 1735 (Fam), [2014] Fam 35.

40 *ND v KP (ex parte application)* [2011] EWHC 457 (Fam), [2011] 2 FLR 662; *UL v BK; C v C* [2015] EWHC 2795 (Fam), [2016] Fam Law 20; *Goyal v Goyal;* and *Tobias v Tobias* [2017] EWFC 46, [2017] 4 WLR 146.

is a specialist matrimonial tool. The applications can be made together in the alternative.

10.34 The statutory language under s 423 differs from that of MCA 1973, s 37 and, depending on the particular set of facts, it may be easier to obtain orders under one section than the other. However, in most cases, an application pursuant to the IA 1986 will add nothing to an application pursuant to s 37[41].

10.35 The operation of s 423, which has unlimited extra-territorial effect[42], requires:

A transaction at an undervalue to be entered into by a person.	+	The transaction in question to have been entered into with the requisite purpose.

10.36 Where the two key requirements are fulfilled, the court has a wide discretion to:

Restore the position to what it would have been had the transaction not been entered into.	+	Protect the interests of persons who are victims of the transaction.

10.37 Section 423 is intended to be a wide-ranging anti-avoidance remedy[43]. Its predecessor was s 172 of the Law of Property Act 1925. This means that:

- the remedy is not confined to cases where the respondent is insolvent[44];
- there is no need for insolvency proceedings.

The remedy has been scarcely used in the context of trusts but was recently considered and applied in *AAZ v BBZ sub nom Akhmedov v Ahkmedova*[45], the facts of which are set out above at **10.11** in the context of MCA 1973, s 37.

> In *AAZ v BBZ*, the wife sought orders under MCA 1973, s 37 and IA 1986, s 423 in the alternative. Since the disposition was a paradigm s 37 case, there was no strict need to rely on s 423 but Haddon-Cave J opted to make an order on both bases in order to aid enforcement.

41 *Mubarak v Mubarik* [2007] EWHC 220 (Fam), [2007] 2 FLR 364.

42 See *Re Paramount Airways Ltd (in administration)* [1993] Ch 223, [1992] 3 All ER 1, CA and more recently *AAZ v BBZ* [2016] EWHC 3234 (Fam), [2018] 1 FLR 153.

43 *B v IB (Order to set aside disposition under Insolvency Act)* [2013] EWHC 3755, [2014] 2 FLR 273: a widow was allowed to proceed with an application under s 423 to set aside a gift of shares made before the husband's death, even though he was not insolvent.

44 *B v IB (Order to set aside disposition under Insolvency Act)* [2013] EWHC 3755, [2014] 2 FLR 273.

45 The court has since made further consequential orders setting aside other dispositions made by or on behalf of the husband. See [2016] EWHC 3361 (Fam), [2017] 2 FCR 461 and [2018] EWFC 23.

Transactions at an undervalue

10.38 Section 423 requires the transaction to have been at an undervalue. For this purpose, a person enters into a transaction at an undervalue if:

- he makes a gift to the other person or he otherwise enters into a transaction with the other on terms that provide for him to receive no consideration;
- he enters into a transaction with the other in consideration of marriage or the formation of a civil partnership; or
- he enters into a transaction with the other for a consideration the value of which, in money or money's worth, is significantly less than the value, in money or money's worth, of the consideration provided by himself.

10.39 A transfer of property at full market value will make the transaction immune from this provision, but a transfer for less than market value may be vulnerable to be set aside. In many cases it will be easier to prove that a transaction has taken place 'at an undervalue' for the purposes of s 423 than to prove an absence of 'valuable consideration' for the purposes of MCA 1973, s 37(4).

10.40 Section 423 applies to disposals of property, subject to limitation, made either[46]:

Prior to the making of a final order.	+	Following the making of a final order when enforcement of that order is sought (including in relation to costs).

Onward transactions by third parties

10.41 Whilst it is debatable whether MCA 1973, s 37 can be used to set aside transactions made from third party to third party[47], there is no doubt that s 423 can be used for that purpose so long as the statutory criteria are established.

10.42 Section 425(5) establishes that an order may affect the property of, or impose any obligation on, any person whether or not he is the person with whom the debtor entered into the transaction, but such an order:

Cannot prejudice any interest in property acquired from a person other than the debtor in good faith, for value and without notice of the relevant circumstances, or prejudice any interest deriving from such an interest.	+	Cannot require a person who received a benefit from the transaction in good faith, for value and without notice of the relevant circumstances to pay any sum unless he was a party to the transaction.

46 *Trowbridge v Trowbridge* [2002] EWHC 3114 (Ch), [2003] 2 FLR 231, David Richards QC.

47 In *Ansari v Ansari* [2008] EWCA Civ 1456, [2010] Fam 1, the Court of Appeal expressed the view that s 37 was broad enough in its scope to permit subsequent disposals to be set aside.

The requisite intention

10.43 An order may only be made if the court is satisfied that it was entered into by a party for one of the following purposes:

Putting assets beyond the reach of a person who is making, or may at some time make, a claim against them.	/	Otherwise prejudicing the interests of such a person in relation to the claim which they are making or may make.

10.44 It is thus necessary to prove that the person who entered into the transaction did so with the requisite purpose. In contrast to the position under MCA 1973, s 37, there is no presumption as to the 'purpose' under s 423 and so the 'purpose' will need to be proved on the balance of probabilities. However, s 423 is a useful adjunct to MCA 1973, s 37 in a case where a party cannot prove that the other intended to defeat *their* claim specifically as opposed to those of other creditors.

10.45 The applicant need not show that one of the statutory purposes was the only or dominant purpose behind the transaction, merely that the person who performed the transaction was substantially motivated by one of those purposes[48]. 'Purpose' in this context has been held to carry the same subjective meaning as the word 'intention' under MCA 1973, s 37[49].

Who may apply and to which court

10.46 There are restrictions on who may apply. Section 424 provides that an application under s 423 may be made by a victim of the transaction[50].

10.47 A victim of the transaction is generally defined as a person who is, or is capable of being, prejudiced by the transaction[51] and is wide enough not to be restricted to creditors with present or actual debts. There does not have to be a connection between the purpose of the transaction and the specific prejudice caused to the victim[52]. Thus, a party will be a 'victim' of the transaction if (judged in retrospect) it adversely affects their claims, even if they were not the contemporaneous object of the other party's requisite intention.

10.48 The application may be made to the High Court or a court which has bankruptcy jurisdiction over the respondent[53].

48 *IRC v Hashmi* [2002] EWCA Civ 981, [2002] 2 BCLC 489, CA.

49 *Trowbridge v Trowbridge* [2002] EWHC 3114 (Ch), [2003] 2 FLR 231; *Mubarak v Mubarik* [2007] EWHC 220 (Fam), [2007] 2 FLR 364.

50 It also includes provision for a variety of individuals to apply. ie where the debtor has been made bankrupt or where the victim of the transaction is bound by an approved voluntary arrangement.

51 IA 1986, s 423(5).

52 *Hill v Spread Trustees Co Ltd and Another* [2006] EWCA Civ 542, [2007] 1 WLR 2404, CA.

53 IA 1986, s 423(4).

Orders which may be made

10.49 The court has broad powers to make whatever orders it sees fit upon such an application but is not bound to do so. Without prejudice to that broad discretion, s 425 provides examples of orders that may be made with respect to such a transaction under s 423.

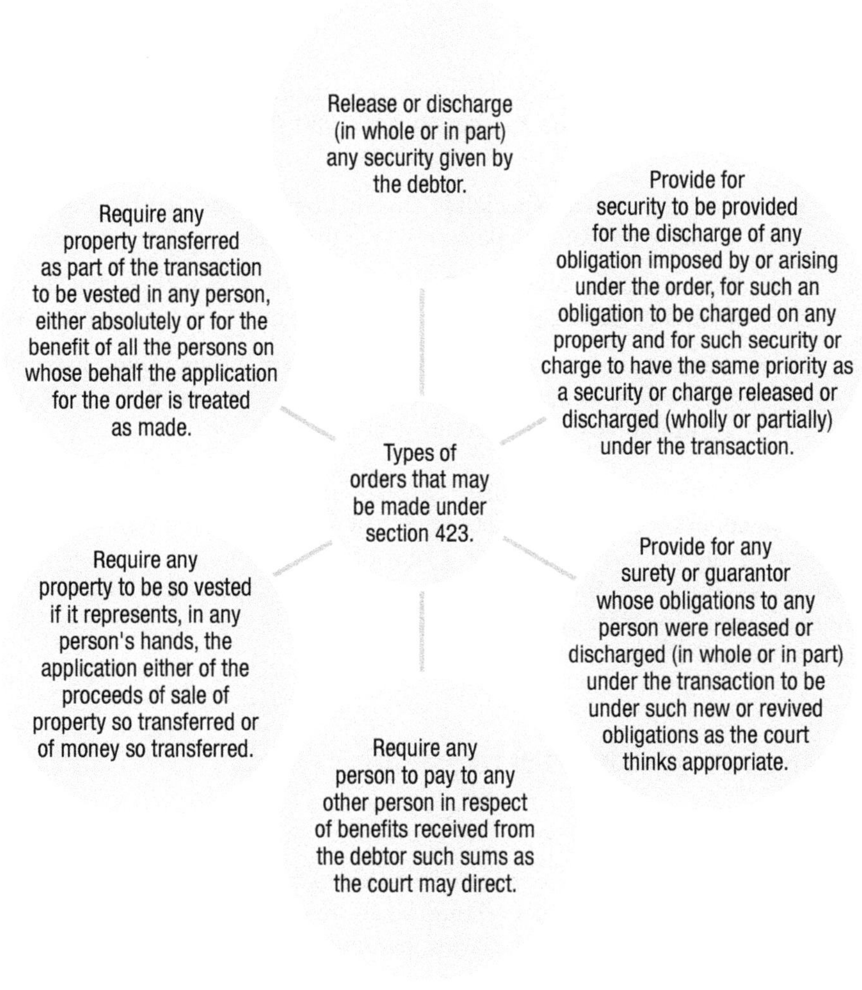

10.50 The objective of making the order is, so far as is practicable, both to restore the position to what it would have been if the transaction had not been entered into and to protect the interests of the victim(s) of it[54].

10.51 Section 423 cannot be used to put the applicant in a better position that he or she would have been had the transaction not occurred[55].

54 IA 1986, s 423(2); *Chohan v Saggar* [1994] BCC 134, CA.
55 *Ram v Ram and Others* [2004] EWCA Civ 1452, [2005] 2 FLR 63, CA.

In *Ram v Ram and Others*, a husband had disposed of property at an undervalue before becoming bankrupcy. It was held that the wife could not seek to have the property re-vested in the husband's name, so that she could obtain financial relief from him as she did not have provable debts; instead, the property would vest in the husband's trustee in bankruptcy.

Limitation

10.52 Practitioners should also be aware that claims under s 423 are subject to time limits pursuant to the Limitation Act 1980 (LA 1980)[56]. The relevant provisions state:

> '8 (1) An action upon a specialty[57] shall not be brought after the expiration of 12 years from the date on which the cause of action accrued.
>
> (2) Subsection (1) above shall not affect any action for which a shorter period of limitation is prescribed by any other provision of this Act.
>
> 9 (1) An action to recover any sum recoverable by virtue of any enactment shall not be brought after the expiration of six years from the date on which the cause of action accrued…'

10.53 Thus, the time limit is either 12 years under s 8(1) or, six years under s 9(1) depending on the remedy sought. So, in the context of s 423, where the substance of the claim is to recover a sum of money, the period is six years; otherwise the time limit for setting aside transactions is 12 years. However, the limitation period for such claims may be postponed by operation of LA 1980, s 32, ie, in cases of fraud, concealment or mistake.

E. REMEDIES AGAINST TRUSTEES

Overview

10.54 Although this book is concerned with trusts within the context of financial remedy proceedings, practitioners should be aware of the more general remedies available against trustees and fiduciaries, particularly where there is a breach of trust and/or of duty that may reduce the resources available for consideration.

10.55 A breach of trust occurs if a trustee does any act which they ought not to do and/or fails to do any act which they ought to do. Breaches may comprise a trustee dishonestly embezzling funds or failing to perform the duties considered below.

56 *Hill v Spread Trustee Co Ltd* [2006] EWCA Civ 542, [2007] 1 WLR 2404, CA.

57 This applies to a contract executed as a deed and claims on a statute (though its importance has been considerably diminished by section 9).

10.56 If the breach of trust has caused loss to the trust fund, the beneficiaries may sue the trustees for compensation to restore the trust fund to what it would have been had there been no breach. Claims against the trustees for compensation are personal or *in personam.* Some breaches, however, may involve the trustee taking trust property. In such a case, the beneficiaries may bring a proprietary claim to recover it or any substitute property. Such claims are proprietary or *in rem.*

10.57 Trustees who breach their duties may be assisted by others or may transfer property to others in breach of trust or fiduciary duty. There may also be potential claims against these third parties, often called 'strangers' but this is beyond the scope of this book.

Duties and powers

10.58 As legal owners of trust property, and subject to the terms of the trust, trustees have wide powers including[58]:

Making distributions to beneficiaries.	+	Making any loan or investment that they could make if they were absolutely entitled to the assets of the trust.

10.59 Those powers, however, are fettered by duties. Trustees' duties are laid down by statute, particularly the Trustee Act 2000 ('TA 2000'), and general law[59] though can be modified by trust instrument. In fulfilling these duties, trustees must exercise the appropriate standard of care.

10.60 The duties are multifarious, and trustees owe duties, including:

- On appointment, to ensure that:
  - They are properly appointed;
  - They become familiar with the terms of the trust;
  - They inquire into past business of the trust to discover any breaches; and
  - They take appropriate action to remedy any breaches.
- Following their appointment, they also have duties:
  - To observe the terms of the trust;
  - To make distributions to the correct beneficiaries;
  - To exercise such care and skill in respect of their administration of the trust as is reasonable in the circumstances[60];
  - To make authorised investments only and to have regard to the standard investment criteria[61];

58 TA 2000, s 3.
59 NB including fiduciary duties and obligations.
60 TA 2000, s 1 and Sch 1.
61 TA 2000, s 4.

- To obtain and consider proper advice about the way they should exercise their powers of investment (unless they reasonably conclude that in the circumstances it is unnecessary or inappropriate to do so)[62];
- To provide information to beneficiaries[63] and keep trust accounts showing how the trust fund is invested and the movement of trust assets[64];
- To consider whether to exercise their powers and discretions;
- To act in the best interests of all beneficiaries and to act impartially between beneficiaries;
- To act personally, ie, to play an active role in the administration of the trust, unless they have authority to delegate[65]; and
- Not to place themselves in a position where their personal interest conflicts with their duties and not to make an unauthorised profit[66].

Personal claim for compensation against a trustee

10.61 In order to sue a trustee[67] for compensation for breach of trust, a beneficiary must prove that:

The trustee has breached one or more of his duties.	+	That breach has caused loss to the trust.

In *Nestle v National Westminster Bank Plc* [1993] 1 WLR 1260, CA, the bank trustee had breached its duty of care when investing the trust fund by failing to review the investments regularly. However, the claimant beneficiary was unsuccessful because there was no evidence that the trust fund would have performed better under the management of a trustee reviewing regularly. It thus could not be shown that the breach had caused any loss to the fund.

10.62 A trustee against whom a claim is made for breach of trust may be able to rely upon various possible defences:

- Knowledge and consent of a beneficiary: Trustees will have a defence where the beneficiary was *sui juris* and gave consent freely with full knowledge of the relevant facts though the beneficiary need not know that what they are agreeing to is a breach *per se*[68].
- Acting honestly and reasonably: Section 61 of the Trustee Act 1925 provides that the court can relieve trustees of liability (wholly or in part) if they acted

62 TA 2000, s 5.
63 This may include a beneficiary's entitlements, the trust documents and the trust accounts.
64 See *Schmidt v Rosewood Trust Ltd* [2003] UKPC 26, [2003] 2 AC 709.
65 See *Pilkington v IRC* [1964] AC 612, HL. There is provision to delegate to co-trustees (or other agents) on a formal basis under the TA 2000, Trustee Act 1925, the Powers of Attorney Act 1971 and the Trustee Delegation Act 1999.
66 See for instance *Boardman v Phipps* [1967] 2 AC 46, HL.
67 Trustees who have breached their duties are jointly and severally liable.
68 *Re Pauling's Settlement Trust* [1964] Ch 303, [1963] 3 WLR 742.

honestly and reasonably and ought fairly to be excused in respect of the breach.

- Express exclusion clause: Such a clause may relieve trustees from liability for negligent or innocent breaches but will be void insofar as it tries to exclude liability for fraudulent breaches[69].
- Limitation and laches: Under s 21 of the LA 1980, actions in respect of any breach of trust cannot be brought after the expiration of six years from the date on which the cause of action accrued. No period of limitation shall apply to an action in respect of any fraudulent breach or proprietary claim. However, the equitable doctrine of laches should be considered in cases where there is no statutory limitation period pursuant to s 26(2). In essence, the courts will not allow a claim to succeed where it would be inequitable to do so.

Equitable proprietary claim against a trustee

10.63 Beneficiaries may bring proprietary claims to recover trust property which a trustee has misappropriated or used to acquire an unauthorised profit. For a trustee to act in this way is a breach of fiduciary duty and so equity's response is to impose a constructive trust over the relevant assets[70].

10.64 Beneficiaries are entitled at their option to either assert their beneficial ownership or to bring a personal claim against the trustee for breach of trust. They will normally exercise the option in a way most advantageous to them. For instance, an advantage of a proprietary claim is that if the trustee is bankrupt, a beneficiary's claim will have priority over other creditors. If the property has increased in value, again, it would be advantageous to bring a proprietary claim and assert a beneficial interest over the profit. On the other hand, if the property is worth less than the original asset, beneficiaries may wish to bring a personal claim.

10.65 Such claims against trustees are only possible if the trustee still holds the trust property or replacement property. A claim will fail if the trustee has 'dissipated' the property, ie, spent it in such a way that it is no longer represented by any asset. In some cases, the trustee may have removed trust property and changed its form, ie, by converting money into shares. In such cases reliance may be placed upon the doctrine of tracing, a detailed consideration of which is beyond the scope of this book.

69 *Armitage v Nurse* [1998] Ch. 241, [1997] 3 WLR 1046.
70 *See FHR European Ventures LLP v Cedar Capital Partners LLC* [2014] UKSC 45, [2015] AC 250, SC.

CHAPTER 11

Enforcement

Content at a Glance:

A. Introduction
- What orders will the court make?
- 'Telescoping' and piercing the corporate veil

B. Methods of enforcement
- International instruments
- Maintenance orders
- Common law systems: orders *in personam* vs orders *in rem*
- Findings of 'sham'
- Variation of the settlement

C. Offshore Legislation: 'firewall' provisions
- Cayman Islands
- Jersey
- Guernsey

D. Conclusion

A. INTRODUCTION

11.1 This Chapter should be read in conjunction with **Chapters 3** and **4**, which deal in detail with considerations as to the jurisdiction of the English court to make orders in relation to trusts in financial relief proceedings, both from the English perspective and from the perspective of another jurisdiction in which the trustee and/or the trust assets are based.

11.2 There is a degree of crossover between the question of jurisdiction to make the order and whether or not that order is then enforceable[1].

11.3 Enforcement is likely to be more straightforward if the court is dealing with a fully 'English' trust, namely one whose governing law is English law, whose trustees are in England and whose trust property is situated in England[2].

1 See paras **3.33–3.37** above: the English court will not make orders (even if it has jurisdiction to do so) where there is clear evidence that those orders will not be recognised and enforced in the relevant foreign jurisdiction.

2 See the discussions in **Chapter 3**, Section D as to the *situs* of the trust assets, the governing law of the trust and **Chapter 4** on submission to the jurisdiction.

> *AB v CB*
>
> [2014] EWHC 2998 (Fam), [2015] 2 FLR 25[3]
>
> H and W married for nine years and had one child. H's family were wealthy farmers and landowners. The parties lived in a farmhouse owned by H's father. During the marriage the farmhouse was settled on discretionary trust with H as the principal beneficiary. W was not a beneficiary.
>
> The trustees, who included H's father, were joined to the proceedings by consent. The dispute centred on whether the trust was a nuptial settlement capable of variation under the MCA 1973 and, if so, whether the property within the trust was H's right to occupy, or the value of the farmhouse itself. Mostyn J varied the trust and ordered £157,000 to be paid to W (50% of the net value of the farmhouse), the majority to be held on trust for her by independent trustees for the remainder of her life, then revert back to the original family trust. If the lump sum was not paid within a certain timeframe, the farmhouse would have to be sold.

11.4 When a trust is not an 'English' trust in the sense described above, problems with jurisdiction may arise and practitioners are likely to encounter issues of enforceability, especially if an offshore trust is governed by the law of a jurisdiction which has implemented 'firewall' legislation to protect trusts. The fact that the English court might assert jurisdiction to make orders in relation to that trust may ultimately be fruitless if the jurisdiction in which orders must be enforced refuses to enforce them.

11.5 This Chapter will address enforcement issues that may arise in respect of trusts with a 'foreign' element. It does not deal with other more conventional remedies that may be available to enforce orders in purely 'English' cases, which might include charging orders, attachment of earnings orders, third party debt orders, injunctions, orders to facilitate a transfer of property or orders for committal.

What orders will the court make?

11.6 The court's powers under the Matrimonial Causes Act 1973 ('MCA 1973') have been discussed in **Chapter 2**. However, it is worth noting the types of capital orders the court has the power to make as set out below:

3 Upheld on appeal to the Court of Appeal, reported at [2016] 1 FLR 437, CA.

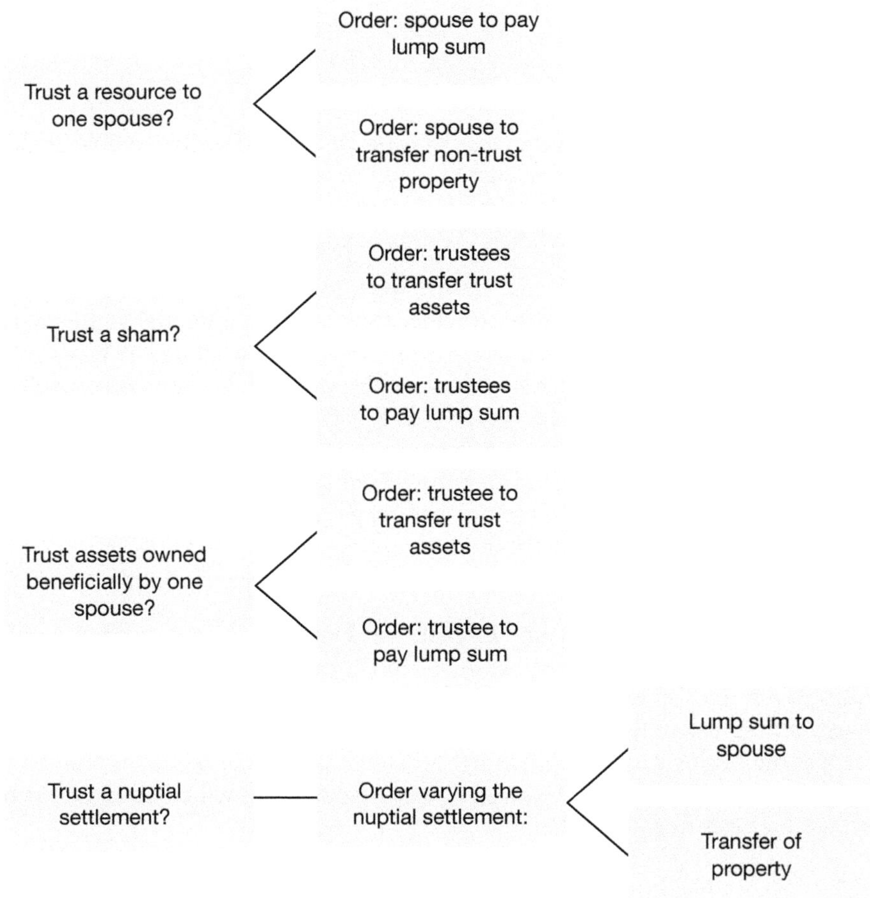

11.7 A lump sum order made against a spouse does not bind a trustee even if is made on the basis that the trustee is likely to make funds available to the paying spouse. This topic is addressed in **Chapter 7**. Such orders are not capable of being enforced against trustees. If no enforcement remedies are available against the paying spouse the order may in practice prove worthless.

11.8 In other cases, including where nuptial settlements are varied, orders may be made personally or *in personam* against trustees. Such orders might even require a trustee to take various steps including varying the trust so as to insert a beneficiary or making a payment to or for the benefit of a beneficiary.

11.9 Enforcing an order against trustees based outside the jurisdiction is fraught with difficulties, especially if the trustees are prevented from complying with the order as a result of a decision of their local court.

'Telescoping' and piercing the corporate veil

11.10 **Chapter 8**[4] addresses the principle of 'telescoping' whereby the courts make an order extracting assets from a trust structure and transfer them to a party in circumstances where the assets are not directly owned by the trustee, but instead held in a complex corporate structure in which the trustee holds shares[5].

11.11 The power to make such orders against a trustee has been brought into serious doubt by the decision of the Supreme Court in *Prest v Petrodel Resources Ltd & Others*[6]. Where orders are sought against underlying assets in a trust structure, the only option may be to seek to persuade a court that the properties legally owned by the relevant company are in fact held on resulting trust and belong beneficially to one of the parties by virtue of the particular circumstances in which the properties came to be vested in them (as was the case in *Prest*[7]). The principles relevant to such an application are discussed in **Chapter 7**.

B. METHODS OF ENFORCEMENT

International instruments

11.12 In an ideal world there would be a system of bilateral or multilateral treaties or agreements to assist with the enforcement of an order made following financial remedy proceedings. Unfortunately that is not the case.

11.13 Although Council Regulation (EC) No 4/2009 ('the Maintenance Regulation') enables a party to enforce in EU Member States orders for 'maintenance', the scope of the Regulation excludes a party's '*rights in property arising out of a matrimonial relationship*'[8].

4 At section H.
5 See for example *Hope v Krejci* [2012] EWHC 1780 (Fam), [2013] 1 FLR 182.
6 [2013] 2 AC 415, SC. It is notable that in refusing permission to appeal out of time in the *Hope v Krejci* case, Gloster LJ accepted that the 'shortcut approach' Mostyn J had adopted at first instance had been 'disproved' by the Supreme Court in *Prest* but that, in reality, the judge would have found that the assets were held beneficially by the husband on resulting trust. Note that in *DR v GR (Financial Remedy: Variation of Overseas Trust)* [2013] EWHC 1196 (Fam); [2013] 2 FLR 1534 Mostyn J defended his decision in *Hope v Krejci* in light of the Court of Appeal's decision in *Prest*, albeit prior to the publication of the Supreme Court's decision.
7 (As above), para 43 onwards.
8 The same is true for the Lugano Convention 2007 (article 1), Brussels Regulation recast (EU) 1215/2012 (art 2) and Brussels 1968 Convention (article 1). Note that some countries do have reciprocal enforcement arrangements with England, but that these tend to be specific to orders for the payment of a sum of money. For example, the Judgments (Reciprocal Enforcement) (Jersey) Law 1960 applies to England and applies to a final and conclusive order for the payment of a sum of money by the superior court.

Maintenance orders

11.14 The corollary of the above is that if an order, or part of an order, falls within the definition of 'maintenance' then it can be directly enforced in all other EU Member States[9] and Gibraltar[10].

11.15 The definition of 'maintenance' is very broad[11] and it is not defined within the Maintenance Regulation itself. Two authorities are key in this regard: *Van den Boogaard v Laumen*[12] and *Moore v Moore*[13].

Van den Boogaard v Laumen

H and W married in the Netherlands and agreed after the marriage to alter their community of property regime to one based on separation of goods. They divorced in London and the English court made a financial relief award to W of capitalised spousal periodical payments, including a transfer of property and a lump sum.

W sought to enforce the order in the Netherlands. A reference was made to the ECJ as to whether the orders for transfer of property and a lump sum represented 'maintenance' or 'rights in property arising out of a matrimonial relationship'[14].

The ECJ held that the orders did fall under the heading of 'maintenance'. The points of principle arising are discussed in *Moore v Moore* below. The important thing to note was the fundamental conclusion that 'maintenance' is not confined to periodical payments.

Moore v Moore

H and W were married for five years, but in a relationship for more than 15 years. They had three children. They had moved to Spain from England for tax reasons. H obtained a divorce in Spain (after some jurisdictional wrangling).

9 See the cases of *EDG v RR* [2014] EWHC 816 (Fam), [2015] 1 FLR 270; *S v S* [2016] EWHC 88 (Fam), [2017] 1 FLR 394 and the preliminary ruling of the ECJ in *MS v PS* (Case 283/16), [2017] 4 WLR 72.

10 Incorporated into Gibraltar's domestic Maintenance Act by the Maintenance Act (Amendment) Regulations 2010. Further, the Lugano Convention 2007 applies to Switzerland, Iceland, Denmark and Norway in addition to all EU Member States.

11 See recital 11 to the Regulation itself: 'the scope of this Regulation should cover all maintenance obligations arising from a family relationship, parentage, marriage or affinity… For the purposes of this Regulation, the term 'maintenance regulation; should be interpreted autonomously.'

12 (Case 220/95), [1997] QB 759, Court of Justice of the European Communities.

13 [2007] EWCA Civ 361, [2007] 2 FLR 339.

14 Note that this case concerned the interpretation of the 1968 Brussels Convention, which was replaced by Regulation (EC) no 44/2001 ('Brussels I'), which has now been replaced by the Maintenance Regulation.

The question became whether an application by H in the Spanish court, which pre-dated W's application for financial relief in England, was a claim for maintenance within the meaning of the applicable Regulation.[15]

Lawrence Collins LJ summarised the principles from *Van den Boogaard* as follows at para 80:

'– whether a claim is for maintenance depends upon an autonomous interpretation of the term; the label under national law is not decisive;

– payment of a lump sum or transfer of property may be in the nature of maintenance if it is intended to ensure the support of a spouse;

– payment of a lump sum or transfer of property which serves only the purpose of a division of property or compensation for non-material damage is not in the nature of maintenance;

– a payment or transfer of property intended as a division of assets will concern "rights in property arising out of a matrimonial relationship";

– whether a claim relates to maintenance will depend on its purpose, and in particular whether it is designed to enable one spouse to provide for himself or herself or if the needs and resources of each of the spouses are taken into consideration in the determination of its amount, or where the capital sum set is designed to ensure a pre-determined level of income;

– where the provision is solely concerned with dividing property between the spouses, the decision will be concerned with rights in property arising out of a matrimonial relationship and will not therefore be enforceable under [the Maintenance Regulation].'

11.16 In other words, an order is properly classified as an order for maintenance if it is a needs-based award, but not an award founded on the entitlement to share in the fruits of the matrimonial partnership[16].

11.17 Thus, it is possible that an order varying a nuptial settlement so as to provide for a lump sum to meet a party's housing needs, or to represent an award of capitalised spousal maintenance would fall well within the definition of maintenance and thus within the remit of the Maintenance Regulation. To assist with enforceability, it would be beneficial to include on the face of any final order

15 By the time of this case Brussels I had replaced the 1968 Convention.

16 See *Agbaje v Agbaje* [2010] UKSC 13, [2010] 1 AC 628, per Lord Collins at para 57: 'a transfer of property may be in the nature of maintenance if it is intended to ensure the support of a spouse; but a transfer of property which serves only the purpose of a division of property is not in the nature of maintenance, and concerns rights in property arising out of a matrimonial relationship.' See also *DB v PB (Financial Provision)* [2016] EWHC 3431 (Fam), [2017] 4 WLR 44 at para 45 onwards.

a declaration that identified provisions within the order are intended to fall within the definition of 'maintenance' for the purposes of the Maintenance Regulation.

Common law systems: orders *in personam* vs orders *in rem*

11.18 A judgment or an order *in personam* is one which requires its object to do a particular thing. For example, an order that a spouse pays to the other spouse a lump sum, or transfers a particular property.

11.19 A judgment or an order *in rem* is one which determines the rights in the property or thing itself. For example, a declaration that property held by a company is actually held beneficially by a respondent husband in financial relief proceedings.

11.20 The distinction may or may not be obvious. For example, a finding that a trust is a sham and that the trust assets are in fact owned by one of the spouses is likely to be a judgment *in rem*; yet, as part of any order the court makes, there are inevitably going to be orders *in personam* as against the trustees requiring them to make certain payments, or transfer certain assets to one or both of the spouses to satisfy the substantive order[17].

11.21 The importance of the distinction is that a judgment *in personam* can be enforced against a foreign trustee in their 'home' jurisdiction assuming that they have submitted to the jurisdiction of the English court[18]. However, a judgment *in rem* (ie, one that purports to affect the underlying trust assets themselves) can only operate if those assets are situated in the jurisdiction of England and Wales.

11.22 Thus, while the English court in financial relief proceedings can assert jurisdiction to make an order *in rem* which affects the underlying trust assets, where those assets are offshore there may be little point in doing so in the absence of a means of enforcement. Under common at least law that judgment *in rem* is not capable of enforcement.

Findings of 'sham'

11.23 The law applicable to the court's assessment of a settlement as a sham has been considered in **Chapter 7**, but if such a finding is sought it is important to consider whether the 'home' court of the foreign trust will recognise that declaration and enforce any order made flowing from it *even if* the trustees have submitted to the jurisdiction.

17 There are some interesting judgments on when a court will consider an order *in rem* to bind the parties *in personam*: *Pattni v Ali* [2006] UKPC 51, [2007] 2 AC 85, which has recently been applied in *Chen v Ng* [2017] UKPC 27, [2018] P&CR DG 2.

18 As to which see **Chapter 4** on submission to the jurisdiction. Of course, if the trustees reside in the jurisdiction then they do not need to 'submit' personally.

Minwalla v Minwalla [2004] EWHC 2823 (Fam), [2005] 1 FLR 771 – England

In the matter of the Fountain Trust [2005] JLR 359 – Jersey

In the English court, Singer J found the Fountain Trust to be a sham trust, ordered that it be set aside, declared the husband to be the beneficial owner of all the trust assets, ordered the husband to transfer some of those assets to the wife and ordered the Jersey trustees to effect those transfers 'subject to any contrary requirement of Jersey Law'[19].

The Royal Court in Jersey was unimpressed with this approach, in particular the application of English law in determining whether the trust was a sham, given that the trust deed provided for the governing law of the trust to be Jersey Law[20]. It said as follows at para 18:

> 'We think that there are important distinctions to be drawn between a finding that a Jersey trust is a post-nuptial settlement, and therefore liable to be varied, and a finding that a Jersey trust is a sham. The right to seek a variation is one which derives from the matrimonial regime of the jurisdiction which dissolves the marriage…There is, so far as we are aware, no such statutory power to declare a foreign trust to be a sham. Furthermore, a decision to seek a variation of a trust in order to give effect to an order under a matrimonial jurisdiction is qualitatively different from a decision to declare a trust to be a sham. Under the law of Jersey, a sham trust requires that the settlor and trustee have not only a subjective intention that the deed is not to create the legal rights and obligations which it purports to create, but also a common intention to mislead. It is a serious matter to find that a professional trustee in Jersey has been party to a sham. It is a finding, moreover, which might well have adverse consequences under the statutory regime which regulates the activities of professional trustees in Jersey and which, incidentally, is absent in England and Wales. It is a finding which requires, so far as Jersey is concerned, a careful analysis under the rules applicable in this jurisdiction. As a matter of generality, we would regard an assumption of jurisdiction by a foreign court to declare a Jersey trust a sham to be exorbitant and we would be reluctant to enforce any judgment based upon such an assumption.'

The Jersey court nevertheless (clearly influenced by the husband's behaviour and the fact that the trustees had submitted to the English jurisdiction) enforced the order in the interests of comity.

19 Note that the trustees had submitted to the jurisdiction of the English court, for which they were heavily criticised (see **Chapter 4**, para **4.9**, including footnote 8).

20 At para 17. As to the importance of the governing law of a trust, see **Chapter 3**.

11.24 It should not be assumed, therefore, that a foreign court will accept an English court's finding that a trust is a sham.

Variation of the settlement

11.25 In *BJ v MJ (Financial Order: Overseas Trust)*[21] Mostyn J said as follows:

> 'The variation powers extend to making outright provision to the applicant, and may even be exercised where the trust is offshore, although, following well-established principle, the court will be unlikely to make a variation order where both the trust and its assets are overseas unless it is satisfied that the order would be implemented by the court exercising effective control over the trust (*Goff v Goff* [1934] P 107, *Hamlin v Hamlin* [1986] Fam 11)[22].'

11.26 Specific cases are discussed below in relation to various offshore jurisdictions. These suggest that an order of the English court purporting to vary an offshore trust is unlikely, as a matter of principle, to be accepted with open arms in the home court of that trust. In Jersey, for example, the Royal Court has said it would be '*an exorbitant exercise of jurisdiction for a foreign court to purport...to vary the terms of a Jersey settlement...*'[23]. Notably, that statement even pre-dated the coming into force of the Jersey firewall provisions (discussed below).

C. OFFSHORE LEGISLATION: 'FIREWALL' PROVISIONS

Cayman Islands

11.27 The firewall legislation introduced in the Cayman Islands was the first of its kind and has subsequently been adopted by a number of other jurisdictions. The relevant legislation initially enacted was the Trusts (Foreign Element) Law 1987. This was then consolidated into the Trusts Law (2011 Revision) and more recently into the Trusts Law (2017 Revision)[24]. The crucial sections for these purposes are contained in Part VII of the Law, titled 'Trusts – Foreign Element'.

21 [2011] EWHC 2708 (Fam), [2012] 1 FLR 667.

22 See paras **3.34–3.36** in **Chapter 3**: it has long been established that the English court will not make orders (even if it has jurisdiction to do so) where there is clear evidence that those orders will not be recognised and enforced in the relevant foreign jurisdiction.

23 *In the matter of the Fountain Trust* [2005] JLR 359, para 27. But note in **Chapter 3** that the English Court has held that it *does* have jurisdiction to do so: eg *C v C (Variation of Post-Nuptial Settlement: Company Shares)* [2003] EWHC 1222 (Fam), [2003] 2 FLR 493, FD.

24 The 2017 Revision did not change any of the provisions relevant to this discussion as were contained in the 2011 Revision. The text of the legislation can be found in full on the Cayman government website: http://www.gov.ky/portal/pls/portal/docs/1/12420394.PDF

11.28 The full text of Part VII of the Law is contained in the Materials at the conclusion of this book. In brief the Law provides for the following:

1 Section 89 provides that the governing law of the trust will be ascertained from the terms of the trust deed in the first instance and that if the trust expressly selects Cayman law as the governing law of the trust that is 'valid, effective and conclusive regardless of any other circumstances.'

2 Section 90 provides that all questions listed in the section which arise with regard to a trust governed by Cayman law are to be determined in accordance with Cayman law without reference to the laws of any other jurisdictions with which the trust may be connected. Crucially, this applies to questions concerning the validity of the trust, the administration of the trust and the existence and extent of powers, conferred or retained, including powers of variation or revocation of the trust.

3 Section 91 excludes any foreign law.

4 Section 93 prevents a foreign judgment being recognised, enforced or giving rise to an estoppel insofar as it is inconsistent with section 91.

11.29 As a matter of Cayman law, therefore, if an English family court applying English law purports to vary the terms or the operation of a Cayman Islands Trust, the trustees are likely to be in breach of their obligations if they comply with the order.

11.30 In the leading Cayman case of *RBS Coutts (Cayman) Ltd v W*[25] Henderson J explained:

> 'An order of the Hong Kong court purporting to effect a variation of the trust, whether in a matrimonial proceeding or otherwise, cannot be recognised by the trustee. That is so even if the trustee were to submit to the jurisdiction of the Hong Kong court. A trust in the Cayman Islands can only be varied in accordance with the law of the Cayman Islands and only by a court of the Cayman Islands.'

11.31 The approach in *RBS Coutts (Cayman) Ltd v W* was followed in *In the Matter of the A Trust*[26] in which the Grand Court took the view that it was not in the best interests of the beneficiaries of a STAR Trust to submit to the jurisdiction of the English High Court in respect of a variation application in financial relief proceedings.

11.32 Cayman Islands cases almost always concern 'STAR trusts'. These are statutory trusts unique to the Cayman Islands and derive their name from the Special Trusts (Alternative Regime) Law 1997[27]. They have their own specific requirements for formation and operation, and as such present real difficulties

25 (2010) 14 ITELR 557, at para 23. This case is discussed in **Chapter 4** at para **4.24**.
26 (1 December 2016, unreported).
27 Now embedded into the Trusts Law itself.

when it comes to the enforcement of English orders. Some features of a STAR trusts include the following[28]:

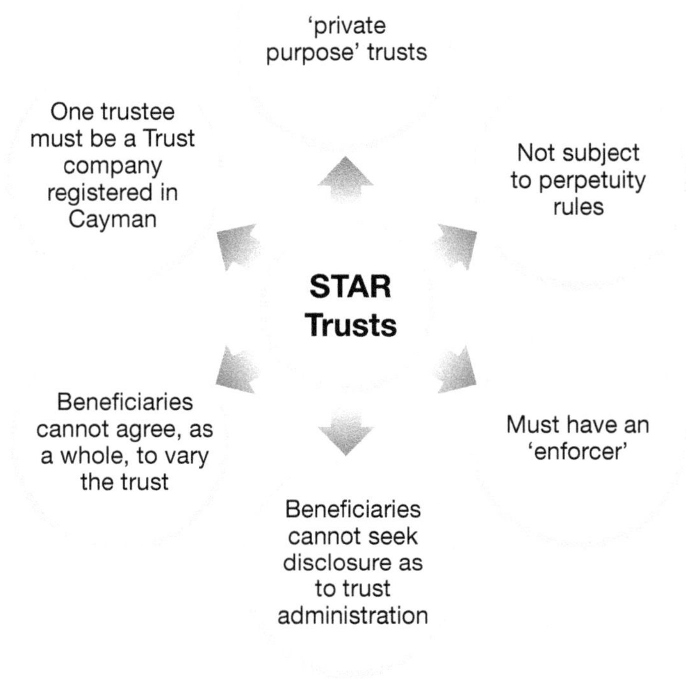

Jersey

11.33 Jersey's firewall provisions are contained within Article 9 of the Trusts (Jersey) Law 1984, as amended (most recently by the Trusts (Amendment No 7) (Jersey) Law 2018).

11.34 The full text of Article 9 of the legislation is contained in the Materials at the conclusion of this book. Most crucially for these purposes:

1 Sub-paragraph (1) provides that any question concerning the validity of a trust, its administration, the existence and extent of the powers conferred (including variation etc), the exercise by a foreign court of any power to vary the terms of a trust, and the nature and extent of any beneficial rights or interests in trust property shall all be determined in accordance with Jersey law.

28 Note that an 'enforcer' in the diagram below is a nominated person within the trust instrument who is the only person/body able to enforce the terms of the trust and none of the beneficiaries is able to do so absent a court order. Also this removes the beneficiaries' rights to seek disclosure as to the administration of the trust by the trustees.

2 Sub-paragraph (4) provides that no judgment of a foreign court with respect to a trust shall be enforceable or given effect in such a way as would be inconsistent with Article 9.

11.35 In the case of *Mubarak* the Jersey Royal Court addressed head-on the question of whether it would enforce an order of the English court varying the terms of a Jersey settlement.

Mubarak v Mubarik

[2008] JRC 136, [2009] 1 FLR 664

An order of Holman J in the English court varied a Jersey trust so as to require the trustees to pay to W all sums owing to her under a previous lump sum order made by Bodey J with which H had not complied (c.£5m).

The trust owned all the issued share capital of a holding company for a group of international jewellery companies. The Jersey Court was respectful of Holman J's variation order:

> 'A reading of the judgment of Holman J shows that he was very conscious of the fact that the trust is governed by the law of Jersey and he specifically accepted that, as a general rule, it would be an exorbitant exercise of jurisdiction for the Family Division to vary the terms of a Jersey trust… However, he felt that, in the light of H's prolonged recalcitrance, he had no alternative but to make the order and this court can well understand why he came to that conclusion.'

The Jersey Court doubted that an order varying a foreign trust was capable of enforcement under the common law[29]. After a discussion of the Jersey case law a distinction was drawn between a variation that altered the terms of the trust deed itself ('alteration') and a variation which the trustees could have executed by exercising an existing power within the trust deed ('variation'). The Jersey court had no inherent jurisdiction to do the former[30].

The Jersey firewall provisions[31] came into being in October 2006 and provided that a variation of a Jersey trust had to be determined in accordance with Jersey law (article 9(4)), yet the English court applied English law to a variation application under the MCA 1973[32]. This did not necessarily preclude, however, the Jersey court exercising a discretion in respect of the English order and directing the trustee to carry out those transfers as envisaged by

29 Paras 36–40.

30 Paras 58–68.

31 Trusts (Jersey) Law 1984 as amended by the Trusts (Amendment No 4) (Jersey) Law 2006, nb. now amended by the Trusts (Amendment No 7) (Jersey) Law 2018. Discussed later on in this Chapter at paras **11.37–11.38**.

32 See *Charalambous v Charalambous* [2004] EWCA Civ 1030, [2005] Fam 250 and **Chapter 3** at para **3.5** and **3.50–3.51**.

the English order (subject to that not amounting to an 'alteration' as opposed to a 'variation')[33].

This case was decided on an entirely different ground, however, namely that all the beneficiaries to a trust may 'alter' it[34]. H had consented to the alteration of the trust contained within the Holman J order and all other beneficiaries, who were not minors or unborn, also agreed. The court approved the alteration as being for the benefit of the minor and unborn beneficiaries of the trust[35].

11.36 The Jersey Court of Appeal upheld the decision of the Royal Court in *Mubarak*[36]. It remains good law and thus the scope for enforcing in Jersey an English order that purports to vary a nuptial settlement under English law (where such a variation goes outside the scope of the existing trust documents) would seem to be highly limited. Any references to 'comity' and 'discretion' in cases such as *the Fountain Trust*[37] or in *re H Trust*[38] must be read in that light, especially as they pre-date the substantial amendment to the Jersey firewall provisions in October 2006.

11.37 The decision in *Mubarak* that by reason of Article 9(4) the Jersey court could not enforce an English order 'altering' a Jersey trust beyond the scope of its existing trust document already had far-reaching consequences. However, it is important to note it was also founded on an old version of Article 9 that did not expressly deal with a foreign court's order purporting to vary an English trust.

11.38 By way of the Trusts (Amendment No 5) (Jersey) Law 2012, a new Article 9(1)(f) was inserted which reads:

> '9 (1) any question concerning … (f) the exercise or purported exercise by a foreign court of any statutory or non-statutory power to vary the terms of a trust… shall be determined in accordance with the law of Jersey and no rule of foreign law shall affect such question.'

11.39 Thus, similarly to the Cayman Islands, an order of the English court purporting to vary the terms of a Jersey trust by applying the English law will fall foul of both the principles of *Mubarak* and the provisions of Article 9(1)(f) of the 1984 Trusts Law.

33 Para 76.
34 *Saunders v Vautier* (1841) 4 Beav 115, (1841) 49 ER 282.
35 Pursuant to its powers to do so under the 1984 Jersey Law, article 47. See paras 81–101.
36 [2009] JCA 196, [2009] WTLR 1543, CA (Jersey).
37 [2005] JLR 359, discussed above.
38 [2006] JLR 280 at paras 12–13, discussed in **Chapter 4** at paras **4.12** and **4.21–4.22**,

Guernsey

11.40 Guernsey adopted similar firewall provisions to Cayman and Jersey when it implemented the Trusts (Guernsey) Law 2007. Section 14 covers the 'application of Guernsey law to questions of validity'.

11.41 The full text of section 14 is contained in the Materials at the conclusion of this book, but for these purposes the Guernsey firewall provisions are almost identical to the Jersey provisions save in one respect.

11.42 What is remarkable about Guernsey firewall legislation, as compared to its equivalent in Jersey or Cayman, is the provision of s 14(1)(d) which refers to the Guernsey court having exclusive jurisdiction over the '*extent of any functions in respect of the trust, including (without limitation) powers of variation, revocation and appointment, and the validity of the exercise of any such function*' in respect of a Guernsey Trust[39]. This, in theory, is a wider firewall even than the ones which feature in the legislation of those other jurisdictions.

11.43 The only case to consider the Guernsey firewall provisions was *A Limited FURBS ('re A Ltd')*[40] which adopted the Jersey jurisprudence on when (if ever) a trustee of a Guernsey trust should be permitted to submit to a foreign jurisdiction. In that case, described as 'exceptional' by the Guernsey court, the trustee was directed to submit because the trust was barely discretionary and in reality the trustee exercised only a 'mechanical' role within the administration of the trust[41]. In all other circumstances, the court was of the view that it would not be appropriate for a trustee to submit to the jurisdiction of a foreign court where to do so would likely conflict with the firewall provisions contained in the 2007 Act.

D. CONCLUSION

11.44 In a case involving a trust with a foreign element the English court *can* assert jurisdiction to make orders in respect of that trust (pursuant to its wide-ranging powers under the MCA 1973) and it will apply English law in doing so.

11.45 Where the foreign court in the jurisdiction in which that trust is based, or in which an order must be enforced against the trustees *in personam*, is a common law jurisdiction then it may be – following from the common law rules as set out above in this Chapter and in **Chapter 3** on jurisdiction – that the

39 A Guernsey Trust is defined in s 3 of the 2007 Act as being a trust the 'proper law of which is the law of Guernsey' either by reference to the express or implied choice of law within the terms of the trust, or the law with which the trust has its closest connection (situs of trust assets, place of administration of the trust etc.) see **Chapter 3** for a discussion as to the meaning of 'proper law' or 'governing law' of a trust.

40 [2017] 21/2017.

41 See the discussion of the case in **Chapter 4** at para **4.23**.

order can be recognised and enforced. However, more often than not a foreign jurisdiction will have enacted its own laws to protect trusts set up within its jurisdiction and intended to be governed by its 'home' laws as its governing or proper law. This is a matter of common sense: settlors are obviously more likely to choose a jurisdiction in which to settle their trust that will protect their trust from attempts by courts of other jurisdictions to interfere with the administration of the trust and/or seek to vary/alter its underlying terms and the distribution of the trust assets.

11.46 A spouse is likely to be faced with substantial difficulties when seeking to enforce an order against trustees of a trust governed by the law of a jurisdiction with firewall legislation. If the English court cannot be satisfied that a variation order will be enforced by the trust's 'home' court, it is at least arguable that the order should not be made at all[42].

11.47 It is not just Cayman, Jersey and Guernsey which have such legislation, but Bermuda, Gibraltar, the Isle of Man, the Cook Islands, the Bahamas and others. The importance, therefore, to an English law matrimonial practitioner to seek advice from a legal professional in the trust's home jurisdiction as early as possible is self-evident. The need for trustees of that trust – when made aware of an application in financial remedy proceedings which may affect that trust – to make an application for directions before the home court is also self-evident[43].

42 See the citation from Mostyn J in *BJ v MJ (Financial Order: Overseas Trust)* [2011] EWHC 2708 (Fam), [2012] 1 FLR 667 at para **11.25** above: 'the court will be unlikely to make a variation order where both the trust and its assets are overseas unless it is satisfied that the order would be implemented by the court exercising effective control over the trust (*Goff v Goff* [1934] P 107, *Hamlin v Hamlin* [1986] Fam 11).'
43 And discussed in **Chapter 3**.

Materials

INSOLVENCY ACT 1986

PART XVI
PROVISIONS AGAINST DEBT AVOIDANCE (ENGLAND AND WALES ONLY)

423 Transactions defrauding creditors.

(1) This section relates to transactions entered into at an undervalue; and a person enters into such a transaction with another person if—
   (a) he makes a gift to the other person or he otherwise enters into a transaction with the other on terms that provide for him to receive no consideration;
   (b) he enters into a transaction with the other in consideration of marriage [or the formation of a civil partnership][1]; or
   (c) he enters into a transaction with the other for a consideration the value of which, in money or money's worth, is significantly less than the value, in money or money's worth, of the consideration provided by himself.

(2) Where a person has entered into such a transaction, the court may, if satisfied under the next subsection, make such order as it thinks fit for—
   (a) restoring the position to what it would have been if the transaction had not been entered into, and
   (b) protecting the interests of persons who are victims of the transaction.

(3) In the case of a person entering into such a transaction, an order shall only be made if the court is satisfied that it was entered into by him for the purpose—
   (a) of putting assets beyond the reach of a person who is making, or may at some time make, a claim against him, or
   (b) of otherwise prejudicing the interests of such a person in relation to the claim which he is making or may make.

(4) In this section 'the court' means the High Court or—
   (a) if the person entering into the transaction is an individual, any other court which would have jurisdiction in relation to a bankruptcy petition relating to him;
   (b) if that person is a body capable of being wound up under Part IV or V of this Act, any other court having jurisdiction to wind it up.

(5) In relation to a transaction at an undervalue, references here and below to a victim of the transaction are to a person who is, or is capable of being, prejudiced by it; and in the following two sections the person entering into the transaction is referred to as 'the debtor'.

Amendment

1 Inserted by the Civil Partnership Act 2004, s 261(1), Sch 27, para 121.

424 Those who may apply for an order under s. 423.

(1) An application for an order under section 423 shall not be made in relation to a transaction except—
  (a) in a case where the debtor has been [made][1] bankrupt or is a body corporate which is being wound up or [is in administration][2], by the official receiver, by the trustee of the bankrupt's estate or the liquidator or administrator of the body corporate or (with the leave of the court) by a victim of the transaction;
  (b) in a case where a victim of the transaction is bound by a voluntary arrangement approved under Part I or Part VIII of this Act, by the supervisor of the voluntary arrangement or by any person who (whether or not so bound) is such a victim; or
  (c) in any other case, by a victim of the transaction.

(2) An application made under any of the paragraphs of subsection (1) is to be treated as made on behalf of every victim of the transaction.

Amendments

1 Substituted by the Enterprise and Regulatory Reform Act 2013, s 71(3), Sch 19, paras 1, 61.
2 Substituted subject to transitional provisions specified in the Enterprise Act 2002 (Commencement No. 4 and Transitional Provisions and Savings) Order 2003, SI 2003/2093, art 3 by the Enterprise Act 2002, s 248(3), Sch 17, paras 9, 36.

425 Provision which may be made by order under s. 423.

(1) Without prejudice to the generality of section 423, an order made under that section with respect to a transaction may (subject as follows)—
  (a) require any property transferred as part of the transaction to be vested in any person, either absolutely or for the benefit of all the persons on whose behalf the application for the order is treated as made;
  (b) require any property to be so vested if it represents, in any person's hands, the application either of the proceeds of sale of property so transferred or of money so transferred;
  (c) release or discharge (in whole or in part) any security given by the debtor;
  (d) require any person to pay to any other person in respect of benefits received from the debtor such sums as the court may direct;
  (e) provide for any surety or guarantor whose obligations to any person were released or discharged (in whole or in part) under the transaction to be under such new or revived obligations as the court thinks appropriate;
  (f) provide for security to be provided for the discharge of any obligation imposed by or arising under the order, for such an obligation to be

charged on any property and for such security or charge to have the same priority as a security or charge released or discharged (in whole or in part) under the transaction.

(2) An order under section 423 may affect the property of, or impose any obligation on, any person whether or not he is the person with whom the debtor entered into the transaction; but such an order—

(a) shall not prejudice any interest in property which was acquired from a person other than the debtor and was acquired in good faith, for value and without notice of the relevant circumstances, or prejudice any interest deriving from such an interest, and

(b) shall not require a person who received a benefit from the transaction in good faith, for value and without notice of the relevant circumstances to pay any sum unless he was a party to the transaction.

(3) For the purposes of this section the relevant circumstances in relation to a transaction are the circumstances by virtue of which an order under section 423 may be made in respect of the transaction.

(4) In this section 'security' means any mortgage, charge, lien or other security.

LIMITATION ACT 1980

PART I
ORDINARY TIME LIMITS FOR DIFFERENT CLASSES OF ACTION

General rule for actions on a specialty

8 *Time limit for actions on a specialty.*

(1) An action upon a specialty shall not be brought after the expiration of twelve years from the date on which the cause of action accrued.

(2) Subsection (1) above shall not affect any action for which a shorter period of limitation is prescribed by any other provision of this Act.

Actions for sums recoverable by statute

9 *Time limit for actions for sums recoverable by statute.*

(1) An action to recover any sum recoverable by virtue of any enactment shall not be brought after the expiration of six years from the date on which the cause of action accrued.

(2) Subsection (1) above shall not affect any action to which section 10 of this Act applies.

Actions in respect of trust property or the personal estate of deceased persons

21 *Time limit for actions in respect of trust property.*

(1) No period of limitation prescribed by this Act shall apply to an action by a beneficiary under a trust, being an action—
   (a) in respect of any fraud or fraudulent breach of trust to which the trustee was a party or privy; or
   (b) to recover from the trustee trust property or the proceeds of trust property in the possession of the trustee, or previously received by the trustee and converted to his use.

(2) Where a trustee who is also a beneficiary under the trust receives or retains trust property or its proceeds as his share on a distribution of trust property under the trust, his liability in any action brought by virtue of subsection (1)(b) above to recover that property or its proceeds after the expiration of the period of limitation prescribed by this Act for bringing an action to recover trust property shall be limited to the excess over his proper share.

This subsection only applies if the trustee acted honestly and reasonably in making the distribution

(3) Subject to the preceding provisions of this section, an action by a beneficiary to recover trust property or in respect of any breach of trust, not being an

action for which a period of limitation is prescribed by any other provision of this Act, shall not be brought after the expiration of six years from the date on which the right of action accrued.

For the purposes of this subsection, the right of action shall not be treated as having accrued to any beneficiary entitled to a future interest in the trust property until the interest fell into possession.

(4) No beneficiary as against whom there would be a good defence under this Act shall derive any greater or other benefit from a judgment or order obtained by any other beneficiary than he could have obtained if he had brought the action and this Act had been pleaded in defence.

PART II
EXTENSION OR EXCLUSION OF ORDINARY TIME LIMITS

Fraud, concealment and mistake

32 Postponement of limitation period in case of fraud, concealment or mistake.

(1) Subject to [subsections (3) and (4A)][1] below, where in the case of any action for which a period of limitation is prescribed by this Act, either—
   (a) the action is based upon the fraud of the defendant; or
   (b) any fact relevant to the plaintiff's right of action has been deliberately concealed from him by the defendant; or
   (c) the action is for relief from the consequences of a mistake;

the period of limitation shall not begin to run until the plaintiff has discovered the fraud, concealment or mistake (as the case may be) or could with reasonable diligence have discovered it.

References in this subsection to the defendant include references to the defendant's agent and to any person through whom the defendant claims and his agent.

(2) For the purposes of subsection (1) above, deliberate commission of a breach of duty in circumstances in which it is unlikely to be discovered for some time amounts to deliberate concealment of the facts involved in that breach of duty.

(3) Nothing in this section shall enable any action—
   (a) to recover, or recover the value of, any property; or
   (b) to enforce any charge against, or set aside any transaction affecting, any property;

to be brought against the purchaser of the property or any person claiming through him in any case where the property has been purchased for valuable consideration by an innocent third party since the fraud or concealment or (as the case may be) the transaction in which the mistake was made took place.

(4) A purchaser is an innocent third party for the purposes of this section—
   (a) in the case of fraud or concealment of any fact relevant to the plaintiff's right of action, if he was not a party to the fraud or (as the case may be) to the concealment of that fact and did not at the time of the purchase know or have reason to believe that the fraud or concealment had taken place; and
   (b) in the case of mistake, if he did not at the time of the purchase know or have reason to believe that the mistake had been made.

[(4A) Subsection (1) above shall not apply in relation to the time limit prescribed by section 11A(3) of this Act or in relation to that time limit as applied by virtue of section 12(1) of this Act.][2]

[(5) Sections 14A and 14B of this Act shall not apply to any action to which subsection (1)(b) above applies (and accordingly the period of limitation referred to in that subsection, in any case to which either of those sections would otherwise apply, is the period applicable under section 2 of this Act).][3]

Amendments

1 Substituted by the Consumer Protection Act 1987, s 6(6), Sch 1, para 5(a).
2 Inserted by the Consumer Protection Act 1987, s 6(6), Sch 1, para 5(b).
3 Inserted by the Latent Damage Act 1986, s 2(2).

MATRIMONIAL CAUSES ACT 1973

PART I
DIVORCE, NULLITY AND OTHER MATRIMONIAL SUITS

Divorce

1 Divorce on breakdown of marriage.

(1) Subject to section 3 below, a petition for divorce may be presented to the court by either party to a marriage on the ground that the marriage has broken down irretrievably.

(2) The court hearing a petition for divorce shall not hold the marriage to have broken down irretrievably unless the petitioner satisfies the court of one or more of the following facts, that is to say—

(a) that the respondent has committed adultery and the petitioner finds it intolerable to live with the respondent;

(b) that the respondent has behaved in such a way that the petitioner cannot reasonably be expected to live with the respondent;

(c) that the respondent has deserted the petitioner for a continuous period of at least two years immediately preceding the presentation of the petition;

(d) that the parties to the marriage have lived apart for a continuous period of at least two years immediately preceding the presentation of the petition (hereafter in this Act referred to as 'two years' separation') and the respondent consents to a decree being granted;

(e) that the parties to the marriage have lived apart for a continuous period of at least five years immediately preceding the presentation of the petition (hereafter in this Act referred to as 'five years' separation').

(3) On a petition for divorce it shall be the duty of the court to inquire, so far as it reasonably can, into the facts alleged by the petitioner and into any facts alleged by the respondent.

(4) If the court is satisfied on the evidence of any such fact as is mentioned in subsection (2) above, then, unless it is satisfied on all the evidence that the marriage has not broken down irretrievably, it shall, subject to [section 5][1] below, grant a decree of divorce.

(5) Every decree of divorce shall in the first instance be a decree nisi and shall not be made absolute before the expiration of six months from its grant unless the High Court by general order from time to time fixes a shorter period, or unless in any particular case the court in which the proceedings are for the time being pending from time to time by special order fixes a shorter period than the period otherwise applicable for the time being by virtue of this subsection.

[(6) Only conduct between the respondent and a person of the opposite sex may constitute adultery for the purposes of this section.][2]

Amendments

1 Substituted by the Matrimonial and Family Proceedings Act 1984, s 46(1), Sch 1, para 10.
2 Inserted by the Marriage (Same Sex Couples) Act 2013, s 11(4), Sch 4, para 3.

2 *Supplemental provisions as to facts raising presumption of breakdown.*

(1) One party to a marriage shall not be entitled to rely for the purposes of section 1(2)(a) above on adultery committed by the other if, after it became known to him that the other had committed that adultery, the parties have lived with each other for a period exceeding, or periods together exceeding, six months.

(2) Where the parties to a marriage have lived with each other after it became known to one party that the other had committed adultery, but subsection (1) above does not apply, in any proceedings for divorce in which the petitioner relies on that adultery the fact that the parties have lived with each other after that time shall be disregarded in determining for the purposes of section 1(2)(a) above whether the petitioner finds it intolerable to live with the respondent.

(3) Where in any proceedings for divorce the petitioner alleges that the respondent has behaved in such a way that the petitioner cannot reasonably be expected to live with him, but the parties to the marriage have lived with each other for a period or periods after the date of the occurrence of the final incident relied on by the petitioner and held by the court to support his allegation, that fact shall be disregarded in determining for the purposes of section 1(2)(b) above whether the petitioner cannot reasonably be expected to live with the respondent if the length of that period or of those periods together was six months or less.

(4) For the purposes of section 1(2)(c) above the court may treat a period of desertion as having continued at a time when the deserting party was incapable of continuing the necessary intention if the evidence before the court is such that, had that party not been so incapable, the court would have inferred that his desertion continued at that time.

(5) In considering for the purposes of section 1(2) above whether the period for which the respondent has deserted the petitioner or the period for which the parties to a marriage have lived apart has been continuous, no account shall be taken of any one period (not exceeding six months) or of any two or more periods (not exceeding six months in all) during which the parties resumed living with each other, but no period during which the parties lived with each other shall count as part of the period of desertion or of the period for which the parties to the marriage lived apart, as the case may be.

(6) For the purposes of section 1(2)(d) and (e) above and this section a husband and wife shall be treated as living apart unless they are living with each other in the same household, and references in this section to the parties to a marriage living with each other shall be construed as references to their living with each other in the same household.

(7) Provision shall be made by rules of court for the purpose of ensuring that where in pursuance of section 1(2)(d) above the petitioner alleges that the respondent consents to a decree being granted the respondent has been given such information as will enable him to understand the consequences to him of his consenting to a decree being granted and the steps which he must take to indicate that he consents to the grant of a decree.

[3 *Bar on petitions for divorce within one year of marriage.*

(1) No petition for divorce shall be presented to the court before the expiration of the period of one year from the date of the marriage.

(2) Nothing in this section shall prohibit the presentation of a petition based on matters which occurred before the expiration of that period.][1]

Amendment

1 Substituted by the Matrimonial and Family Proceedings Act 1984, s 1.

4 *Divorce not precluded by previous judicial separation.*

(1) A person shall not be prevented from presenting a petition for divorce, or the court from granting a decree of divorce, by reason only that the petitioner or respondent has at any time, on the same facts or substantially the same facts as those proved in support of the petition, been granted a decree of judicial separation or an order under, or having effect as if made under, the Matrimonial Proceedings (Magistrates' Courts) Act 1960 [or Part I of the Domestic Proceedings and Magistrates' Courts Act 1978][1] or any corresponding enactments in force in Northern Ireland, the Isle of Man or any of the Channel Islands.

(2) On a petition for divorce in such a case as is mentioned in subsection (1) above, the court may treat the decree or order as sufficient proof of any adultery, desertion or other fact by reference to which it was granted, but shall not grant a decree of divorce without receiving evidence from the petitioner.

(3) Where a petition for divorce in such a case follows a decree of judicial separation or [(subject to sub-section (5) below)][2] an order containing a provision exempting one party to the marriage from the obligation to cohabit with the other, for the purposes of that petition a period of desertion immediately preceding the institution of the proceedings for the decree or order shall, if the parties have not resumed cohabitation and the decree or order has been continuously in force since it was granted, be deemed immediately to precede the presentation of the petition.

[(4) For the purposes of section 1(2)(c) above the court may treat as a period during which the respondent has deserted the petitioner any of the following periods, that is to say—

(a) any period during which there is in force an injunction granted by the High Court[, the family court or the county court][3] which excludes the respondent from the matrimonial home;

(b) any period during which there is in force an order made by the High Court or a county court under [section 1 or 9 of the Matrimonial Homes Act 1983][4] which prohibits the exercise by the respondent of the right to occupy a dwelling-house in which the applicant and the respondent have or at any time have had a matrimonial home;

(c) any period during which there is in force an order made by a magistrates' court under section 16(3) of the Domestic Proceedings and Magistrates' Courts Act 1978 which requires the respondent to leave the matrimonial home or prohibits the respondent from entering the matrimonial home.

(5) Where—

(a) a petition for divorce is presented after the date on which Part I of the Domestic Proceedings and Magistrates' Courts Act 1978 comes into force, and

(b) an order made under the Matrimonial Proceedings (Magistrates' Courts) Act 1960 containing a provision exempting the petitioner from the obligation to cohabit with the respondent is in force on that date,

then, for the purposes of section 1(2)(c) above, the court may treat a period during which such a provision was included in that order (whether before or after that date) as a period during which the respondent has deserted the petitioner.]

Amendments

1 Inserted by the Domestic Proceedings and Magistrates' Courts Act 1978, s 89(2)(a), Sch 2, para 38.
2 Inserted by the Domestic Proceedings and Magistrates' Courts Act 1978, s 62.
3 Substituted by the Crime and Courts Act 2013, s 17(6), Sch 11, paras 58, 59.
4 Substituted by the Matrimonial Homes Act 1983, s 12(1), Sch 2.

5 *Refusal of decree in five year separation cases on grounds of grave hardship to respondent.*

(1) The respondent to a petition for divorce in which the petitioner alleges five years' separation may oppose the grant of a decree on the ground that the dissolution of the marriage will result in grave financial or other hardship to him and that it would in all the circumstances be wrong to dissolve the marriage.

(2) Where the grant of a decree is opposed by virtue of this section, then—

(a) if the court finds that the petitioner is entitled to rely in support of his petition on the fact of five years' separation and makes no such finding as to any other fact mentioned in section 1(2) above, and

(b) if apart from this section the court would grant a decree on the petition, the court shall consider all the circumstances, including the conduct of the parties to the marriage and the interests of those parties and of any children or other persons concerned, and if of opinion that the dissolution of the marriage will result in grave financial or other hardship to the respondent and that it would in all the circumstances be wrong to dissolve the marriage it shall dismiss the petition.

(3) For the purposes of this section hardship shall include the loss of the chance of acquiring any benefit which the respondent might acquire if the marriage were not dissolved.

6 *Attempts at reconciliation of parties to marriage.*

(1) Provision shall be made by rules of court for requiring the [legal representative][1] acting for a petitioner for divorce to certify whether he has discussed with the petitioner the possibility of a reconciliation and given him the names and addresses of persons qualified to help effect a reconciliation between parties to a marriage who have become estranged.

(2) If at any stage of proceedings for divorce it appears to the court that there is a reasonable possibility of a reconciliation between the parties to the marriage, the court may adjourn the proceedings for such period as it thinks fit to enable attempts to be made to effect such a reconciliation.

The power conferred by the foregoing provision is additional to any other power of the court to adjourn proceedings.

Amendment

1 Substituted by the Legal Services Act 2007, s 208(1), Sch 21, para 29.

7 *Consideration by the court of certain agreements or arrangements.*

Provision may be made by rules of court for enabling the parties to a marriage, or either of them, on application made either before or after the presentation of a petition for divorce, to refer to the court any agreement or arrangement made or proposed to be made between them, being an agreement or arrangement which relates to, arises out of, or is connected with, the proceedings for divorce which are contemplated or, as the case may be, have begun, and for enabling the court to express an opinion, should it think it desirable to do so, as to the reasonableness of the agreement or arrangement and to give such directions, if any, in the matter as it thinks fit.

8 *Intervention of Queen's Proctor.*

(1) In the case of a petition for divorce—

(a) the court may, if it thinks fit, direct all necessary papers in the matter to be sent to the Queen's Proctor, who shall under the directions of the Attorney-General instruct counsel to argue before the court any question in relation to the matter which the court considers it necessary or expedient to have fully argued;

(b) any person may at any time during the progress of the proceedings or before the decree nisi is made absolute give information to the Queen's Proctor on any matter material to the due decision of the case, and the Queen's Proctor may thereupon take such steps as the Attorney-General considers necessary or expedient.

(2) Where the Queen's Proctor intervenes or shows cause against a decree nisi in any proceedings for divorce, the court may make such order as may be just as to the payment by other parties to the proceedings of the costs incurred by him in so doing or as to the payment by him of any costs incurred by any of those parties by reason of his so doing.

(3) The Queen's Proctor shall be entitled to charge as part of the expenses of his office—

(a) the costs of any proceedings under subsection (1)(a) above;

(b) where his reasonable costs of intervening or showing cause as mentioned in subsection (2) above are not fully satisfied by any order under that subsection, the amount of the difference;

(c) if the Treasury so directs, any costs which he pays to any parties under an order made under subsection (2).

9 *Proceedings after decree nisi: general powers of court.*

(1) Where a decree of divorce has been granted but not made absolute, then, without prejudice to section 8 above, any person (excluding a party to the proceedings other than the Queen's Proctor) may show cause why the decree should not be made absolute by reason of material facts not having been brought before the court; and in such a case the court may—

(a) notwithstanding anything in section 1(5) above (but subject to [section][1] 10(2) to (4) …[2] below) make the decree absolute; or

(b) rescind the decree; or

(c) require further inquiry; or

(d) otherwise deal with the case as it thinks fit.

(2) Where a decree of divorce has been granted and no application for it to be made absolute has been made by the party to whom it was granted, then, at any time after the expiration of three months from the earliest date on which that party could have made such an application, the party against whom it was granted may make an application to the court, and on that application the court may exercise any of the powers mentioned in paragraphs (a) to (d) of subsection (1) above.

Amendments

1 Substituted by the Children and Families Act 2014, s 17(2), (3)(a).

2 Repealed by the Children and Families Act 2014, s 17(2), (3)(b).

10 Proceedings after decree nisi: special protection for respondent in separation cases.

(1) Where in any case the court has granted a decree of divorce on the basis of a finding that the petitioner was entitled to rely in support of his petition on the fact of two years' separation coupled with the respondent's consent to a decree being granted and has made no such finding as to any other fact mentioned in section 1(2) above, the court may, on an application made by the respondent at any time before the decree is made absolute, rescind the decree if it is satisfied that the petitioner misled the respondent (whether intentionally or unintentionally) about any matter which the respondent took into account in deciding to give his consent.

(2) The following provisions of this section apply where—
- (a) the respondent to a petition for divorce in which the petitioner alleged two years' or five years' separation coupled, in the former case, with the respondent's consent to a decree being granted, has applied to the court for consideration under subsection (3) below of his financial position after the divorce; and
- (b) the court has granted a decree on the petition on the basis of a finding that the petitioner was entitled to rely in support of his petition on the fact of two years' or five years' separation (as the case may be) and has made no such finding as to any other fact mentioned in section 1(2) above.

(3) The court hearing an application by the respondent under subsection (2) above shall consider all the circumstances, including the age, health, conduct, earning capacity, financial resources and financial obligations of each of the parties, and the financial position of the respondent, as having regard to the divorce, it is likely to be after the death of the petitioner should the petitioner die first; and, subject to subsection (4) below, the court shall not make the decree absolute unless it is satisfied—
- (a) that the petitioner should not be required to make any financial provision for the respondent, or
- (b) that the financial provision made by the petitioner for the respondent is reasonable and fair or the best that can be made in the circumstances.

(4) The court may if it thinks fit makes the decree absolute notwithstanding the requirements of subsection (3) above if—
- (a) it appears that there are circumstances making it desirable that the decree should be made absolute without delay, and
- (b) the court has obtained a satisfactory undertaking from the petitioner that he will make such financial provision for the respondent as the court may approve.

[10A Proceedings after decree nisi: religious marriage

(1) This section applies if a decree of divorce has been granted but not made absolute and the parties to the marriage concerned—

(a) were married in accordance with—
(i) the usages of the Jews, or
(ii) any other prescribed religious usages; and
(b) must co-operate if the marriage is to be dissolved in accordance with those usages.

(2) On the application of either party, the court may order that a decree of divorce is not to be made absolute until a declaration made by both parties that they have taken such steps as are required to dissolve the marriage in accordance with those usages is produced to the court.

(3) An order under subsection (2)—
(a) may be made only if the court is satisfied that in all the circumstances of the case it is just and reasonable to do so; and
(b) may be revoked at any time.

(4) A declaration of a kind mentioned in subsection (2)—
(a) must be in a specified form;
(b) must, in specified cases, be accompanied by such documents as may be specified; and
(c) must, in specified cases, satisfy such other requirements as may be specified.

(5) The validity of a decree of divorce made by reference to such a declaration is not to be affected by any inaccuracy in that declaration.

(6) 'Prescribed' means prescribed in an order made by the Lord Chancellor [after consulting the Lord Chief Justice][1] and such an order—
(a) must be made by statutory instrument;
(b) shall be subject to annulment in pursuance of a resolution of either House of Parliament.

(7) 'Specified' means specified in rules of court.

[(8) The Lord Chief Justice may nominate a judicial office holder (as defined in section 109(4) of the Constitutional Reform Act 2005) to exercise his functions under this section.][1]][2]

Amendments

1 Inserted by the Constitutional Reform Act 2005, s 15(1), Sch 4, para 76.
2 Inserted by the Divorce (Religious Marriages) Act 2002, s 1(1).

Nullity

11 Grounds on which a marriage is void.

A marriage celebrated after 31st July 1971[, other than a marriage to which section 12A applies,]1 shall be void on the following grounds only, that is to say—
(a) that it is not a valid marriage under the provisions of the [Marriage Acts 1949 to 1986][2] (that is to say where—

(i) the parties are within the prohibited degrees of relationship;
(ii) either party is under the age of sixteen; or
(iii) the parties have intermarried in disregard of certain requirements as to the formation of marriage);

(b) that at the time of the marriage either party was already lawfully married [or a civil partner][3];
(c) …[4]
(d) in the case of a polygamous marriage entered into outside England and Wales, that either party was at the time of the marriage domiciled in England and Wales.

For the purposes of paragraph (d) of this subsection a marriage [is not polygamous if]5 at its inception neither party has any spouse additional to the other.

Amendments

1 Inserted by the Marriage (Same Sex Couples) Act 2013 (Consequential and Contrary Provisions and Scotland) and Marriage and Civil Partnership (Scotland) Act 2014 (Consequential Provisions) Order 2014, SI 2014/3168, art 2, Schedule, para 6(1), (2).
2 Substituted by the Marriage (Prohibited Degrees of Relationship) Act 1986, s 6(4).
3 Inserted by the Civil Partnership Act 2004, s 261(1), Sch 27, para 40.
4 Repealed by the Marriage (Same Sex Couples) Act 2013, s 17(4), Sch 7, paras 26, 27.
5 Substituted by the Private International Law (Miscellaneous Provisions) Act 1995, s 8(2), Schedule, para 2(1), (2).

12 Grounds on which a marriage is voidable.

[(1)][1] A marriage celebrated after 31st July 1971[, other than a marriage to which section 12A applies,][2] shall be voidable on the following grounds only, that is to say—

(a) that the marriage has not been consummated owing to the incapacity of either party to consummate it;
(b) that the marriage has not been consummated owing to the wilful refusal of the respondent to consummate it;
(c) that either party to the marriage did not validly consent to it, whether in consequence of duress, mistake, unsoundness of mind or otherwise;
(d) that at the time of the marriage either party, though capable of giving a valid consent, was suffering (whether continuously or intermittently) from mental disorder within the meaning of the Mental Health Act 1983 of such a kind or to such an extent as to be unfitted for marriage;
(e) that at the time of the marriage the respondent was suffering from venereal disease in a communicable form;
(f) that at the time of the marriage the respondent was pregnant by some person other than the petitioner;
[(g) that an interim gender recognition certificate under the Gender Recognition Act 2004 has, after the time of the marriage, been issued to either party to the marriage;][3]
[(h) that the respondent is a person whose gender at the time of the marriage had become the acquired gender under the Gender Recognition Act 2004.][4]

[(2) Paragraphs (a) and (b) of subsection (1) do not apply to the marriage of a same sex couple.][1]

Amendments

1 Inserted by the Marriage (Same Sex Couples) Act 2013, s 11(4), Sch 4, para 4.

2 Inserted by the Marriage (Same Sex Couples) Act 2013 (Consequential and Contrary Provisions and Scotland) and Marriage and Civil Partnership (Scotland) Act 2014 (Consequential Provisions) Order 2014, SI 2014/3168, art 2, Schedule, para 6(1), (3).

3 Substituted by the Gender Recognition Act 2004, s 4(4), Sch 2, paras 1, 2.

4 Substituted by the Gender Recognition Act 2004, s 11, Sch 4, paras 4, 5.

[12A Grounds on which a marriage converted from a civil partnership is void or voidable

(1) This section applies to a marriage which has been converted, or is purported to have been converted, from a civil partnership under section 9 of the 2013 Act and regulations made under that section.

(2) A marriage which results from the purported conversion of a void civil partnership is void.

(3) A marriage which results from the conversion of a civil partnership is voidable if any of paragraphs (c) to (h) of section 12(1) applied at the date from which the marriage is treated as having subsisted in accordance with section 9(6) of the 2013 Act.

(4) In this section, the '2013 Act' means the Marriage (Same Sex Couples) Act 2013.][1]

Amendment

1 Inserted by the Marriage (Same Sex Couples) Act 2013 (Consequential and Contrary Provisions and Scotland) and Marriage and Civil Partnership (Scotland) Act 2014 (Consequential Provisions) Order 2014, SI 2014/3168, art 2, Schedule, para 6(1), (4).

13 Bars to relief where marriage is voidable.

(1) The court shall not, in proceedings instituted after 31st July 1971, grant a decree of nullity on the ground that a marriage is voidable if the respondent satisfies the court—

- (a) that the petitioner, with knowledge that it was open to him to have the marriage avoided, so conducted himself in relation to the respondent as to lead the respondent reasonably to believe that he would not seek to do so; and
- (b) that it would be unjust to the respondent to grant the decree.

[(2) Without prejudice to subsection (1) above, the court shall not grant a decree of nullity by virtue of section 12 above on the grounds mentioned in paragraph (c), (d), (e)[, (f) or (h)][1] of that section unless—

(a) it is satisfied that proceedings were instituted within the period of three years from the date of the marriage, or
(b) leave for the institution of proceedings after the expiration of that period has been granted under subsection (4) below.][2]

[(2A) Without prejudice to subsection (1) above, the court shall not grant a decree of nullity by virtue of section 12 above on the ground mentioned in paragraph (g) of that section unless it is satisfied that proceedings were instituted within the period of six months from the date of issue of the interim gender recognition certificate.][3]

(3) Without prejudice to subsections (1) and (2) above, the court shall not grant a decree of nullity by virtue of section 12 above on the grounds mentioned in paragraph (e)[, (f) or (h)][1] of that section unless it is satisfied that the petitioner was at the time of the marriage ignorant of the facts alleged.

[(4) In the case of proceedings for the grant of a decree of a nullity by virtue of section 12 above on the grounds mentioned in paragraph (c), (d), (e)[, (f) or (h)][1] of that section, a judge of the court may, on an application made to him, grant leave for the institution of proceedings after the expiration of the period of three years from the date of the marriage if—
(a) he is satisfied that the petitioner has at some time during that period suffered from mental disorder within the meaning of the Mental Health Act 1983, and
(b) he considers that in all the circumstances of the case it would be just to grant leave for the institution of proceedings.

(5) An application for leave under subsection (4) above may be made after the expiration of the period of three years from the date of the marriage.][4]

Amendments

1 Substituted by the Gender Recognition Act 2004, s 11, Sch 4, paras 4, 6.
2 Substituted by the Matrimonial and Family Proceedings Act 1984, s 2(1), (2).
3 Substituted by the Gender Recognition Act 2004, s 4(4), Sch 2, paras 1, 3.
4 Inserted by the Matrimonial and Family Proceedings Act 1984, s 2(1), (3).

14 Marriages governed by foreign law or celebrated abroad under English law.

(1) [Subject to subsection (3) where][1], apart from this Act, any matter affecting the validity of a marriage would fall to be determined (in accordance with the rules of private international law) by reference to the law of a country outside England and Wales, nothing in section 11, 12 or 13(1) above shall—
(a) preclude the determination of that matter as aforesaid; or
(b) require the application to the marriage of the grounds or bar there mentioned except so far as applicable in accordance with those rules.

(2) In the case of a marriage which purports to have been celebrated under the Foreign Marriage Acts 1892 to 1947 or has taken place outside

England and Wales and purports to be a marriage under common law, section 11 above is without prejudice to any ground on which the marriage may be void under those Acts or, as the case may be, by virtue of the rules governing the celebration of marriages outside England and Wales under common law.

[(3) No marriage is to be treated as valid by virtue of subsection (1) if, at the time when it purports to have been celebrated, either party was already a civil partner.][1]

Amendments

1 Inserted by the Civil Partnership Act 2004, s 261(1), Sch 27, para 41.

15 Application of ss. 1(5), 8 and 9 to nullity proceedings.

Sections 1(5), 8 and 9 above shall apply in relation to proceedings for nullity of marriage as if for any reference in those provisions to divorce there were substituted a reference to nullity of marriage.

16 Effect of decree of nullity in case of voidable marriage.

A decree of nullity granted after 31st July 1971 in respect of a voidable marriage shall operate to annul the marriage only as respects any time after the decree has been made absolute, and the marriage shall, notwithstanding the decree, be treated as if it had existed up to that time.

Other matrimonial suits

17 Judicial separation.

(1) A petition for judicial separation may be presented to the court by either party to a marriage on the ground that any such fact as is mentioned in section 1(2) above exists, and the provisions of section 2 above shall apply accordingly for the purposes of a petition for judicial separation alleging any such fact, as they apply in relation to a petition for divorce alleging that fact.

(2) On a petition for judicial separation it shall be the duty of the court to inquire, so far as it reasonably can, into the facts alleged by the petitioner and into any facts alleged by the respondent, but the court shall not be concerned to consider whether the marriage has broken down irretrievably, and if it is satisfied on the evidence of any such fact as is mentioned in section 1(2) above it shall ...[1] grant a decree of judicial separation.

(3) Sections 6 and 7 above shall apply for the purpose of encouraging the reconciliation of parties to proceedings for judicial separation and of enabling the parties to a marriage to refer to the court for its opinion an

agreement or arrangement relevant to actual or contemplated proceedings for judicial separation, as they apply in relation to proceedings for divorce.

Amendment

1 Repealed by the Children and Families Act 2014, s 17(2), (4).

18 Effects of judicial separation.

(1) Where the court grants a decree of judicial separation it shall no longer be obligatory for the petitioner to cohabit with the respondent.

(2) If while a decree of judicial separation is in force and the separation is continuing either of the parties to the marriage dies intestate as respects all or any of his or her real or personal property, the property as respects which he or she died intestate shall devolve as if the other party to the marriage had then been dead.

(3) Notwithstanding anything in section 2(1)(a) of the Matrimonial Proceedings (Magistrates' Courts) Act 1960, a provision in force under an order made, or having effect as if made, under that section exempting one party to a marriage from the obligation to cohabit with the other shall not have effect as a decree of judicial separation for the purposes of subsection (2) above.

19 ...[1]

...[1]

Amendment

1 Repealed by the Presumption of Death Act 2013, s 16(3), Sch 2, para 1.

General

20 Relief for respondent in divorce proceedings.

If in any proceedings for divorce the respondent alleges and proves any such fact as is mentioned in subsection (2) of section 1 above (treating the respondent as the petitioner and the petitioner as the respondent for the purposes of that subsection) the court may give to the respondent the relief to which he would have been entitled if he had presented a petition seeking that relief.

PART II
FINANCIAL RELIEF FOR PARTIES TO MARRIAGE AND CHILDREN OF FAMILY

Financial provision and property adjustment orders

21 Financial provision and property adjustment orders.

(1) The financial provision orders for the purposes of this Act are the orders for periodical or lump sum provision available (subject to the provisions of this Act) under section 23 below for the purpose of adjusting the financial position of the parties to a marriage and any children of the family in connection with proceedings for divorce, nullity of marriage or judicial separation and under section 27(6) below on proof of neglect by one party to a marriage to provide, or to make a proper contribution towards, reasonable maintenance for the other or a child of the family, that is to say—

(a) any order for periodical payments in favour of a party to a marriage under section 23(1)(a) or 27(6)(a) or in favour of a child of the family under section 23(1)(d), (2) or (4) or 27(6)(d);

(b) any order for secured periodical payments in favour of a party to a marriage under section 23(1)(b) or 27(6)(b) or in favour of a child of the family under section 23(1)(e), (2) or (4) or 27(6)(e); and

(c) any order for lump sum provision in favour of a party to a marriage under section 23(1)(c) or 27(6)(c) or in favour of a child of the family under section 23(1)(f), (2) or (4) or 27(6)(f);

and references in this Act (except in paragraphs 17(1) and 23 of Schedule 1 below) to periodical payments orders, secured periodical payments orders, and orders for the payment of a lump sum are references to all or some of the financial provision orders requiring the sort of financial provision in question according as the context of each reference may require.

(2) The property adjustment orders for the purposes of this Act are the orders dealing with property rights available (subject to the provisions of this Act) under section 24 below for the purpose of adjusting the financial position of the parties to a marriage and any children of the family on or after the grant of a decree of divorce, nullity of marriage or judicial separation, that is to say—

(a) any order under subsection (1)(a) of that section for a transfer of property;

(b) any order under subsection (1)(b) of that section for a settlement of property; and

(c) any order under subsection (1)(c) or (d) of that section for a variation of settlement.

[21A Pension sharing orders.

(1) For the purposes of this Act, a pension sharing order is an order which—

(a) provides that one party's—

(i) shareable rights under a specified pension arrangement, or

(ii) shareable state scheme rights,

be subject to pension sharing for the benefit of the other party, and

(b) specifies the percentage value to be transferred.

(2) In subsection (1) above—

(a) the reference to shareable rights under a pension arrangement is to rights in relation to which pension sharing is available under Chapter I of Part IV of the Welfare Reform and Pensions Act 1999, or under corresponding Northern Ireland legislation,

(b) the reference to shareable state scheme rights is to rights in relation to which pension sharing is available under Chapter II of Part IV of the Welfare Reform and Pensions Act 1999, or under corresponding Northern Ireland legislation, and

(c) 'party' means a party to a marriage.][1]

Amendment

1 Inserted by the Welfare Reform and Pensions Act 1999, s 19, Sch 3, paras 1, 2.

Ancillary relief in connection with divorce proceedings, etc.

22 *Maintenance pending suit.*

[(1)][1] On a petition for divorce, nullity of marriage or judicial separation, the court may make an order for maintenance pending suit, that is to say, an order requiring either party to the marriage to make to the other such periodical payments for his or her maintenance and for such term, being a term beginning not earlier than the date of the presentation of the petition and ending with the date of the determination of the suit, as the court thinks reasonable.

[(2) An order under this section may not require a party to a marriage to pay to the other party any amount in respect of legal services for the purposes of the proceedings.

(3) In subsection (2) 'legal services' has the same meaning as in section 22ZA.][1]

Amendments

1 Inserted by the Legal Aid, Sentencing and Punishment of Offenders Act 2012, s 49(1).

[22ZA Orders for payment in respect of legal services

(1) In proceedings for divorce, nullity of marriage or judicial separation, the court may make an order or orders requiring one party to the marriage to pay to the other ('the applicant') an amount for the purpose of enabling the applicant to obtain legal services for the purposes of the proceedings.

(2) The court may also make such an order or orders in proceedings under this Part for financial relief in connection with proceedings for divorce, nullity of marriage or judicial separation.

(3) The court must not make an order under this section unless it is satisfied that, without the amount, the applicant would not reasonably be able to obtain appropriate legal services for the purposes of the proceedings or any part of the proceedings.

(4) For the purposes of subsection (3), the court must be satisfied, in particular, that—

(a) the applicant is not reasonably able to secure a loan to pay for the services, and

(b) the applicant is unlikely to be able to obtain the services by granting a charge over any assets recovered in the proceedings.

(5) An order under this section may be made for the purpose of enabling the applicant to obtain legal services of a specified description, including legal services provided in a specified period or for the purposes of a specified part of the proceedings.

(6) An order under this section may—

(a) provide for the payment of all or part of the amount by instalments of specified amounts, and

(b) require the instalments to be secured to the satisfaction of the court.

(7) An order under this section may direct that payment of all or part of the amount is to be deferred.

(8) The court may at any time in the proceedings vary an order made under this section if it considers that there has been a material change of circumstances since the order was made.

(9) For the purposes of the assessment of costs in the proceedings, the applicant's costs are to be treated as reduced by any amount paid to the applicant pursuant to an order under this section for the purposes of those proceedings.

(10) In this section 'legal services', in relation to proceedings, means the following types of services—

(a) providing advice as to how the law applies in the particular circumstances,

(b) providing advice and assistance in relation to the proceedings,

(c) providing other advice and assistance in relation to the settlement or other resolution of the dispute that is the subject of the proceedings, and

(d) providing advice and assistance in relation to the enforcement of decisions in the proceedings or as part of the settlement or resolution of the dispute,

and they include, in particular, advice and assistance in the form of representation and any form of dispute resolution, including mediation.

(11) In subsections (5) and (6) 'specified' means specified in the order concerned.][1]

Amendment

1 Inserted by the Legal Aid, Sentencing and Punishment of Offenders Act 2012, s 49(2).

[22ZB Matters to which court is to have regard in deciding how to exercise power under section 22ZA

(1) When considering whether to make or vary an order under section 22ZA, the court must have regard to—
   (a) the income, earning capacity, property and other financial resources which each of the applicant and the paying party has or is likely to have in the foreseeable future,
   (b) the financial needs, obligations and responsibilities which each of the applicant and the paying party has or is likely to have in the foreseeable future,
   (c) the subject matter of the proceedings, including the matters in issue in them,
   (d) whether the paying party is legally represented in the proceedings,
   (e) any steps taken by the applicant to avoid all or part of the proceedings, whether by proposing or considering mediation or otherwise,
   (f) the applicant's conduct in relation to the proceedings,
   (g) any amount owed by the applicant to the paying party in respect of costs in the proceedings or other proceedings to which both the applicant and the paying party are or were party, and
   (h) the effect of the order or variation on the paying party.

(2) In subsection (1)(a) 'earning capacity', in relation to the applicant or the paying party, includes any increase in earning capacity which, in the opinion of the court, it would be reasonable to expect the applicant or the paying party to take steps to acquire.

(3) For the purposes of subsection (1)(h), the court must have regard, in particular, to whether the making or variation of the order is likely to—
   (a) cause undue hardship to the paying party, or
   (b) prevent the paying party from obtaining legal services for the purposes of the proceedings.

(4) The Lord Chancellor may by order amend this section by adding to, omitting or varying the matters mentioned in subsections (1) to (3).

(5) An order under subsection (4) must be made by statutory instrument.

(6) A statutory instrument containing an order under subsection (4) may not be made unless a draft of the instrument has been laid before, and approved by a resolution of, each House of Parliament.

(7) In this section 'legal services' has the same meaning as in section 22ZA.][1]

Amendment

1 Inserted by the Legal Aid, Sentencing and Punishment of Offenders Act 2012, s 50.

23 Financial provision orders in connection with divorce proceedings, etc.

(1) On granting a decree of divorce, a decree of nullity of marriage or a decree of judicial separation or at any time thereafter (whether, in the case of a decree of divorce or of nullity of marriage, before or after the decree is made absolute), the court may make any one or more of the following orders, that is to say—

  (a) an order that either party to the marriage shall make to the other such periodical payments, for such term, as may be specified in the order;
  (b) an order that either party to the marriage shall secure to the other to the satisfaction of the court such periodical payments, for such term, as may be so specified;
  (c) an order that either party to the marriage shall pay to the other such lump sum or sums as may be so specified;
  (d) an order that a party to the marriage shall make to such person as may be specified in the order for the benefit of a child of the family, or to such a child, such periodical payments, for such term, as may be so specified;
  (e) an order that a party to the marriage shall secure to such person as may be so specified for the benefit of such a child, or to such a child, to the satisfaction of the court, such periodical payments, for such term, as may be so specified;
  (f) an order that a party to the marriage shall pay to such person as may be so specified for the benefit of such a child, or to such a child, such lump sum as may be so specified;

subject, however, in the case of an order under paragraph (d), (e) or (f) above, to the restrictions imposed by section 29(1) and (3) below on the making of financial provision orders in favour of children who have attained the age of eighteen.

(2) The court may also, subject to those restrictions, make any one or more of the orders mentioned in subsection (1)(d), (e) and (f) above—

  (a) in any proceedings for divorce, nullity of marriage or judicial separation, before granting a decree; and
  (b) where any such proceedings are dismissed after the beginning of the trial, either forthwith or within a reasonable period after the dismissal.

(3) Without prejudice to the generality of subsection (1)(c) or (f) above—

(a) an order under this section that a party to a marriage shall pay a lump sum to the other party may be made for the purpose of enabling that other party to meet any liabilities or expenses reasonably incurred by him or her in maintaining himself or herself or any child of the family before making an application for an order under this section in his or her favour;

(b) an order under this section for the payment of a lump sum to or for the benefit of a child of the family may be made for the purpose of enabling any liabilities or expenses reasonably incurred by or for the benefit of that child before the making of an application for an order under this section in his favour to be met; and

(c) an order under this section for the payment of a lump sum may provide for the payment of that sum by instalments of such amount as may be specified in the order and may require the payment of the instalments to be secured to the satisfaction of the court.

(4) The power of the court under subsection (1) or (2)(a) above to make an order in favour of a child of the family shall be exercisable from time to time; and where the court makes an order in favour of a child under subsection (2)(b) above, it may from time to time, subject to the restrictions mentioned in subsection (1) above, make a further order in his favour of any of the kinds mentioned in subsection (1)(d), (e) or (f) above.

(5) Without prejudice to the power to give a direction under section 30 below for the settlement of an instrument by conveyancing counsel, where an order is made under subsection (1)(a), (b) or (c) above on or after granting a decree of divorce or nullity of marriage, neither the order nor any settlement made in pursuance of the order shall take effect unless the decree has been made absolute.

[(6) Where the court—

(a) makes an order under this section for the payment of a lump sum; and

(b) directs—

(i) that payment of that sum or any part of it shall be deferred; or

(ii) that that sum or any part of it shall be paid by instalments,

the court may order that the amount deferred or the instalments shall carry interest at such rate as may be specified by the order from such date, not earlier than the date of the order, as may be so specified, until the date when payment of it is due.][1]

Amendment

1 Inserted by the Administration of Justice Act 1982, s 16.

24 Property adjustment orders in connection with divorce proceedings, etc.

(1) On granting a decree of divorce, a decree of nullity of marriage or a decree of judicial separation or at any time thereafter (whether, in the case of a decree of divorce or of nullity of marriage, before or after the decree is

made absolute), the court may make any one or more of the following orders, that is to say—

(a) an order that a party to the marriage shall transfer to the other party, to any child of the family or to such person as may be specified in the order for the benefit of such a child such property as may be so specified, being property to which the first-mentioned party is entitled, either in possession or reversion;

(b) an order that a settlement of such property as may be so specified, being property to which a party to the marriage is so entitled, be made to the satisfaction of the court for the benefit of the other party to the marriage and of the children of the family or either or any of them;

(c) an order varying for the benefit of the parties to the marriage and of the children of the family or either or any of them any ante-nuptial or post-nuptial settlement (including such a settlement made by will or codicil) made on the parties to the marriage[, other than one in the form of a pension arrangement (within the meaning of section 25D below)][1];

(d) an order extinguishing or reducing the interest of either of the parties to the marriage under any such settlement[, other than one in the form of a pension arrangement (within the meaning of section 25D below)][1];

subject, however, in the case of an order under paragraph (a) above, to the restrictions imposed by section 29(1) and (3) below on the making of orders for a transfer of property in favour of children who have attained the age of eighteen.

(2) The court may make an order under subsection (1)(c) above notwithstanding that there are no children of the family.

(3) Without prejudice to the power to give a direction under section 30 below for the settlement of an instrument by conveyancing counsel, where an order is made under this section on or after granting a decree of divorce or nullity of marriage, neither the order nor any settlement made in pursuance of the order shall take effect unless the decree has been made absolute.

Amendments

1 Inserted by the Welfare Reform and Pensions Act 1999, s 19, Sch 3, paras 1, 3.

[24A Orders for sale of property.

(1) Where the court makes [an order under section 22ZA or makes][1] under section 23 or 24 of this Act a secured periodical payments order, an order for the payment of a lump sum or a property adjustment order, then, on making that order or at any time thereafter, the court may make a further order for the sale of such property as may be specified in the order, being property in which or in the proceeds of sale of which either or both of the

parties to the marriage has or have a beneficial interest, either in possession or reversion.

(2) Any order made under subsection (1) above may contain such consequential or supplementary provisions as the court thinks fit and, without prejudice to the generality of the foregoing provision, may include—

(a) provision requiring the making of a payment out of the proceeds of sale of the property to which the order relates, and

(b) provision requiring any such property to be offered for sale to a person, or class of persons, specified in the order.

(3) Where an order is made under subsection (1) above on or after the grant of a decree of divorce or nullity of marriage, the order shall not take effect unless the decree has been made absolute.

(4) Where an order is made under subsection (1) above, the court may direct that the order, or such provision thereof as the court may specify, shall not take effect until the occurrence of an event specified by the court or the expiration of a period so specified.

(5) Where an order under subsection (1) above contains a provision requiring the proceeds of sale of the property to which the order relates to be used to secure periodical payments to a party to the marriage, the order shall cease to have effect on the death or re-marriage of[, or formation of a civil partnership by,][2] that person.

[(6) Where a party to a marriage has a beneficial interest in any property, or in the proceeds of sale thereof, and some other person who is not a party to the marriage also has a beneficial interest in that property or in the proceeds of sale thereof, then, before deciding whether to make an order under this section in relation to that property, it shall be the duty of the court to give that other person an opportunity to make representations with respect to the order; and any representations made by that other person shall be included among the circumstances to which the court is required to have regard under section 25(1) below.][3]][4]

Amendments

1 Inserted by the Legal Aid, Sentencing and Punishment of Offenders Act 2012, s 51.
2 Inserted by the Civil Partnership Act 2004, s 261(1), Sch 27, para 42.
3 Inserted by the Matrimonial and Family Proceedings Act 1984, s 46(1), Sch 1, para 11.
4 Inserted by the Matrimonial Homes and Property Act 1981, s 7.

[24B Pension sharing orders in connection with divorce proceedings etc.

(1) On granting a decree of divorce or a decree of nullity of marriage or at any time thereafter (whether before or after the decree is made absolute), the court may, on an application made under this section, make one or more pension sharing orders in relation to the marriage.

(2) A pension sharing order under this section is not to take effect unless the decree on or after which it is made has been made absolute.

(3) A pension sharing order under this section may not be made in relation to a pension arrangement which—
(a) is the subject of a pension sharing order in relation to the marriage, or
(b) has been the subject of pension sharing between the parties to the marriage.

(4) A pension sharing order under this section may not be made in relation to shareable state scheme rights if—
(a) such rights are the subject of a pension sharing order in relation to the marriage, or
(b) such rights have been the subject of pension sharing between the parties to the marriage.

(5) A pension sharing order under this section may not be made in relation to the rights of a person under a pension arrangement if there is in force a requirement imposed by virtue of section 25B or 25C below which relates to benefits or future benefits to which he is entitled under the pension arrangement.][1]

Amendment

1 Inserted by the Welfare Reform and Pensions Act 1999, s 19, Sch 3, paras 1, 4.

[24C Pension sharing orders: duty to stay.

(1) No pension sharing order may be made so as to take effect before the end of such period after the making of the order as may be prescribed by regulations made by the Lord Chancellor.

(2) The power to make regulations under this section shall be exercisable by statutory instrument which shall be subject to annulment in pursuance of a resolution of either House of Parliament.][1]

Amendment

1 Inserted by the Welfare Reform and Pensions Act 1999, s 19, Sch 3, paras 1, 4.

[24D Pension sharing orders: apportionment of charges.

If a pension sharing order relates to rights under a pension arrangement, the court may include in the order provision about the apportionment between the parties of any charge under section 41 of the Welfare Reform and Pensions Act 1999 (charges in respect of pension sharing costs), or under corresponding Northern Ireland legislation.][1]

Amendment

1 Inserted by the Welfare Reform and Pensions Act 1999, s 19, Sch 3, paras 1, 4.

[24E Pension compensation sharing orders in connection with divorce proceedings

(1) On granting a decree of divorce or a decree of nullity of marriage or at any time thereafter (whether before or after the decree is made absolute), the court may, on an application made under this section, make a pension compensation sharing order in relation to the marriage.

(2) A pension compensation sharing order under this section is not to take effect unless the decree on or after which it is made has been made absolute.

(3) A pension compensation sharing order under this section may not be made in relation to rights to PPF compensation that—
  (a) are the subject of pension attachment,
  (b) derive from rights under a pension scheme that were the subject of pension sharing between the parties to the marriage,
  (c) are the subject of pension compensation attachment, or
  (d) are or have been the subject of pension compensation sharing between the parties to the marriage.

(4) For the purposes of subsection (3)(a), rights to PPF compensation 'are the subject of pension attachment' if any of the following three conditions is met.

(5) The first condition is that—
  (a) the rights derive from rights under a pension scheme in relation to which an order was made under section 23 imposing a requirement by virtue of section 25B(4), and
  (b) that order, as modified under section 25E(3), remains in force.

(6) The second condition is that—
  (a) the rights derive from rights under a pension scheme in relation to which an order was made under section 23 imposing a requirement by virtue of section 25B(7), and
  (b) that order—
    (i) has been complied with, or
    (ii) has not been complied with and, as modified under section 25E(5), remains in force.

(7) The third condition is that—
  (a) the rights derive from rights under a pension scheme in relation to which an order was made under section 23 imposing a requirement by virtue of section 25C, and
  (b) that order remains in force.

(8) For the purposes of subsection (3)(b), rights under a pension scheme 'were the subject of pension sharing between the parties to the marriage' if the rights were at any time the subject of a pension sharing order in relation to the marriage or a previous marriage between the same parties.

(9) For the purposes of subsection (3)(c), rights to PPF compensation 'are the subject of pension compensation attachment' if there is in force a requirement imposed by virtue of section 25F relating to them.

(10) For the purposes of subsection (3)(d), rights to PPF compensation 'are or have been the subject of pension compensation sharing between the parties to the marriage' if they are or have ever been the subject of a pension compensation sharing order in relation to the marriage or a previous marriage between the same parties.][1]

Amendment

1 Inserted by the Pensions Act 2008, s 120, Sch 6, paras 1, 3.

[24F Pension compensation sharing orders: duty to stay

(1) No pension compensation sharing order may be made so as to take effect before the end of such period after the making of the order as may be prescribed by regulations made by the Lord Chancellor.

(2) The power to make regulations under this section shall be exercisable by statutory instrument which shall be subject to annulment in pursuance of a resolution of either House of Parliament.][1]

Amendment

1 Inserted by the Pensions Act 2008, s 120, Sch 6, paras 1, 3.

[24G Pension compensation sharing orders: apportionment of charges

The court may include in a pension compensation sharing order provision about the apportionment between the parties of any charge under section 117 of the Pensions Act 2008 (charges in respect of pension compensation sharing costs), or under corresponding Northern Ireland legislation.][1]

Amendment

1 Inserted by the Pensions Act 2008, s 120, Sch 6, paras 1, 3.

[25 Matters to which court is to have regard in deciding how to exercise its powers under ss. 23, 24[, 24A, 24B and 24E][1]

(1) It shall be the duty of the court in deciding whether to exercise its powers under section 23, 24[, 24A[, 24B or 24E][1]][2] above and, if so, in what manner, to have regard to all the circumstances of the case, first consideration being given to the welfare while a minor of any child of the family who has not attained the age of eighteen.

(2) As regards the exercise of the powers of the court under section 23(1)(a), (b) or (c), 24[, 24A[, 24B or 24E][1]][2] above in relation to a party to the marriage, the court shall in particular have regard to the following matters—

(a) the income, earning capacity, property and other financial resources which each of the parties to the marriage has or is likely to have in the foreseeable future, including in the case of earning capacity any increase in that capacity which it would in the opinion of the court be reasonable to expect a party to the marriage to take steps to acquire;

(b) the financial needs, obligations and responsibilities which each of the parties to the marriage has or is likely to have in the foreseeable future;

(c) the standard of living enjoyed by the family before the breakdown of the marriage;

(d) the age of each party to the marriage and the duration of the marriage;

(e) any physical or mental disability of either of the parties to the marriage;

(f) the contributions which each of the parties has made or is likely in the foreseeable future to make to the welfare of the family, including any contribution by looking after the home or caring for the family;

(g) the conduct of each of the parties, if that conduct is such that it would in the opinion of the court be inequitable to disregard it;

(h) in the case of proceedings for divorce or nullity of marriage, the value to each of the parties to the marriage of any benefit …[3] which, by reason of the dissolution or annulment of the marriage, that party will lose the chance of acquiring.

(3) As regards the exercise of the powers of the court under section 23(1)(d) or, (e) or (f), (2) (4), 24 or 24A above in relation to a child of the family, the court shall in particular have regard to the following matters—

(a) the financial needs of the child;

(b) the income, earning capacity (if any), property and other financial resources of the child;

(c) any physical or mental disability of the child;

(d) the manner in which he was being and in which the parties to the marriage expected him to be educated or trained;

(e) the considerations mentioned in relation to the parties to the marriage in paragraphs (a), (b), (c) and (e) of subsection (2) above.

(4) As regards the exercise of the powers of the court under section 23(1)(d), (e) or (f), (2) or (4), 24 or 24A above against a party to a marriage in favour of a child of the family who is not the child of that party, the court shall also have regard—

(a) to whether that party assumed any responsibility for the child's maintenance, and, if so, to the extent to which, and the basis upon which, that party assumed such responsibility and to the length of time for which that party discharged such responsibility;

(b) to whether in assuming and discharging such responsibility that party did so knowing that the child was not his or her own;

(c) to the liability of any other person to maintain the child.][4]

Amendments

1 Substituted by the Pensions Act 2008, s 120, Sch 6, paras 1, 4.

2 Substituted by the Welfare Reform and Pensions Act 1999, s 19, Sch 3, paras 1, 5.

3 Repealed by the Pensions Act 1995, s 166(2).

4 Substituted by the Matrimonial and Family Proceedings Act 1984, s 3.

[25A Exercise of court's powers in favour of party to marriage on decree of divorce or nullity of marriage.

(1) Where on or after the grant of a decree of divorce or nullity of marriage the court decides to exercise its powers under section 23(1)(a), (b) or (c), 24[, 24A[, 24B or 24E][1]][2] above in favour of a party to the marriage, it shall be the duty of the court to consider whether it would be appropriate so to exercise those powers that the financial obligations of each party towards the other will be terminated as soon after the grant of the decree as the court considers just and reasonable.

(2) Where the court decides in such a case to make a periodical payments or secured periodical payments order in favour of a party to the marriage, the court shall in particular consider whether it would be appropriate to require those payments to be made or secured only for such term as would in the opinion of the court be sufficient to enable the party in whose favour the order is made to adjust without undue hardship to the termination of his or her financial dependence on the other party.

(3) Where on or after the grant of a decree of divorce or nullity of marriage an application is made by a party to the marriage for a periodical payments or secured periodical payments order in his or her favour, then, if the court considers that no continuing obligation should be imposed on either party to make or secure periodical payments in favour of the other, the court may dismiss the application with a direction that the applicant shall not be entitled to make any further application in relation to that marriage for an order under section 23(1)(a) or (b) above.][3]

Amendments

1 Substituted by the Pensions Act 2008, s 120, Sch 6, paras 1, 5.
2 Substituted by the Welfare Reform and Pensions Act 1999, s 19, Sch 3, paras 1, 5.
3 Substituted by the Matrimonial and Family Proceedings Act 1984, s 3.

[25B Pensions.

(1) The matters to which the court is to have regard under section 25(2) above include—

(a) in the case of paragraph (a) , any benefits under a pension [arrangement][1] which a party to the marriage has or is likely to have, and

(b) in the case of paragraph (h) , any benefits under a pension [arrangement][1] which, by reason of the dissolution or annulment of the marriage, a party to the marriage will lose the chance of acquiring, and, accordingly, in relation to benefits under a pension [arrangement][1], section 25(2)(a) above shall have effect as if 'in the foreseeable future' were omitted.

(2) ...[2]

(3) The following provisions apply where, having regard to any benefits under a pension [arrangement][1], the court determines to make an order under section 23 above.

(4) To the extent to which the order is made having regard to any benefits under a pension [arrangement][1], the order may require the [person responsible for][1] the pension [arrangement][1] in question, if at any time any payment in respect of any benefits under the [arrangement][1] becomes due to the party with pension rights, to make a payment for the benefit of the other party.

[(5) The order must express the amount of any payment required to be made by virtue of subsection (4) above as a percentage of the payment which becomes due to the party with pension rights.][1]

(6) Any such payment by the [person responsible for the arrangement][1]—

(a) shall discharge so much of [his][1] liability to the party with pension rights as corresponds to the amount of the payment, and

(b) shall be treated for all purposes as a payment made by the party with pension rights in or towards the discharge of his liability under the order.

(7) Where the party with pension rights [has a right of commutation under the arrangement, the order may require him to exercise it to any extent][1]; and this section applies to [any payment due in consequence of commutation][1] in pursuance of the order as it applies to other payments in respect of benefits under the [arrangement][1].

[(7A) The power conferred by subsection (7) above may not be exercised for the purpose of commuting a benefit payable to the party with pension rights to a benefit payable to the other party.

(7B) The power conferred by subsection (4) or (7) above may not be exercised in relation to a pension arrangement which—

(a) is the subject of a pension sharing order in relation to the marriage, or

(b) has been the subject of pension sharing between the parties to the marriage.

(7C) In subsection (1) above, references to benefits under a pension arrangement include any benefits by way of pension, whether under a pension arrangement or not.][3]][4]

Amendments

1 Substituted by the Welfare Reform and Pensions Act 1999, s 21, Sch 4, para 1(1), (2), (4)-(8).

2 Repealed by the Welfare Reform and Pensions Act 1999, s 21, Sch 4, para 1(1), (3).

3 Inserted by the Welfare Reform and Pensions Act 1999, s 21, Sch 4, para 1(1), (9).

4 Inserted by the Pensions Act 1995, s 166(1).

[25C Pensions: lump sums.

(1) The power of the court under section 23 above to order a party to a marriage to pay a lump sum to the other party includes, where the benefits which the party with pension rights has or is likely to have under a pension [arrangement][1] include any lump sum payable in respect of his death, power to make any of the following provision by the order.

(2) The court may—
   (a) if the [person responsible for the pension arrangement in question has][1] power to determine the person to whom the sum, or any part of it, is to be paid, require [him][1] to pay the whole or part of that sum, when it becomes due, to the other party,
   (b) if the party with pension rights has power to nominate the person to whom the sum, or any part of it, is to be paid, require the party with pension rights to nominate the other party in respect of the whole or part of that sum,
   (c) in any other case, require the [person responsible for the pension arrangement][1] in question to pay the whole or part of that sum, when it becomes due, for the benefit of the other party instead of to the person to whom, apart from the order, it would be paid.

(3) Any payment by the [person responsible for the arrangement][1] under an order made under section 23 above by virtue of this section shall discharge so much of [his][1] liability in respect of the party with pension rights as corresponds to the amount of the payment.

[(4) The powers conferred by this section may not be exercised in relation to a pension arrangement which—
   (a) is the subject of a pension sharing order in relation to the marriage, or
   (b) has been the subject of pension sharing between the parties to the marriage.][2]][3]

Amendments

1 Substituted by the Welfare Reform and Pensions Act 1999, s 21, Sch 4, para 2(1)-(4).
2 Inserted by the Welfare Reform and Pensions Act 1999, s 21, Sch 4, para 2(1), (5).
3 Inserted by the Pensions Act 1995, s 166(1).

[25D Pensions: supplementary.

[(1) Where—
   (a) an order made under section 23 above by virtue of section 25B or 25C above imposes any requirement on the person responsible for a pension arrangement ('the first arrangement') and the party with pension rights acquires rights under another pension arrangement ('the new arrangement') which are derived (directly or indirectly) from the whole of his rights under the first arrangement, and
   (b) the person responsible for the new arrangement has been given notice in accordance with regulations made by the Lord Chancellor,

the order shall have effect as if it had been made instead in respect of the person responsible for the new arrangement.][1]

(2) [The Lord Chancellor may by regulations][1]—

(a) in relation to any provision of sections 25B or 25C above which authorises the court making an order under section 23 above to require the [person responsible for a pension arrangement][1] to make a payment for the benefit of the other party, make provision as to the person to whom, and the terms on which, the payment is to be made,

[(ab) make, in relation to payment under a mistaken belief as to the continuation in force of a provision included by virtue of section 25B or 25C above in an order under section 23 above, provision about the rights or liabilities of the payer, the payee or the person to whom the payment was due,][2]

(b) require notices to be given in respect of changes of circumstances relevant to such orders which include provision made by virtue of sections 25B and 25C above,

[(ba) make provision for the person responsible for a pension arrangement to be discharged in prescribed circumstances from a requirement imposed by virtue of section 25B or 25C above,][2]

(c) …[3]

(d) …[3]

[(e) make provision about calculation and verification in relation to the valuation of—

(i) benefits under a pension arrangement, or

(ii) shareable state scheme rights,

for the purposes of the court's functions in connection with the exercise of any of its powers under this Part of this Act.][1]

…3

[(2A) Regulations under subsection (2)(e) above may include—

(a) provision for calculation or verification in accordance with guidance from time to time prepared by a prescribed person, and

(b) provision by reference to regulations under section 30 or 49(4) of the Welfare Reform and Pensions Act 1999.

(2B) Regulations under subsection (2) above may make different provision for different cases.

(2C) Power to make regulations under this section shall be exercisable by statutory instrument which shall be subject to annulment in pursuance of a resolution of either House of Parliament.][2]

[(3) In this section and sections 25B and 25C above—

'occupational pension scheme' has the same meaning as in the Pension Schemes Act 1993;

'the party with pension rights' means the party to the marriage who has or is likely to have benefits under a pension arrangement and 'the other party' means the other party to the marriage;

'pension arrangement' means—
- (a) an occupational pension scheme,
- (b) a personal pension scheme,
- (c) a retirement annuity contract,
- (d) an annuity or insurance policy purchased, or transferred, for the purpose of giving effect to rights under an occupational pension scheme or a personal pension scheme, and
- (e) an annuity purchased, or entered into, for the purpose of discharging liability in respect of a pension credit under section 29(1)(b) of the Welfare Reform and Pensions Act 1999 or under corresponding Northern Ireland legislation;

'personal pension scheme' has the same meaning as in the Pension Schemes Act 1993;

'prescribed' means prescribed by regulations;

'retirement annuity contract' means a contract or scheme approved under Chapter III of Part XIV of the Income and Corporation Taxes Act 1988;

'shareable state scheme rights' has the same meaning as in section 21A(1) above; and

'trustees or managers', in relation to an occupational pension scheme or a personal pension scheme, means—
- (a) in the case of a scheme established under a trust, the trustees of the scheme, and
- (b) in any other case, the managers of the scheme.

(4) In this section and sections 25B and 25C above, references to the person responsible for a pension arrangement are—
- (a) in the case of an occupational pension scheme or a personal pension scheme, to the trustees or managers of the scheme,
- (b) in the case of a retirement annuity contract or an annuity falling within paragraph (d) or (e) of the definition of 'pension arrangement' above, the provider of the annuity, and
- (c) in the case of an insurance policy falling within paragraph (d) of the definition of that expression, the insurer.][1]][4]

Amendments

1 Substituted by the Welfare Reform and Pensions Act 1999, s 21, Sch 4, para 3(1), (2), (3)(a), (b), (f), (5).
2 Inserted by the Welfare Reform and Pensions Act 1999, s 21, Sch 4, para 3(1), (3)(c), (d), (4).
3 Repealed by the Welfare Reform and Pensions Act 1999, s 21, Sch 4, para 3(1), (3)(e), (g).
4 Inserted by the Pensions Act 1995, s 166(1).

[25E The Pension Protection Fund

(1) The matters to which the court is to have regard under section 25(2) include–

(a) in the case of paragraph (a), any PPF compensation to which a party to the marriage is or is likely to be entitled, and
(b) in the case of paragraph (h), any PPF compensation which, by reason of the dissolution or annulment of the marriage, a party to the marriage will lose the chance of acquiring entitlement to,

and, accordingly, in relation to PPF compensation, section 25(2)(a) shall have effect as if 'in the foreseeable future' were omitted.

(2) Subsection (3) applies in relation to an order under section 23 so far as it includes provision made by virtue of section 25B(4) which–
(a) imposed requirements on the trustees or managers of an occupational pension scheme for which the Board has assumed responsibility in accordance with Chapter 3 of Part 2 of the Pensions Act 2004 (pension protection) or any provision in force in Northern Ireland corresponding to that Chapter, and
(b) was made before the trustees or managers of the scheme received the transfer notice in relation to the scheme.

(3) The order is to have effect from the time when the trustees or managers of the scheme receive the transfer notice–
(a) as if, except in prescribed descriptions of case–
(i) references in the order to the trustees or managers of the scheme were references to the Board, and
(ii) references in the order to any pension or lump sum to which the party with pension rights is or may become entitled under the scheme were references to any PPF compensation to which that person is or may become entitled in respect of the pension or lump sum, and
(b) subject to such other modifications as may be prescribed.

(4) Subsection (5) applies to an order under section 23 if–
(a) it includes provision made by virtue of section 25B(7) which requires the party with pension rights to exercise his right of commutation under an occupational pension scheme to any extent, and
(b) before the requirement is complied with the Board has assumed responsibility for the scheme as mentioned in subsection (2)(a).

(5) From the time the trustees or managers of the scheme receive the transfer notice, the order is to have effect with such modifications as may be prescribed.

(6) Regulations may modify section 25C as it applies in relation to an occupational pension scheme at any time when there is an assessment period in relation to the scheme.

(7) Where the court makes a pension sharing order in respect of a person's shareable rights under an occupational pension scheme, or an order which includes provision made by virtue of section 25B(4) or (7) in relation to such a scheme, the Board subsequently assuming responsibility for the scheme as mentioned in subsection (2)(a) does not affect–

(a) the powers of the court under section 31 to vary or discharge the order or to suspend or revive any provision of it, or

(b) on an appeal, the powers of the appeal court to affirm, reinstate, set aside or vary the order.

(8) Regulations may make such consequential modifications of any provision of, or made by virtue of, this Part as appear to the Lord Chancellor necessary or expedient to give effect to the provisions of this section.

(9) In this section–

'assessment period' means an assessment period within the meaning of Part 2 of the Pensions Act 2004 (pension protection) (see sections 132 and 159 of that Act) or an equivalent period under any provision in force in Northern Ireland corresponding to that Part;

'the Board' means the Board of the Pension Protection Fund;

'occupational pension scheme' has the same meaning as in the Pension Schemes Act 1993;

'prescribed' means prescribed by regulations;

...[1]

'regulations' means regulations made by the Lord Chancellor;

'shareable rights' are rights in relation to which pension sharing is available under Chapter 1 of Part 4 of the Welfare Reform and Pensions Act 1999 or any provision in force in Northern Ireland corresponding to that Chapter;

'transfer notice' has the same meaning as in section 160 of the Pensions Act 2004 or any corresponding provision in force in Northern Ireland.

(10) Any power to make regulations under this section is exercisable by statutory instrument, which shall be subject to annulment in pursuance of a resolution of either House of Parliament.][2]

Amendments

1 Repealed by the Pensions Act 2008, ss 120, 148, Sch 6, paras 1, 6, Sch 11, Pt 4.
2 Inserted by the Pensions Act 2004, s 319(1), Sch 12, para 3.

[25F *Attachment of pension compensation*

(1) This section applies where, having regard to any PPF compensation to which a party to the marriage is or is likely to be entitled, the court determines to make an order under section 23.

(2) To the extent to which the order is made having regard to such compensation, the order may require the Board of the Pension Protection Fund, if at any time any payment in respect of PPF compensation becomes due to the party with compensation rights, to make a payment for the benefit of the other party.

(3) The order must express the amount of any payment required to be made by virtue of subsection (2) as a percentage of the payment which becomes due to the party with compensation rights.

(4) Any such payment by the Board of the Pension Protection Fund—
  (a) shall discharge so much of its liability to the party with compensation rights as corresponds to the amount of the payment, and
  (b) shall be treated for all purposes as a payment made by the party with compensation rights in or towards the discharge of that party's liability under the order.

(5) Where the party with compensation rights has a right to commute any PPF compensation, the order may require that party to exercise it to any extent; and this section applies to any payment due in consequence of commutation in pursuance of the order as it applies to other payments in respect of PPF compensation.

(6) The power conferred by subsection (5) may not be exercised for the purpose of commuting compensation payable to the party with compensation rights to compensation payable to the other party.

(7) The power conferred by subsection (2) or (5) may not be exercised in relation to rights to PPF compensation that—
  (a) derive from rights under a pension scheme that were at any time the subject of a pension sharing order in relation to the marriage, or a previous marriage between the same parties, or
  (b) are or have ever been the subject of a pension compensation sharing order in relation to the marriage or a previous marriage between the same parties.][1]

Amendment

1 Inserted by the Pensions Act 2008, s 120, Sch 6, paras 1, 7.

[25G Pension compensation: supplementary

(1) The Lord Chancellor may by regulations—
  (a) make provision, in relation to any provision of section 25F which authorises the court making an order under section 23 to require the Board of the Pension Protection Fund to make a payment for the benefit of the other party, as to the person to whom, and the terms on which, the payment is to be made;
  (b) make provision, in relation to payment under a mistaken belief as to the continuation in force of a provision included by virtue of section 25F in an order under section 23, about the rights or liabilities of the payer, the payee or the person to whom the payment was due;
  (c) require notices to be given in respect of changes of circumstances relevant to orders under section 23 which include provision made by virtue of section 25F;

(d) make provision for the Board of the Pension Protection Fund to be discharged in prescribed circumstances from a requirement imposed by virtue of section 25F;

(e) make provision about calculation and verification in relation to the valuation of PPF compensation for the purposes of the court's functions in connection with the exercise of any of its powers under this Part.

(2) Regulations under subsection (1)(e) may include—

(a) provision for calculation or verification in accordance with guidance from time to time prepared by a prescribed person;

(b) provision by reference to regulations under section 112 of the Pensions Act 2008.

(3) Regulations under subsection (1) may make different provision for different cases.

(4) The power to make regulations under subsection (1) is exercisable by statutory instrument which shall be subject to annulment in pursuance of a resolution of either House of Parliament.

(5) In this section and section 25F—

'the party with compensation rights' means the party to the marriage who is or is likely to be entitled to PPF compensation, and 'the other party' means the other party to the marriage;

'prescribed' means prescribed by regulations.][1]

Amendment

1 Inserted by the Pensions Act 2008, s 120, Sch 6, paras 1, 7.

26 *Commencement of proceedings for ancillary relief, etc.*

(1) Where a petition for divorce, nullity of marriage or judicial separation has been presented, then, subject to subsection (2) below, proceedings for maintenance pending suit under section 22 above, for a financial provision order under section 23 above, or for a property adjustment order may be begun, subject to and in accordance with rules of court, at any time after the presentation of the petition.

(2) Rules of court may provide, in such cases as may be prescribed by the rules—

(a) that applications for any such relief as is mentioned in subsection (1) above shall be made in the petition or answer; and

(b) that applications for any such relief which are not so made, or are not made until after the expiration of such period following the presentation of the petition or filing of the answer as may be so prescribed, shall be made only with the leave of the court.

Financial provision in case of neglect to maintain

27 *Financial provision orders, etc., in case of neglect by party to marriage to maintain other party or child of the family.*

[(1) Either party to a marriage may apply to the court for an order under this section on the ground that the other party to the marriage (in this section referred to as the respondent)—

(a) has failed to provide reasonable maintenance for the applicant, or

(b) has failed to provide, or to make a proper contribution towards, reasonable maintenance for any child of the family.][1]

[(2) The court may not entertain an application under this section unless it has jurisdiction to do so by virtue of the Maintenance Regulation and Schedule 6 to the Civil Jurisdiction and Judgments (Maintenance) Regulations 2011.][2]

[[(3) Where an application under this section is made on the ground mentioned in subsection (1)(a) above, then, in deciding—

(a) whether the respondent has failed to provide reasonable maintenance for the applicant, and

(b) what order, if any, to make under this section in favour of the applicant,

the court shall have regard to all the circumstances of the case including the matters mentioned in section 25(2) above, and where an application is also made under this section in respect of a child of the family who has not attained the age of eighteen, first consideration shall be given to the welfare of the child while a minor.][3]

(3A) Where an application under this section is made on the ground mentioned in subsection (1)(b) above then, in deciding—

(a) whether the respondent has failed to provide, or to make a proper contribution towards, reasonable maintenance for the child of the family to whom the application relates, and

(b) what order, if any, to make under this section in favour of the child,

the court shall have regard to all the circumstances of the case including the matters mentioned in [section 25(3)(a) to (e)][4] above, and where the child of the family to whom the application relates is not the child of the respondent, including also the matters mentioned in [section 25(4)][4] above.

(3B) In relation to an application under this section on the ground mentioned in subsection (1)(a) above, [section 25(2)(c) above][4] shall have effect as if for the reference therein to the breakdown of the marriage there were substituted a reference to the failure to provide reasonable maintenance for the applicant, and in relation to an application under this section on the ground mentioned in subsection (1)(b) above, [section 25(2)(c) above (as it applies by virtue of section 25(3)(e) above)][4] shall have effect as if for the reference therein to the breakdown of the marriage there were substituted a reference to the failure to provide, or to make a proper contribution towards, reasonable maintenance for the child of the family to whom the application relates.][1]

(4) ...[5]

(5) Where on an application under this section it appears to the court that the applicant or any child of the family to whom the application relates is in immediate need of financial assistance, but it is not yet possible to determine what order, if any, should be made on the application, the court may make an interim order for maintenance, that is to say, an order requiring the respondent to make to the applicant until the determination of the application such periodical payments as the court thinks reasonable.

(6) Where on an application under this section the applicant satisfies the court of any ground mentioned in subsection (1) above, the court may make [any one or more of the following orders][1], that is to say—
  (a) an order that the respondent shall make to the applicant such periodical payments, for such term, as may be specified in the order;
  (b) an order that the respondent shall secure to the applicant, to the satisfaction of the court, such periodical payments, for such term, as may be so specified;
  (c) an order that the respondent shall pay to the applicant such lump sum as may be so specified;
  (d) an order that the respondent shall make to such person as may be specified in the order for the benefit of the child to whom the application relates, or to that child, such periodical payments, for such term, as may be so specified;
  (e) an order that the respondent shall secure to such person as may be so specified for the benefit of that child, or to that child, to the satisfaction of the court, such periodical payments, for such term, as may be so specified;
  (f) an order that the respondent shall pay to such person as may be so specified for the benefit of that child, or to that child, such lump sum as may be so specified;

subject, however, in the case of an order under paragraph (d), (e) or (f) above, to the restrictions imposed by section 29(1) and (3) below on the making of financial provision orders in favour of children who have attained the age of eighteen.

[(6A) An application for the variation under section 31 of this Act of a periodical payments order or secured periodical payments order made under this section in favour of a child may, if the child has attained the age of sixteen, be made by the child himself.

[(6B) Where a periodical payments order made in favour of a child under this section ceases to have effect on the date on which the child attains the age of sixteen or at any time after that date but before or on the date on which he attains the age of eighteen, then if, on an application made to the court for an order under this subsection, it appears to the court that—
  (a) the child is, will be or (if an order were made under this subsection) would be receiving instruction at an educational establishment or undergoing training for a trade, profession or vocation, whether or not he also is, will be or would be in gainful employment; or

(b) there are special circumstances which justify the making of an order under this subsection,

the court shall have power by order to revive the first mentioned order from such date as the court may specify, not being earlier than the date of the making of the application, and to exercise its power under section 31 of this Act in relation to any order so revived.][6]][7]

(7) Without prejudice to the generality of subsection (6)(c) or (f) above, an order under this section for the payment of a lump sum—

(a) may be made for the purpose of enabling any liabilities or expenses reasonably incurred in maintaining the applicant or any child of the family to whom the application relates before the making of the application to be met;

(b) may provide for the payment of that sum by instalments of such amount as may be specified in the order and may require the payment of the instalments to be secured to the satisfaction of the court.

(8) …[8]

Amendments

1 Substituted by the Domestic Proceedings and Magistrates' Courts Act 1978, s 63(1)-(3).

2 Substituted by the Civil Jurisdiction and Judgments (Maintenance) Regulations 2011, SI 2011/1484, reg 9, Sch 7, para 6(1), (2).

3 Substituted by the Matrimonial and Family Proceedings Act 1984, s 4.

4 Substituted by the Matrimonial and Family Proceedings Act 1984, s 46(1), Sch 1, para 12.

5 Repealed by virtue of the Domestic Proceedings and Magistrates' Courts Act 1978, s 63(2).

6 Substituted by the Family Law Reform Act 1987, s 33(1), Sch 2, para 52.

7 Inserted by the Domestic Proceedings and Magistrates' Courts Act 1978, s 63(4).

8 Repealed by the Domestic Proceedings and Magistrates' Courts Act 1978, ss 63(5), 89(2)(b), Sch 3.

Additional provisions with respect to financial provision and property adjustment orders

28 Duration of continuing financial provision orders in favour of party to marriage, and effect of remarriage [or formation of civil partnership][1].

(1) [Subject in the case of an order made on or after the grant of a decree of divorce or nullity of marriage to the provisions of sections 25A(2) above and 31(7) below, the term to be specified in a periodical payments or secured periodical payments order in favour of a party to a marriage shall be such term as the court thinks fit, except that the term shall not begin before or extend beyond the following limits][2], that is to say—

(a) in the case of a periodical payments order, the term shall begin not earlier than the date of the making of an application for the order, and shall be so defined as not to extend beyond the death of either of the parties to the marriage or, where the order is made on or after the grant of a decree of divorce or nullity of marriage, the remarriage of[, or formation of a civil partnership by,][1] the party in whose favour the order is made; and

(b) in the case of a secured periodical payments order, the term shall begin not earlier than the date of the making of an application for the order, and shall be so defined as not to extend beyond the death or, where the order is made on or after the grant of such a decree, the remarriage of[, or formation of a civil partnership by,][1] the party in whose favour the order is made.

[(1A) Where a periodical payments or secured periodical payments order in favour of a party to a marriage is made on or after the grant of a decree of divorce or nullity of marriage, the court may direct that that party shall not be entitled to apply under section 31 below for the extension of the term specified in the order.][3]

(2) Where a periodical payments or secured periodical payments order in favour of a party to a marriage is made otherwise than on or after the grant of a decree of divorce or nullity of marriage, and the marriage in question is subsequently dissolved or annulled but the order continues in force, the order shall, notwithstanding anything in it, cease to have effect on the remarriage of[, or formation of a civil partnership by,][1] that party, except in relation to any arrears due under it on the date of the remarriage [or formation of the civil partnership][1].

(3) If after the grant of a decree dissolving or annulling a marriage either party to that marriage remarries [whether at any time before or after the commencement of this Act][3] [or forms a civil partnership][1], that party shall not be entitled to apply, by reference to the grant of that decree, for a financial provision order in his or her favour, or for a property adjustment order, against the other party to that marriage.

Amendments

1 Inserted by the Civil Partnership Act 2004, s 261(1), Sch 27, para 43.
2 Substituted by the Matrimonial and Family Proceedings Act 1984, s 5(1).
3 Inserted by the Matrimonial and Family Proceedings Act 1984, s 5(2), (3).

29 *Duration of continuing financial provision orders in favour of children, and age limit on making certain orders in their favour.*

(1) Subject to subsection (3) below, no financial provision order and no order for a transfer of property under section 24(1)(a) above shall be made in favour of a child who has attained the age of eighteen.

(2) The term to be specified in a periodical payments or secured periodical payments order in favour of a child may begin with the date of the making of an application for the order in question or any later date [or a date ascertained in accordance with subsection (5) or (6) below][1] but—

(a) shall not in the first instance extend beyond the date of the birthday of the child next following his attaining the upper limit of the compulsory school age [(construed in accordance with section 8 of the Education Act 1996)][2] [unless the court considers that in the circumstances of the case the welfare of the child requires that it should extend to a later date][3]; and

(b) shall not in any event, subject to subsection (3) below, extend beyond the date of the child's eighteenth birthday.

(3) Subsection (1) above, and paragraph (b) of subsection (2), shall not apply in the case of a child, if it appears to the court that—

(a) the child is, or will be, or if an order were made without complying with either or both of those provisions would be, receiving instruction at an educational establishment or undergoing training for a trade, profession or vocation, whether or not he is also, or will also be, in gainful employment; or

(b) there are special circumstances which justify the making of an order without complying with either or both of those provisions.

(4) Any periodical payments order in favour of a child shall, notwithstanding anything in the order, cease to have effect on the death of the person liable to make payments under the order, except in relation to any arrears due under the order on the date of the death.

[(5) Where—

(a) a [maintenance calculation][4] ('the [current calculation][4]') is in force with respect to a child; and

(b) an application is made under Part II of this Act for a periodical payments or secured periodical payments order in favour of that child—

(i) in accordance with section 8 of the Child Support Act 19917, and

(ii) before the end of the period of 6 months beginning with the making of the [current calculation][4]

the term to be specified in any such order made on that application may be expressed to begin on, or at any time after, the earliest permitted date.

(6) For the purposes of subsection (5) above, 'the earliest permitted date' is whichever is the later of—

(a) the date 6 months before the application is made; or

(b) the date on which the [current calculation][4] took effect or, where successive [maintenance calculations][4] have been continuously in force with respect to a child, on which the first of [those calculations][4] took effect.

(7) Where—

(a) a [maintenance calculation][4] ceases to have effect …[5] by or under any provision of the Child Support Act 1991; and

(b) an application is made, before the end of the period of 6 months beginning with the relevant date, for a periodical payments or secured periodical payments order in favour of a child with respect to whom that [maintenance calculation][4] was in force immediately before it ceased to have effect ...[5],

the term to be specified in any such order made on that application may begin with the date on which that [maintenance calculation]4 ceased to have effect ...[5], or any later date.

(8) In subsection (7)(b) above—
- (a) where the [maintenance calculation][4] ceased to have effect, the relevant date is the date on which it so ceased; ...[5]
- (b) ...[5]][6]

Amendments

1 Inserted by the Maintenance Orders (Backdating) Order 1993, SI 1993/623, art 2, Sch 1, para 1.
2 Substituted by the Education Act 1996, s 582(1), Sch 37, para 136.
3 Substituted by the Matrimonial and Family Proceedings Act 1984, s 5(4).
4 Substituted by the Child Support, Pensions and Social Security Act 2000, s 26, Sch 3, para 3(1), (2).
5 Repealed by the Child Support, Pensions and Social Security Act 2000, s 85, Sch 9, Pt I.
6 Inserted by the Maintenance Orders (Backdating) Order 1993, SI 1993/623, art 2, Sch 1, para 2.

30 Direction for settlement of instrument for securing payments or effecting property adjustment.

Where the court decides to make a financial provision order requiring any payments to be secured or a property adjustment order—
- (a) it may direct that the matter be referred to one of the conveyancing counsel of the court for him to settle a proper instrument to be executed by all necessary parties; and
- (b) where the order is to be made in proceedings for divorce, nullity of marriage or judicial separation it may, if it thinks fit, defer the grant of the decree in question until the instrument has been duly executed.

Variation, discharge and enforcement of certain orders, etc.

31 Variation, discharge, etc., of certain orders for financial relief.

(1) Where the court has made an order to which this section applies, then, subject to the provisions of this section [and of section 28(1A) above][1], the court shall have power to vary or discharge the order or to suspend any provision thereof temporarily and to revive the operation of any provision so suspended.

(2) This section applies to the following orders, that is to say—
- (a) any order for maintenance pending suit and any interim order for maintenance;
- (b) any periodical payments order;
- (c) any secured periodical payments order;

(d) any order made by virtue of section 23(3)(c) or 27(7)(b) above (provision for payment of a lump sum by instalments);

[(dd) any deferred order made by virtue of section 23(1)(c) (lump sums) which includes provision made by virtue of—

(i) section 25B(4) , …[2]

(ii) section 25C, [or][3]

[(iii) section 25F(2),][3]

(provision in respect of pension rights [or pension compensation rights][3])][4]

(e) any order for a settlement of property under section 24(1)(b) or for a variation of settlement under section 24(1)(c) or (d) above, being an order made on or after the grant of a decree of judicial separation.

[(f) any order made under section 24A(1) above for the sale of property;][5]

[(g) a pension sharing order under section 24B above[, or a pension compensation sharing order under section 24E above,][3] which is made at a time before the decree has been made absolute.][6]

[(2A) Where the court has made an order referred to in subsection (2)(a), (b) or (c) above, then, subject to the provisions of this section, the court shall have power to remit the payment of any arrears due under the order or of any part thereof.][7]

[(2B) Where the court has made an order referred to in subsection (2)(dd)(ii) above, this section shall cease to apply to the order on the death of either of the parties to the marriage][4]

(3) The powers exercisable by the court under this section in relation to an order shall be exercisable also in relation to any instrument executed in pursuance of the order.

(4) The court shall not exercise the powers conferred by this section in relation to an order for a settlement under section 24(1)(b) or for a variation of settlement under section 24(1)(c) or (d) above except on an application made in proceedings—

(a) for the rescission of the decree of judicial separation by reference to which the order was made, or

(b) for the dissolution of the marriage in question.

[(4A) In relation to an order which falls within paragraph (g) of subsection (2) above ('the subsection (2) order')—

(a) the powers conferred by this section may be exercised—

(i) only on an application made before the subsection (2) order has or, but for paragraph (b) below, would have taken effect; and

(ii) only if, at the time when the application is made, the decree has not been made absolute; and

(b) an application made in accordance with paragraph (a) above prevents the subsection (2) order from taking effect before the application has been dealt with.

(4B) No variation of a pension sharing order[, or a pension compensation sharing order,][3] shall be made so as to take effect before the decree is made absolute.

(4C) The variation of a pension sharing order[, or a pension compensation sharing order,][3] prevents the order taking effect before the end of such period after the making of the variation as may be prescribed by regulations made by the Lord Chancellor.][6]

(5) [Subject to subsections (7A) to [(7G)][8] below and without prejudice to any power exercisable by virtue of subsection (2)(d), (dd)[, (e) or (g)][8] above or otherwise than by virtue of this section,][9] no property adjustment order [or pension sharing order][3] [or pension compensation sharing order][6] shall be made on an application for the variation of a periodical payments or secured periodical payments order made (whether in favour of a party to a marriage or in favour of a child of the family) under section 23 above, and no order for the payment of a lump sum shall be made on an application for the variation of a periodical payments or secured periodical payments order in favour of a party to a marriage (whether made under section 23 or under section 27 above).

(6) Where the person liable to make payments under a secured periodical payments order has died, an application under this section relating to that order [(and to any order made under section 24A(1) above which requires the proceeds of sale of property to be used for securing those payments) may be made by the person entitled to payments under the periodical payments order][10] or by the personal representatives of the deceased person, but no such application shall, except with the permission of the court, be made after the end of the period of six months from the date on which representation in regard to the estate of that person is first taken out.

[(7) In exercising the powers conferred by this section the court shall have regard to all the circumstances of the case, first consideration being given to the welfare while a minor of any child of the family who has not attained the age of eighteen, and the circumstances of the case shall include any change in any of the matters to which the court was required to have regard when making the order to which the application relates, and—

(a) in the case of a periodical payments or secured periodical payments order made on or after the grant of a decree of divorce or nullity of marriage, the court shall consider whether in all the circumstances and after having regard to any such change it would be appropriate to vary the order so that payments under the order are required to be made or secured only for such further period as will in the opinion of the court be sufficient [(in the light of any proposed exercise by the court, where the marriage has been dissolved, of its powers under subsection (7B) below)][9] to enable the party in whose favour the order was made to adjust without undue hardship to the termination of those payments;

(b) in a case where the party against whom the order was made has died, the circumstances of the case shall also include the changed circumstances resulting from his or her death.][11]

[(7A) Subsection (7B) below applies where, after the dissolution of a marriage, the court—

(a) discharges a periodical payments order or secured periodical payments order made in favour of a party to the marriage; or

(b) varies such an order so that payments under the order are required to be made or secured only for such further period as is determined by the court.

(7B) The court has power, in addition to any power it has apart from this subsection, to make supplemental provision consisting of any of—

(a) an order for the payment of a lump sum in favour of a party to the marriage;

(b) one or more property adjustment orders in favour of a party to the marriage;

[(ba) one or more pension sharing orders;][6]

[(bb) a pension compensation sharing order;][3]

(c) a direction that the party in whose favour the original order discharged or varied was made is not entitled to make any further application for—

(i) a periodical payments or secured periodical payments order, or

(ii) an extension of the period to which the original order is limited by any variation made by the court.

(7C) An order for the payment of a lump sum made under subsection (7B) above may—

(a) provide for the payment of that sum by instalments of such amount as may be specified in the order; and

(b) require the payment of the instalments to be secured to the satisfaction of the court.

(7D) [Section 23(6)][12] above [applies][12] where the court makes an order for the payment of a lump sum under subsection (7B) above as [it applies where the court][12] makes such an order under [section 23][12] above.

(7E) If under subsection (7B) above the court makes more than one property adjustment order in favour of the same party to the marriage, each of those orders must fall within a different paragraph of section 21(2) above.

(7F) Sections 24A and 30 above apply where the court makes a property adjustment order under subsection (7B) above as they apply where it makes such an order under [section 24][12] above.][9]

[(7G) Subsections (3) to (5) of section 24B above apply in relation to a pension sharing order under subsection (7B) above as they apply in relation to a pension sharing order under that section.][6]

[(7H) Subsections (3) to (10) of section 24E above apply in relation to a pension compensation sharing order under subsection (7B) above as they apply in relation to a pension compensation sharing order under that section.][3]

(8) The personal representatives of a deceased person against whom a secured periodical payments order was made shall not be liable for having distributed any part of the estate of the deceased after the expiration of the period of six months referred to in subsection (6) above on the ground that they ought to have taken into account the possibility that the court might permit an application under this section to be made after that period by the person entitled to payments under the order; but this subsection shall not prejudice any power to recover any part of the estate so distributed arising by virtue of the making of an order in pursuance of this section.

[(9) The following are to be left out of account when considering for the purposes of subsection (6) above when representation was first taken out—

(a) a grant limited to settled land or to trust property,

(b) any other grant that does not permit any of the estate to be distributed,

(c) a grant limited to real estate or to personal estate, unless a grant limited to the remainder of the estate has previously been made or is made at the same time,

(d) a grant, or its equivalent, made outside the United Kingdom (but see subsection (9A) below).

(9A) A grant sealed under section 2 of the Colonial Probates Act 1892 counts as a grant made in the United Kingdom for the purposes of subsection (9) above, but is to be taken as dated on the date of sealing.][13]

[(10) Where the court, in exercise of its powers under this section, decides to vary or discharge a periodical payments or secured periodical payments order, then, subject to section 28(1) and (2) above, the court shall have power to direct that the variation or discharge shall not take effect until the expiration of such period as may be specified in the order.][1]

[(11) Where—

(a) a periodical payments or secured periodical payments order in favour of more than one child ('the order') is in force;

(b) the order requires payments specified in it to be made to or for the benefit of more than one child without apportioning those payments between them;

(c) a [maintenance calculation][14] ('[the calculation][14]') is made with respect to one or more, but not all, of the children with respect to whom those payments are to be made; and

(d) an application is made, before the end of the period of 6 months beginning with the date on which the assessment was made, for the variation or discharge of the order,

the court may, in exercise of its powers under this section to vary or discharge the order, direct that the variation or discharge shall take effect from the date on which [the calculation]14 took effect or any later date.

(12) Where—
(a) an order ('the child order') of a kind prescribed for the purposes of section 10(1) of the Child Support Act 1991 is affected by a [maintenance calculation][14];
(b) on the date on which the child order became so affected there was in force a periodical payments or secured periodical payments order ('the spousal order') in favour of a party to a marriage having the care of the child in whose favour the child order was made; and
(c) an application is made, before the end of the period of 6 months beginning with the date on which the [maintenance calculation][14] was made, for the spousal order to be varied or discharged,

the court may, in exercise of its powers under this section to vary or discharge the spousal order, direct that the variation or discharge shall take effect from the date on which the child order became so affected or any later date.

(13) For the purposes of subsection (12) above, an order is affected if it ceases to have effect or is modified by or under section 10 of the Child Support Act 1991.

(14) Subsections (11) and (12) above are without prejudice to any other power of the court to direct that the variation of discharge of an order under this section shall take effect from a date earlier than that on which the order for variation or discharge was made.][15]

[(15) The power to make regulations under subsection (4C) above shall be exercisable by statutory instrument which shall be subject to annulment in pursuance of a resolution of either House of Parliament.][6]

Amendments

1 Inserted by the Matrimonial and Family Proceedings Act 1984, s 6(1), (2), (4).
2 Repealed by the Pensions Act 2008, ss 120, 148, Sch 6, paras 1, 8(1), (2)(a), Sch 11, Pt 4.
3 Inserted by the Pensions Act 2008, s 120, Sch 6, paras 1, 8(1), (2)(b)-(d), (3)-(8).
4 Inserted by the Pensions Act 1995, s 166(3).
5 Inserted by the Matrimonial Homes and Property Act 1981, s 8(2)(a).
6 Inserted by the Welfare Reform and Pensions Act 1999, s 19, Sch 3, paras 1, 7(1)-(3), (4)(c), (5)-(7).
7 Inserted by the Administration of Justice Act 1982, s 51.
8 Substituted by the Welfare Reform and Pensions Act 1999, s 19, Sch 3, paras 1, 7(1), (4)(a), (b).
9 Inserted by the Family Law Act 1996, s 66(1), Sch 8, paras 4, 16(1), (5)(a), (6)(b), (7).
10 Substituted by the Matrimonial Homes and Property Act 1981, s 8(2)(b).
11 Substituted by the Matrimonial and Family Proceedings Act 1984, s 6(1), (3).
12 Substituted by the Children and Families Act 2014, s 18(6), (7)(b), (8).
13 Substituted by the Inheritance and Trustees' Powers Act 2014, s 7, Sch 3, para 1.
14 Substituted by the Child Support, Pensions and Social Security Act 2000, s 26, Sch 3, para 3(1), (3).
15 Inserted by the Maintenance Orders (Backdating) Order 1993, SI 1993/623, art 2, Sch 1, para 3.

32 Payment of certain arrears unenforceable without the leave of the court.

(1) A person shall not be entitled to enforce through the High Court or [the family court][1] the payment of any arrears due under an order for maintenance

pending suit, an interim order for maintenance or any financial provision order without the leave of that court if those arrears became due more than twelve months before proceedings to enforce the payment of them are begun.

(2) The court hearing an application for the grant of leave under this section may refuse leave, or may grant leave subject to such restrictions and conditions (including conditions as to the allowing of time for payment or the making of payment by instalments) as that court thinks proper, or may remit the payment of the arrears or of any part thereof.

(3) An application for the grant of leave under this section shall be made in such manner as may be prescribed by rules of court.

Amendment

1 Substituted by the Crime and Courts Act 2013, s 17(6), Sch 11, paras 58, 60.

33 *Orders for repayment in certain cases of sums paid under certain orders.*

(1) Where on an application made under this section in relation to an order to which this section applies it appears to the court that by reason of—
   (a) a change in the circumstances of the person entitled to, or liable to make, payments under the order since the order was made, or
   (b) the changed circumstances resulting from the death of the person so liable,

the amount received by the person entitled to payments under the order in respect of a period after those circumstances changed or after the death of the person liable to make payments under the order, as the case may be, exceeds the amount which the person so liable or his or her personal representatives should have been required to pay, the court may order the respondent to the application to pay to the applicant such sum, not exceeding the amount of the excess, as the court thinks just.

(2) This section applies to the following orders, that is to say—
   (a) any order for maintenance pending suit and any interim order for maintenance;
   (b) any periodical payments order; and
   (c) any secured periodical payments order.

(3) An application under this section may be made by the person liable to make payments under an order to which this section applies or his or her personal representatives and may be made against the person entitled to payments under the order or her or his personal representatives.

(4) An application under this section may be made in proceedings in the High Court or [the family court][1] for—
   (a) the variation or discharge of the order to which this section applies, or
   (b) leave to enforce, or the enforcement of, the payment of arrears under that order;

but when not made in such proceedings shall be made to [the family court][1], and accordingly references in this section to the court are references to the High Court or [the family court][1], as the circumstances require.

(5) …[2]

(6) An order under this section for the payment of any sum may provide for the payment of that sum by instalments of such amount as may be specified in the order.

Amendments

1 Substituted by the Crime and Courts Act 2013, s 17(6), Sch 11, paras 58, 61(1), (2).
2 Repealed by the Crime and Courts Act 2013, s 17(6), Sch 11, paras 58, 61(1), (3).

[Consent orders

33A Consent orders for financial provision or property adjustment.

(1) Notwithstanding anything in the preceding provisions of this Part of this Act, on an application for a consent order for financial relief the court may, unless it has reason to think that there are other circumstances into which it ought to inquire, make an order in the terms agreed on the basis only of the prescribed information furnished with the application.

(2) Subsection (1) above applies to an application for a consent order varying or discharging an order for financial relief as it applies to an application for an order for financial relief.

(3) In this section—

'consent order', in relation to an application for an order, means an order in the terms applied for to which the respondent agrees;

'order for financial relief' means an order under any of sections 23, 24, 24A[, 24B][1] or 27 above; and

'prescribed' means prescribed by rules of court.][2]

Amendments

1 Inserted by the Welfare Reform and Pensions Act 1999, s 19, Sch 3, paras 1, 8.
2 Inserted by the Matrimonial and Family Proceedings Act 1984, s 7.

Maintenance agreements

34 Validity of maintenance agreements.

(1) If a maintenance agreement includes a provision purporting to restrict any right to apply to a court for an order containing financial arrangements, then—

(a) that provision shall be void; but

(b) any other financial arrangements contained in the agreement shall not thereby be rendered void or unenforceable and shall, unless they are void or unenforceable for any other reason (and subject to sections 35 and 36 below), be binding on the parties to the agreement.

(2) In this section and in section 35 below—

'maintenance agreement' means any agreement in writing made, whether before or after the commencement of this Act, between the parties to a marriage, being—

(a) an agreement containing financial arrangements, whether made during the continuance or after the dissolution or annulment of the marriage; or

(b) a separation agreement which contains no financial arrangements in a case where no other agreement in writing between the same parties contains such arrangements;

'financial arrangements' means provisions governing the rights and liabilities towards one another when living separately of the parties to a marriage (including a marriage which has been dissolved or annulled) in respect of the making or securing of payments or the disposition or use of any property, including such rights and liabilities with respect to the maintenance or education of any child, whether or not a child of the family.

35 Alteration of agreements by court during lives of parties.

(1) Where a maintenance agreement is for the time being subsisting and each of the parties to the agreement is for the time being either domiciled or resident in England and Wales, then, subject to [subsections (1A) and (3)][1] below, either party may apply to the court ...[2] for an order under this section.

[(1A) If an application or part of an application relates to a matter where jurisdiction falls to be determined by reference to the jurisdictional requirements of the Maintenance Regulation and Schedule 6 to the Civil Jurisdiction and Judgments (Maintenance) Regulations 2011—

(a) the requirement as to domicile or residence in subsection (1) does not apply to the application or that part of it, but

(b) the court may not entertain the application or that part of it unless it has jurisdiction to do so by virtue of that Regulation and that Schedule.][3]

(2) If the court ...[2] is satisfied either—

(a) that by reason of a change in the circumstances in the light of which any financial arrangements contained in the agreement were made or, as the case may be, financial arrangements were omitted from it (including a change foreseen by the parties when making the agreement), the agreement should be altered so as to make different, or, as the case may be, so as to contain, financial arrangements, or

(b) that the agreement does not contain proper financial arrangements with respect to any child of the family,

then subject to [subsections][4] (4) and (5) below, [the court][4] may by order make such alterations in the agreement—

(i) by varying or revoking any financial arrangements contained in it, or

(ii) by inserting in it financial arrangements for the benefit of one of the parties to the agreement or of a child of the family,

as may appear to [the court][4] to be just having regard to all the circumstances, including, if relevant, the matters mentioned in [section 25(4)][5] above; and the agreement shall have effect thereafter as if any alteration made by the order had been made by agreement between the parties and for valuable consideration.

(3) ...[2]

(4) Where [the court][4] decides to alter, by order under this section, an agreement by inserting provision for the making or securing by one of the parties to the agreement of periodical payments for the maintenance of the other party or by increasing the rate of the periodical payments which the agreement provides shall be made by one of the parties for the maintenance of the other, the term for which the payments or, as the case may be, the additional payments attributable to the increase are to be made under the agreement as altered by the order shall be such term as the court may specify, subject to the following limits, that is to say—

(a) where the payments will not be secured, the term shall be so defined as not to extend beyond the death of either of the parties to the agreement or the remarriage of[, or formation of a civil partnership by,][6] the party to whom the payments are to be made;

(b) where the payments will be secured, the term shall be so defined as not to extend beyond the death or remarriage of[, or formation of a civil partnership by,][6] that party.

(5) Where [the court][4] decides to alter, by order under this section, an agreement by inserting provision for the making or securing by one of the parties to the agreement of periodical payments for the maintenance of a child of the family or by increasing the rate of the periodical payments which the agreement provides shall be made or secured by one of the parties for the maintenance of such a child, then, in deciding the term for which under the agreement as altered by the order the payments, or as the case may be, the additional payments attributable to the increase are to be made or secured for the benefit of the child, the court shall apply the provisions of section 29(2) and (3) above as to age limits as if the order in question were a periodical payments or secured periodical payments order in favour of the child.

(6) For the avoidance of doubt it is hereby declared that nothing in this section or in section 34 above affects any power of a court before which any proceedings between the parties to a maintenance agreement are brought under any other enactment (including a provision of this Act) to make an

order containing financial arrangements or any right of either party to apply for such an order in such proceedings.

Amendments

1 Substituted by the Civil Jurisdiction and Judgments (Maintenance) Regulations 2011, SI 2011/1484, reg 9, Sch 7, para 6(1), (3)(a).
2 Repealed by the Crime and Courts Act 2013, s 17(6), Sch 11, paras 58, 62(1), (2), (3)(a), (4).
3 Inserted by the Civil Jurisdiction and Judgments (Maintenance) Regulations 2011, SI 2011/1484, reg 9, Sch 7, para 6(1), (3)(b).
4 Substituted by the Crime and Courts Act 2013, s 17(6), Sch 11, paras 58, 62(1), (3)(b).
5 Substituted by the Matrimonial and Family Proceedings Act 1984, s 46(1), Sch 1, para 13(a)
6 Inserted by the Civil Partnership Act 2004, s 261(1), Sch 27, para 44.

36 Alteration of agreements by court after death of one party.

(1) Where a maintenance agreement within the meaning of section 34 above provides for the continuation of payments under the agreement after the death of one of the parties and that party dies domiciled in England and Wales, the surviving party or the personal representatives of the deceased party may, subject to subsections (2) and (3) below, apply to the …[1] court for an order under section 35 above.

(2) An application under this section shall not, except with the permission of the …[1] court, be made after the end of the period of six months from the date on which representation in regard to the estate of the deceased is first taken out.

(3) …[1]

(4) If a maintenance agreement is altered by [the court][2] on an application made in pursuance of subsection (1) above, the like consequences shall ensue as if the alteration had been made immediately before the death by agreement between the parties and for valuable consideration.

(5) The provisions of this section shall not render the personal representatives of the deceased liable for having distributed any part of the estate of the deceased after the expiration of the period of six months referred to in subsection (2) above on the ground that they ought to have taken into account the possibility that [the court][2] might permit an application by virtue of this section to be made by the surviving party after that period; but this subsection shall not prejudice any power to recover any part of the estate so distributed arising by virtue of the making of an order in pursuance of this section.

(6) Section 31(9) above shall apply for the purposes of subsection (2) above as it applies for the purposes of subsection (6) of section 31.

(7) …[1]

Amendments

1 Repealed by the Crime and Courts Act 2013, s 17(6), Sch 11, paras 58, 63(1), (2)-(4).
2 Substituted by the Crime and Courts Act 2013, s 17(6), Sch 11, paras 58, 63(1), (5).

Miscellaneous and supplemental

37 Avoidance of transactions intended to prevent or reduce financial relief.

(1) For the purposes of this section 'financial relief' means relief under any of the provisions of sections 22, 23, 24, [24B,][1] 27, 31 (except subsection (6)) and 35 above, and any reference in this section to defeating a person's claim for financial relief is a reference to preventing financial relief from being granted to that person, or to that person for the benefit of a child of the family, or reducing the amount of any financial relief which might be so granted, or frustrating or impeding the enforcement of any order which might be or has been made at his instance under any of those provisions.

(2) Where proceedings for financial relief are brought by one person against another, the court may, on the application of the first-mentioned person—

(a) if it is satisfied that the other party to the proceedings is, with the intention of defeating the claim for financial relief, about to make any disposition or to transfer out of the jurisdiction or otherwise deal with any property, make such order as it thinks fit for restraining the other party from so doing or otherwise for protecting the claim;

(b) if it is satisfied that the other party has, with that intention, made a reviewable disposition and that if the disposition were set aside financial relief or different financial relief would be granted to the applicant, make an order setting aside the disposition;

(c) if it is satisfied, in a case where an order has been obtained under any of the provisions mentioned in subsection (1) above by the applicant against the other party, that the other party has, with that intention, made a reviewable disposition, make an order setting aside the disposition;

and an application for the purposes of paragraph (b) above shall be made in the proceedings for the financial relief in question.

(3) Where the court makes an order under subsection (2)(b) or (c) above setting aside a disposition it shall give such consequential directions as it thinks fit for giving effect to the order (including directions requiring the making of any payments or the disposal of any property).

(4) Any disposition made by the other party to the proceedings for financial relief in question (whether before or after the commencement of those proceedings) as is reviewable disposition for the purposes of subsection (2)(b) and (c) above unless it was made for valuable consideration (other than marriage) to a person who, at the time of the disposition, acted in relation to it in good faith and without notice of any intention on the part of the other party to defeat the applicant's claim for financial relief.

(5) Where an application is made under this section with respect to a disposition which took place less than three years before the date of the application or with respect to a disposition or other dealing with property which is about to take place and the court is satisfied—

(a) in a case falling within subsection (2)(a) or (b) above, that the disposition or other dealing would (apart from this section) have the consequence, or
(b) in a case falling within subsection (2)(c) above, that the disposition has had the consequence,

of defeating the applicant's claim for financial relief, it shall be presumed, unless the contrary is shown, that the person who disposed of or is about to dispose of or deal with the property did so or, as the case may be, is about to do so, with the intention of defeating the applicant's claim for financial relief.

(6) In this section 'disposition' does not include any provision contained in a will or codicil but, with that exception, includes any conveyance, assurance or gift of property of any description, whether made by an instrument or otherwise.

(7) This section does not apply to a disposition made before 1st January 1968.

Amendment

1 Inserted by the Welfare Reform and Pensions Act 1999, s 19, Sch 3, paras 1, 9.

38 Orders for repayment in certain cases of sums paid after cessation of order by reason of remarriage [or formation of civil partnership][1].

(1) Where—
(a) a periodical payments or secured periodical payments order in favour of a party to a marriage (hereafter in this section referred to as 'a payments order') has ceased to have effect by reason of the remarriage of[, or formation of a civil partnership by,][1] that party, and
(b) the person liable to make payments under the order or his or her personal representatives made payments in accordance with it in respect of a period after the date of the remarriage [or formation of the civil partnership][1] in the mistaken belief that the order was still subsisting,

the person so liable or his or her personal representatives shall not be entitled to bring proceedings in respect of a cause of action arising out of the circumstances mentioned in paragraphs (a) and (b) above against the person entitled to payments under the order or her or his personal representatives, but may instead make an application against that person or her or his personal representatives under this section.

(2) On an application under this section the court [to which the application is made][2] may order the respondent to pay to the applicant a sum equal to the amount of the payments made in respect of the period mentioned in subsection (1)(b) above or, if it appears to the court that it would be unjust to make that order, it may either order the respondent to pay to the applicant such lesser sum as it thinks fit or dismiss the application.

(3) An application under this section may be made in proceedings in the High Court or [the family court][3] for leave to enforce, or the enforcement of, payment of arrears under the order in question, but when not made in such proceedings shall be made to [the family court][3]; and accordingly references in this section to the court are references to the High Court or [the family court][3], as the circumstances require.

(4) …[4]

(5) An order under this section for the payment of any sum may provide for the payment of that sum by instalments of such amount as may be specified in the order.

(6) [An officer of the family court,][3] and the collecting officer under an attachment of earnings order made to secure payments under a payments order, shall not be liable—

(a) in the case of [an officer of the family court,][3] for any act done by him[, in pursuance of a payments order requiring payments to be made to the court or an officer of the court,][3] after the date on which that order ceased to have effect by reason of the remarriage of[, or formation of a civil partnership by,][1] the person entitled to payments under it, and

(b) in the case of the collecting officer, for any act done by him after that date in accordance with any enactment or rule of court specifying how payments made to him in compliance with the attachment of earnings order are to be dealt with,

if, but only if, the act was one which he would have been under a duty to do had the payments order not so ceased to have effect and the act was done before notice in writing of the fact that the person so entitled had remarried [or formed a civil partnership]1 was given to him by or on behalf of that person, the person liable to make payments under the payments order or the personal representatives of either of those persons.

(7) In this section 'collecting officer' , in relation to an attachment of earnings order, means the officer of the High Court, [or the officer of the family court,][3] to whom a person makes payments in compliance with the order.

Amendments

1 Inserted by the Civil Partnership Act 2004, s 261(1), Sch 27, para 45.
2 Inserted by the Crime and Courts Act 2013, s 17(6), Sch 11, paras 58, 64(1), (2).
3 Substituted by the Crime and Courts Act 2013, s 17(6), Sch 11, paras 58, 64(1), (3), (5), (6).
4 Repealed by the Crime and Courts Act 2013, s 17(6), Sch 11, paras 58, 64(1), (4).

39 *Settlement, etc. made in compliance with a property adjustment order may be avoided on bankruptcy of settlor.*

The fact that a settlement or transfer of property had to be made in order to comply with a property adjustment order shall not prevent that settlement or transfer from being [a transaction in respect of which an order may be made under [section 339 or 340 of the Insolvency Act 1986][1] (transactions at an undervalue and preferences.)][2]

Amendments

1 Substituted by the Insolvency Act 1986, s 439(2), Sch 14.
2 Substituted by the Insolvency Act 1985, s 235, Sch 8, para 23.

40 Payments, etc., under order made in favour of person suffering from mental disorder.

[(1)][1] Where the court makes an order under this Part of this Act requiring payments (including a lump sum payment) to be made, or property to be transferred, to a party to a marriage and the court is satisfied that the person in whose favour the order is made [('P') lacks capacity (within the meaning of the Mental Capacity Act 2005) in relation to the provisions of the order][2] then, subject to any order, direction or authority made or given in relation to [P under that Act][2], the court may order the payments to be made, or as the case may be, the property to be transferred, to [such person ('D') as it may direct][2] having charge of that person as the court may direct.

[(2) In carrying out any functions of his in relation to an order made under subsection (1), D must act in P's best interests (within the meaning of that Act).][1]

Amendments

1 Inserted by the Mental Capacity Act 2005, s 67(1), Sch 6, para 19.
2 Substituted by the Mental Capacity Act 2005, s 67(1), Sch 6, para 19(a)-(c).

[40A Appeals relating to pension sharing orders which have taken effect.

(1) Subsections (2) and (3) below apply where an appeal against a pension sharing order is begun on or after the day on which the order takes effect.

(2) If the pension sharing order relates to a person's rights under a pension arrangement, the appeal court may not set aside or vary the order if the person responsible for the pension arrangement has acted to his detriment in reliance on the taking effect of the order.

(3) If the pension sharing order relates to a person's shareable state scheme rights, the appeal court may not set aside or vary the order if the Secretary of State has acted to his detriment in reliance on the taking effect of the order.

(4) In determining for the purposes of subsection (2) or (3) above whether a person has acted to his detriment in reliance on the taking effect of the order, the appeal court may disregard any detriment which in its opinion is insignificant.

(5) Where subsection (2) or (3) above applies, the appeal court may make such further orders (including one or more pension sharing orders) as it thinks fit for the purpose of putting the parties in the position it considers appropriate.

(6) Section 24C above only applies to a pension sharing order under this section if the decision of the appeal court can itself be the subject of an appeal.

(7) In subsection (2) above, the reference to the person responsible for the pension arrangement is to be read in accordance with section 25D(4) above.][1]

Amendment

1 Inserted by the Welfare Reform and Pensions Act 1999, s 19, Sch 3, paras 1, 10.

[40B *Appeals relating to pension compensation sharing orders which have taken effect*

(1) This section applies where an appeal against a pension compensation sharing order is begun on or after the day on which the order takes effect.

(2) If the Board of the Pension Protection Fund has acted to its detriment in reliance on the taking effect of the order the appeal court—
  - (a) may not set aside or vary the order;
  - (b) may make such further orders (including a pension compensation sharing order) as it thinks fit for the purpose of putting the parties in the position it considers appropriate.

(3) In determining for the purposes of subsection (2) whether the Board has acted to its detriment the appeal court may disregard any detriment which in the court's opinion is insignificant.

(4) Section 24F (duty to stay) only applies to a pension compensation sharing order under this section if the decision of the appeal court can itself be the subject of an appeal.][1]

Amendment

1 Inserted by the Pensions Act 2008, s 120, Sch 6, paras 1, 9.

MATRIMONIAL AND FAMILY PROCEEDINGS ACT 1984

PART III
FINANCIAL RELIEF IN ENGLAND AND WALES AFTER OVERSEAS DIVORCE ETC.

Applications for financial relief

12 Applications for financial relief after overseas divorce etc.

(1) Where—

(a) a marriage has been dissolved or annulled, or the parties to a marriage have been legally separated, by means of judicial or other proceedings in an overseas country, and

(b) the divorce, annulment or legal separation is entitled to be recognised as valid in England and Wales,

either party to the marriage may apply to the court in the manner prescribed by rules of court for an order for financial relief under this Part of this Act.

(2) If after a marriage has been dissolved or annulled in an overseas country one of the parties to the marriage [forms a subsequent marriage or civil partnership,][1] that party shall not be entitled to make an application in relation to that marriage.

[(3) The reference in subsection (2) above to the forming of a subsequent marriage or civil partnership includes a reference to the forming of a marriage or civil partnership which is by law void or voidable.][1]

(4) In this Part of this Act except sections 19, 23, and 24 'order for financial relief' means an order under section 17 or 22 below of a description referred to in that section.

Amendments

1 Substituted by the Civil Partnership Act 2004, s 261(1), Sch 27, para 90.

13 Leave of the court required for applications for financial relief.

(1) No application for an order for financial relief shall be made under this Part of this Act unless the leave of the court has been obtained in accordance with rules of court; and the court shall not grant leave unless it considers that there is substantial ground for the making of an application for such an order.

(2) The court may grant leave under this section notwithstanding that an order has been made by a court in a country outside England and Wales requiring the other party to the marriage to make any payment or transfer any property to the applicant or a child of the family.

(3) Leave under this section may be granted subject to such conditions as the court thinks fit.

14 Interim orders for maintenance.

(1) Where leave is granted under section 13 above for the making of an application for an order for financial relief and it appears to the court that the applicant or any child of the family is in immediate need of financial assistance, the court may make an interim order for maintenance, that is to say, an order requiring the other party to the marriage to make to the applicant or to the child such periodical payments, and for such term, being a term beginning not earlier than the date of the grant of leave and ending with the date of the determination of the application for an order for financial relief, as the court thinks reasonable.

(2) If it appears to the court that the court has jurisdiction to entertain the application for an order for financial relief by reason only of paragraph (c) of section 15(1) below the court shall not make an interim order under this section.

(3) An interim order under subsection (1) above may be made subject to such conditions as the court thinks fit.

15 Jurisdiction of the court.

(1) Subject to [subsections (1A) and (2)][1] below, the court shall have jurisdiction to entertain an application for an order for financial relief if any of the following jurisdictional requirements are satisfied, that is to say—
  (a) either of the parties to the marriage was domiciled in England and Wales on the date of the application for leave under section 13 above or was so domiciled on the date on which the divorce, annulment or legal separation obtained in the overseas country took effect in that country; or
  (b) either of the parties to the marriage was habitually resident in England and Wales throughout the period of one year ending with the date of the application for leave or was so resident throughout the period of one year ending with the date on which the divorce, annulment or legal separation obtained in the overseas country took effect in that country; or
  (c) either or both of the parties to the marriage had at the date of the application for leave a beneficial interest in possession in a dwelling-house situated in England or Wales which was at some time during the marriage a matrimonial home of the parties to the marriage.

[(1A) If an application or part of an application relates to a matter where jurisdiction falls to be determined by reference to the jurisdictional requirements of the Maintenance Regulation and Schedule 6 to the Civil Jurisdiction and Judgments (Maintenance) Regulations 2011, those requirements are to determine whether the court has jurisdiction to entertain the application or that part of it.][2]

(2) Where the jurisdiction of the court to entertain proceedings under this Part of this Act would fall to be determined by reference to the jurisdictional

requirements imposed by virtue of Part I of the Civil Jurisdiction and Judgments Act 1982 (implementation of certain European conventions) [...[3] or][4] then—

(a) satisfaction of the requirements of subsection (1) above shall not obviate the need to satisfy the requirements imposed by virtue of [...[3]][4] Part I of that Act; and

(b) satisfaction of the requirements imposed by virtue of [...[3]][4] Part I of that Act shall obviate the need to satisfy the requirements of subsection (1) above;

and the court shall entertain or not entertain the proceedings accordingly.

[(3) In this section, 'the Maintenance Regulation' means Council Regulation (EC) No 4/2009 including as applied in relation to Denmark by virtue of the Agreement made on 19th October 2005 between the European Community and the Kingdom of Denmark.][2]

Amendments

1 Substituted by the Civil Jurisdiction and Judgments (Maintenance) Regulations 2011, SI 2011/1484, reg 9, Sch 7, para 10(1), (2)(a).
2 Inserted by the Civil Jurisdiction and Judgments (Maintenance) Regulations 2011, SI 2011/1484, reg 9, Sch 7, para 10(1), (2)(b), (d).
3 Repealed by the Civil Jurisdiction and Judgments (Maintenance) Regulations 2011, SI 2011/1484, reg 9, Sch 7, para 10(1), (2)(c).
4 Inserted by the Civil Jurisdiction and Judgments Order 2001, SI 2001/3929, art 5, Sch 3, paras 18, 19.

16 Duty of the court to consider whether England and Wales is appropriate venue for application.

(1) [Subject to subsection (3),][1] before making an order for financial relief the court shall consider whether in all the circumstances of the case it would be appropriate for such an order to be made by a court in England and Wales, and if the court is not satisfied that it would be appropriate, the court shall dismiss the application.

(2) The court shall in particular have regard to the following matters—

(a) the connection which the parties to the marriage have with England and Wales;

(b) the connection which those parties have with the country in which the marriage was dissolved or annulled or in which they were legally separated;

(c) the connection which those parties have with any other country outside England and Wales;

(d) any financial benefit which the applicant or a child of the family has received, or is likely to receive, in consequence of the divorce, annulment or legal separation, by virtue of any agreement or the operation of the law of a country outside England and Wales;

(e) in a case where an order has been made by a court in a country outside England and Wales requiring the other party to the marriage to make any payment or transfer any property for the benefit of the applicant or a child of the family, the financial relief given by the order and the extent to which the order has been complied with or is likely to be complied with;

(f) any right which the applicant has, or has had, to apply for financial relief from the other party to the marriage under the law of any country outside England and Wales and if the applicant has omitted to exercise that right the reason for that omission;

(g) the availability in England and Wales of any property in respect of which an order under this Part of this Act in favour of the applicant could be made;

(h) the extent to which any order made under this Part of this Act is likely to be enforceable;

(i) the length of time which has elapsed since the date of the divorce, annulment or legal separation.

[(3) If the court has jurisdiction in relation to the application or part of it by virtue of the Maintenance Regulation and Schedule 6 to the Civil Jurisdiction and Judgments (Maintenance) Regulations 2011, the court may not dismiss the application or that part of it on the ground mentioned in subsection (1) if to do so would be inconsistent with the jurisdictional requirements of that Regulation and that Schedule.

(4) In this section, 'the Maintenance Regulation' means Council Regulation (EC) No 4/2009 including as applied in relation to Denmark by virtue of the Agreement made on 19th October 2005 between the European Community and the Kingdom of Denmark.][1]

Amendments

1 Inserted by the Civil Jurisdiction and Judgments (Maintenance) Regulations 2011, SI 2011/1484, reg 9, Sch 7, para 10(1), (3).

Orders for financial provision and property adjustment

17 Orders for financial provision and property adjustment.

[(1) Subject to section 20 below, on an application by a party to a marriage for an order for financial relief under this section, the court may—

(a) make any one or more of the orders which it could make under Part II of the 1973 Act if a decree of divorce, a decree of nullity of marriage or a decree of judicial separation in respect of the marriage had been granted in England and Wales, that is to say—

(i) any order mentioned in section 23(1) of the 1973 Act (financial provision orders); and

(ii) any order mentioned in section 24(1) of that Act (property adjustment orders); and

(b) if the marriage has been dissolved or annulled, make one or more orders each of which would, within the meaning of that Part of that Act, be a pension sharing order in relation to the marriage;

[(c) if the marriage has been dissolved or annulled, make an order which would, within the meaning of that Part of that Act, be a pension compensation sharing order in relation to the marriage.][1]][2]

(2) Subject to section 20 below, where the court makes a secured periodical payments order, an order for the payment of a lump sum or a property adjustment order under subsection (1) above, then, on making that order or at any time thereafter, the court may make any order mentioned in section 24A(1) of the 1973 Act (orders for sale of property) which the court would have power to make if the order under subsection (1) above had been made under Part II of the 1973 Act.

Amendments

1 Inserted by the Pensions Act 2008, s 120, Sch 6, paras 10, 11.
2 Substituted by the Welfare Reform and Pensions Act 1999, s 84(1), Sch 12, paras 2, 3.

18 Matters to which the court is to have regard in exercising its powers under s. 17.

(1) In deciding whether to exercise its powers under section 17 above and, if so, in what manner the court shall act in accordance with this section.

(2) The court shall have regard to all the circumstances of the case, first consideration being given to the welfare while a minor of any child of the family who has not attained the age of eighteen.

(3) As regards the exercise of those powers in relation to a party to the marriage, the court shall in particular have regard to the matters mentioned in section 25(2)(a) to (h) of the 1973 Act and shall be under duties corresponding with those imposed by section 25A(1) and (2) of the 1973 Act where it decides to exercise under section 17 above powers corresponding with the powers referred to in those subsections.

[(3A) The matters to which the court is to have regard under subsection (3) above—

(a) so far as relating to paragraph (a) of section 25(2) of the 1973 Act, include any benefits under a pension arrangement which a party to the marriage has or is likely to have [and any PPF compensation to which a party to the marriage is or is likely to be entitled,][1] (whether or not in the foreseeable future), and

(b) so far as relating to paragraph (h) of that provision, include–

[(i)][1] any benefits under a pension arrangement which, by reason of the dissolution or annulment of the marriage, a party to the marriage will lose the chance of acquiring[, and

(ii) any PPF compensation which, by reason of the dissolution or annulment of the marriage, a party to the marriage will lose the chance of acquiring entitlement to.][1]][2]

(4) As regards the exercise of those powers in relation to a child of the family, the court shall in particular have regard to the matters mentioned in section 25(3)(a) to (e) of the 1973 Act.

(5) As regards the exercise of those powers against a party to the marriage in favour of a child of the family who is not the child of that party, the court shall also have regard to the matters mentioned in section 25(4)(a) to (c) of the 1973 Act.

(6) Where an order has been made by a court outside England and Wales for the making of payments or the transfer of property by a party to the marriage, the court in considering in accordance with this section the financial resources of the other party to the marriage or a child of the family shall have regard to the extent to which that order has been complied with or is likely to be complied with.

[(7) In this section—

(a) 'pension arrangement' has the meaning given by section 25D(3) of the 1973 Act, and

(b) references to benefits under a pension arrangement include any benefits by way of pension, whether under a pension arrangement or not[, and

[(c) 'PPF compensation' means compensation payable under—

(i) Chapter 3 of Part 2 of the Pensions Act 2004 (pension protection) or any regulations or order made under it,

(ii) Chapter 1 of Part 3 of the Pensions Act 2008 (pension compensation sharing) or any regulations or order made under it, or

(iii) any provision corresponding to the provisions mentioned in sub-paragraph (i) or (ii) in force in Northern Ireland.][3]][1]][2]

Amendments

1 Inserted by the Pensions Act 2004, s 319(1), Sch 12, para 4(1), (2).
2 Inserted by the Welfare Reform and Pensions Act 1999, s 22(1)-(3).
3 Substituted by the Pensions Act 2008, s 120, Sch 6, paras 10, 12.

19 Consent orders for financial provision or property adjustment.

(1) Notwithstanding anything in section 18 above, on an application for a consent order for financial relief the court may, unless it has reason to think that there are other circumstances into which it ought to inquire, make an order in the terms agreed on the basis only of the prescribed information furnished with the application.

(2) Subsection (1) above applies to an application for a consent order varying or discharging an order for financial relief as it applies to an application for an order for financial relief.

(3) In this section—

'consent order', in relation to an application for an order, means an order in the terms applied for to which the respondent agrees;

'order for financial relief' means an order under section 17 above; and

'prescribed' means prescribed by rules of court.

20 Restriction of powers of court where jurisdiction depends on matrimonial home in England or Wales.

(1) Where the court has jurisdiction to entertain an application for an order for financial relief by reason only of the situation in England and Wales of a dwelling-house which was a matrimonial home of the parties, the court may make under section 17 above any one or more of the following orders (but no other)—

(a) an order that either party to the marriage shall pay to the other such lump sum as may be specified in the order;

(b) an order that a party to the marriage shall pay to such person as may be so specified for the benefit of a child of the family, or to such a child, such lump sum as may be so specified;

(c) an order that a party to the marriage shall transfer to the other party, to any child of the family or to such person as may be so specified for the benefit of such a child, the interest of the first-mentioned party in the dwelling-house, or such part of that interest as may be so specified;

(d) an order that a settlement of the interest of a party to the marriage in the dwelling-house, or such part of that interest as may be so specified, be made to the satisfaction of the court for the benefit of the other party to the marriage and of the children of the family or either or any of them;

(e) an order varying for the benefit of the parties to the marriage and of the children of the family or either or any of them any ante-nuptial or post-nuptial settlement (including such a settlement made by will or codicil) made on the parties to the marriage so far as that settlement relates to an interest in the dwelling-house;

(f) an order extinguishing or reducing the interest of either of the parties to the marriage under any such settlement so far as that interest is an interest in the dwelling-house;

(g) an order for the sale of the interest of a party to the marriage in the dwelling-house.

(2) Where, in the circumstances mentioned in subsection (1) above, the court makes an order for the payment of a lump sum by a party to the marriage, the amount of the lump sum shall not exceed, or where more than one such order is made the total amount of the lump sums shall not exceed in aggregate, the following amount, that is to say—

(a) if the interest of that party in the dwelling-house is sold in pursuance of an order made under subsection (1)(g) above, the amount of the proceeds of the sale of that interest after deducting therefrom any costs incurred in the sale thereof;

(b) if the interest of that party is not so sold, the amount which in the opinion of the court represents the value of that interest.

(3) Where the interest of a party to the marriage in the dwelling-house is held jointly or in common with any other person or persons—

(a) the reference in subsection (1)(g) above to the interest of a party to the marriage shall be construed as including a reference to the interest of that other person, or the interest of those other persons, in the dwelling-house, and

(b) the reference in subsection (2)(a) above to the amount of the proceeds of a sale ordered under subsection (1)(g) above shall be construed as a reference to that part of those proceeds which is attributable to the interest of that party to the marriage in the dwelling-house.

21 *Application to orders under ss. 14 and 17 of certain provisions of Part II of Matrimonial Causes Act 1973.*

[(1)][1] The following provisions of Part II of the 1973 Act (financial relief for parties to marriage and children of family) shall apply in relation to an order ...[2] under section 14 or 17 above as they apply in relation to a like order ...[2] under that Part of that Act, that is to say—

(a) section 23(3) (provisions as to lump sums);
(b) section 24A(2), (4), (5) and (6) (provisions as to orders for sale);
[(ba) section 24B(3) to (5) (provisions about pension sharing orders in relation to divorce and nullity);
(bb) section 24C (duty to stay pension sharing orders);
(bc) section 24D (apportionment of pension sharing charges);][3]
[(bd) section 25B(3) to (7B) (power, by financial provision order, to attach payments under a pension arrangement, or to require the exercise of a right of commutation under such an arrangement);
(be) section 25C (extension of lump sum powers in relation to death benefits under a pension arrangement);][1]
[(bf) section 25E(2) to (10) (the Pension Protection Fund);][4]
(c) section 28(1) and (2) (duration of continuing financial provision orders in favour of party to marriage);
(d) section 29 (duration of continuing financial provision orders in favour of children, and age limit on making certain orders in their favour);
(e) section 30 (direction for settlement of instrument for securing payments or effecting property adjustment), except paragraph (b);
(f) section 31 (variation, discharge etc. of certain orders for financial relief), except subsection (2)(e) and subsection (4);
(g) section 32 (payment of certain arrears unenforceable without the leave of the court);
(h) section 33 (orders for repayment of sums paid under certain orders);
(i) section 38 (orders for repayment of sums paid after cessation of order by reason of remarriage);
(j) section 39 (settlements etc. made in compliance with a property adjustment order may be avoided on bankruptcy of settlor); and
(k) section 40 (payments etc. under order made in favour of person suffering from mental disorder);
[(l) section 40A (appeals relating to pension sharing orders which have taken effect).][3]

[(2) Subsection (1)(bd) and (be) above shall not apply where the court has jurisdiction to entertain an application for an order for financial relief by reason only of the situation in England or Wales of a dwelling-house which was a matrimonial home of the parties.

(3) Section 25D(1) of the 1973 Act (effect of transfers on orders relating to rights under a pension arrangement) shall apply in relation to an order made under section 17 above by virtue of subsection (1)(bd) or (be) above as it applies in relation to an order made under section 23 of that Act by virtue of section 25B or 25C of the 1973 Act.

(4) The Lord Chancellor may by regulations make for the purposes of this Part of this Act provision corresponding to any provision which may be made by him under subsections (2) to (2B) of section 25D of the 1973 Act.

(5) Power to make regulations under this section shall be exercisable by statutory instrument which shall be subject to annulment in pursuance of a resolution of either House of Parliament.][1]

Amendments

1 Inserted by the Welfare Reform and Pensions Act 1999, s 22(1), (4), (5).
2 Repealed by the Welfare Reform and Pensions Act 1999, ss 84(1), 88, Sch 12, paras 2, 4(a), Sch 13, Pt II.
3 Inserted by the Welfare Reform and Pensions Act 1999, s 84(1), Sch 12, paras 2, 4(b), (c).
4 Inserted by the Pensions Act 2004, s 319(1), Sch 12, para 4(1), (3).

Orders for transfer of tenancies

[22 Powers of court in relation to certain tenancies of dwelling-houses.

(1) This section applies if—
(a) an application is made by a party to a marriage for an order for financial relief; and
(b) one of the parties is entitled, either in his own right or jointly with the other party, to occupy a dwelling-house situated in England or Wales by virtue of a tenancy which is a relevant tenancy within the meaning of Schedule 7 to the Family Law Act 1996 (certain statutory tenancies).

(2) The court may make in relation to that dwelling-house any order which it could make under Part II of that Schedule [if a decree of divorce, a decree of nullity of marriage or a decree of judicial separation has been granted][1] in England and Wales in respect of the marriage.

(3) The provision of paragraph 10, 11 and 14(1) in Part III of that Schedule apply in relation to any order under this section as they apply to any order under Part II of that Schedule.][2]

Amendments

1 Substituted by the Children and Families Act 2014, s 18(6), (7)(a).
2 Substituted by the Family Law Act 1996, s 66(1), Sch 8, para 52.

Avoidance of transactions intended to prevent or reduce financial relief

23 *Avoidance of transactions intended to defeat applications for financial relief.*

(1) For the purposes of this section 'financial relief' means relief under section 14 or 17 above and any reference to defeating a claim by a party to a marriage for financial relief is a reference to preventing financial relief from being granted or reducing the amount of relief which might be granted, or frustrating or impeding the enforcement of any order which might be or has been made under either of those provisions at the instance of that party.

(2) Where leave is granted under section 13 above for the making by a party to a marriage of an application for an order for financial relief under section 17 above, the court may, on an application by that party—
- (a) if it is satisfied that the other party to the marriage is, with the intention of defeating the claim for financial relief, about to make any disposition or to transfer out of the jurisdiction or otherwise deal with any property, make such order as it thinks fit for restraining the other party from so doing or otherwise for protecting the claim;
- (b) if it is satisfied that the other party has, with that intention, made a reviewable disposition and that if the disposition were set aside financial relief or different financial relief would be granted to the applicant, make an order setting aside the disposition.

(3) Where an order for financial relief under section 14 or 17 above has been made by the court at the instance of a party to a marriage, then, on an application made by that party, the court may, if it is satisfied that the other party to the marriage has, with the intention of defeating the claim for financial relief, made a reviewable disposition, make an order setting aside the disposition.

(4) Where the court has jurisdiction to entertain the application for an order for financial relief by reason only of paragraph (c) of section 15(1) above, it shall not make any order under subsection (2) or (3) above in respect of any property other than the dwelling-house concerned.

(5) Where the court makes an order under subsection (2)(b) or (3) above setting aside a disposition it shall give such consequential directions as it thinks fit for giving effect to the order (including directions requiring the making of any payments or the disposal of any property).

(6) Any disposition made by the other party to the marriage (whether before or after the commencement of the application) is a reviewable disposition for the purposes of subsections (2)(b) and (3) above unless it was made for valuable consideration (other than marriage) to a person who, at the time of the disposition, acted in relation to it in good faith and without notice of any intention on the part of the other party to defeat the applicant's claim for financial relief.

(7) Where an application is made under subsection (2) or (3) above with respect to a disposition which took place less than three years before the date of the

application or with respect to a disposition or other dealing with property which is about to take place and the court is satisfied—

(a) in a case falling within subsection (2)(a) or (b) above, that the disposition or other dealing would (apart from this section) have the consequence, or

(b) in a case falling within subsection (3) above, that the disposition has had the consequence,

of defeating a claim by the applicant for financial relief, it shall be presumed, unless the contrary is shown, that the person who disposed of or is about to dispose of or deal with the property did so or, as the case may be, is about to do so, with the intention of defeating the applicant's claim for financial relief.

(8) In this section 'disposition' does not include any provision contained in a will or codicil but, with that exception, includes any conveyance, assurance or gift of property of any description, whether made by an instrument or otherwise.

(9) The preceding provisions of this section are without prejudice to any power of the High Court to grant injunctions under [section 37 of the Senior Courts Act 1981][1].

Amendment

1 Substituted by the Constitutional Reform Act 2005, s 59(5), Sch 11, para 1(2).

24 Prevention of transactions intended to defeat prospective applications for financial relief.

(1) Where, on an application by a party to a marriage, it appears to the court—

(a) that the marriage has been dissolved or annulled, or that the parties to the marriage have been legally separated, by means of judicial or other proceedings in an overseas country; and

(b) that the applicant intends to apply for leave to make an application for an order for financial relief under section 17 above as soon as he or she has been habitually resident in England and Wales for a period of one year; and

(c) that the other party to the marriage is, with the intention of defeating a claim for financial relief, about to make any disposition or to transfer out of the jurisdiction or otherwise deal with any property,

the court may make such order as it thinks fit for restraining the other party from taking such action as is mentioned in paragraph (c) above.

(2) For the purposes of an application under subsection (1) above—

(a) the reference to defeating a claim for financial relief shall be construed in accordance with subsection (1) of section 23 above (omitting the reference to any order which has been made); and

(b) subsections (7) and (8) of section 23 above shall apply as they apply for the purposes of an application under that section.

(3) The preceding provisions of this section are without prejudice to any power of the High Court to grant injunctions under [section 37 of the Senior Courts Act 1981][1].

Amendment

1 Substituted by the Constitutional Reform Act 2005, s 59(5), Sch 11, para 1(2).

Financial provision out of estate of deceased party to marriage

25 Extension of powers under Inheritance (Provision for Family and Dependants) Act 1975 in respect of former spouses.

(1) The Inheritance (Provision for Family and Dependants) Act 1975 shall have effect with the following amendments, being amendments designed to give to persons whose marriages are dissolved or annulled overseas the same rights to apply for provision under that Act (as amended by section 8 of this Act) as persons whose marriages are dissolved or annulled under the 1973 Act.

(2) In section 25(1), for the definition of 'former wife' and 'former husband' there shall be substituted the following definition—

'"former wife" or "former husband" means a person whose marriage with the deceased was during the lifetime of the deceased either—

(a) dissolved or annulled by a decree of divorce or a decree of nullity of marriage granted under the law of any part of the British Islands, or

(b) dissolved or annulled in any country or territory outside the British Islands by a divorce or annulment which is entitled to be recognised as valid by the law of England and Wales;'.

(3) After section 15 (restriction in divorce proceedings etc. of applications under the Act) there shall be inserted the following section—

'15A Restriction imposed in proceedings under Matrimonial and Family Proceedings Act 1984 on application under this Act.

(1) On making an order under section 17 of the Matrimonial and Family Proceedings Act 1984 (orders for financial provision and property adjustment following overseas divorces, etc.) the court, if it considers it just to do so, may, on the application of either party to the marriage, order that the other party to the marriage shall not on the death of the applicant be entitled to apply for an order under section 2 of this Act.

In this subsection "the court" means the High Court or, where a county court has jurisdiction by virtue of Part V of the Matrimonial and Family Proceedings Act 1984, a county court.

(2) Where an order under subsection (1) above has been made with respect to a party to a marriage which has been dissolved or annulled, then, on the death of the other party to that marriage, the court shall not entertain an application under section 2 of this Act made by the first-mentioned party.

(3) Where an order under subsection (1) above has been made with respect to a party to a marriage the parties to which have been legally separated, then, if the other party to the marriage dies while the legal separation is in force, the court shall not entertain an application under section 2 of this Act made by the first-mentioned party.'

Recovery of maintenance in magistrates' courts after overseas divorce etc.

26 ...[1]

...[1]

Amendment

1 Repealed by the Maintenance Orders (Reciprocal Enforcement) Act 1992, s 2(2), Sch 3.

Interpretation

27 Interpretation of Part III.

In this Part of this Act—

'the 1973Act' means the Matrimonial Causes Act 1973;

'child of the family' has the same meaning as in section 52(1) of the 1973 Act;

'the court' means the High Court or [the family court][1];

'dwelling-house' includes any building or part thereof which is occupied as a dwelling, and any yard, garden, garage or outhouse belonging to the dwelling-house and occupied therewith;

'order for financial relief' has the meaning given by section 12(4) above;

'overseas country' means a country or territory outside the British Islands;

'possession' includes receipt of, or the right to receive, rents and profits;

'property adjustment order' means such an order as is specified in section 24(1)(a), (b), (c) or (d) of the 1973 Act;

'rent' does not include mortgage interest;

'secured periodical payments order' means such an order as is specified in section 23(1)(b) or (e) of the 1973 Act.

Amendment

1 Substituted by the Crime and Courts Act 2013, s 17(6), Sch 11, paras 58, 88.

TRUSTEE ACT 1925

PART IV
POWERS OF THE COURT

Jurisdiction to make other Orders

61 *Power to relieve trustee from personal liability.*

If it appears to the court that a trustee, whether appointed by the court or otherwise, is or may be personally liable for any breach of trust, whether the transaction alleged to be a breach of trust occurred before or after the commencement of this Act, but has acted honestly and reasonably, and ought fairly to be excused for the breach of trust and for omitting to obtain the directions of the court in the matter in which he committed such breach, then the court may relieve him either wholly or partly from personal liability for the same.

TRUSTEE ACT 2000

PART I
THE DUTY OF CARE

1 *The duty of care.*

(1) Whenever the duty under this subsection applies to a trustee, he must exercise such care and skill as is reasonable in the circumstances, having regard in particular—
   (a) to any special knowledge or experience that he has or holds himself out as having, and
   (b) if he acts as trustee in the course of a business or profession, to any special knowledge or experience that it is reasonable to expect of a person acting in the course of that kind of business or profession.

(2) In this Act the duty under subsection (1) is called 'the duty of care'.

2 *Application of duty of care.*

Schedule 1 makes provision about when the duty of care applies to a trustee.

SCHEDULE 1
APPLICATION OF DUTY OF CARE
(Section 2)

1 *Investment*

The duty of care applies to a trustee—
   (a) when exercising the general power of investment or any other power of investment, however conferred;
   (b) when carrying out a duty to which he is subject under section 4 or 5 (duties relating to the exercise of a power of investment or to the review of investments).

2 *Acquisition of land*

The duty of care applies to a trustee—
   (a) when exercising the power under section 8 to acquire land;
   (b) when exercising any other power to acquire land, however conferred;
   (c) when exercising any power in relation to land acquired under a power mentioned in sub-paragraph (a) or (b).

3 *Agents, nominees and custodians*

(1) The duty of care applies to a trustee—

(a) when entering into arrangements under which a person is authorised under section 11 to exercise functions as an agent;
(b) when entering into arrangements under which a person is appointed under section 16 to act as a nominee;
(c) when entering into arrangements under which a person is appointed under section 17 or 18 to act as a custodian;
(d) when entering into arrangements under which, under any other power, however conferred, a person is authorised to exercise functions as an agent or is appointed to act as a nominee or custodian;
(e) when carrying out his duties under section 22 (review of agent, nominee or custodian, etc.).

(2) For the purposes of sub-paragraph (1), entering into arrangements under which a person is authorised to exercise functions or is appointed to act as a nominee or custodian includes, in particular—
(a) selecting the person who is to act,
(b) determining any terms on which he is to act, and
(c) if the person is being authorised to exercise asset management functions, the preparation of a policy statement under section 15.

4 *Compounding of liabilities*

The duty of care applies to a trustee—
(a) when exercising the power under section 15 of the Trustee Act 1925 to do any of the things referred to in that section;
(b) when exercising any corresponding power, however conferred.

5 *Insurance*

The duty of care applies to a trustee—
(a) when exercising the power under section 19 of the Trustee Act 1925 to insure property;
(b) when exercising any corresponding power, however conferred.

6 *Reversionary interests, valuations and audit*

The duty of care applies to a trustee—
(a) when exercising the power under section 22(1) or (3) of the Trustee Act 1925 to do any of the things referred to there;
(b) when exercising any corresponding power, however conferred.

7 *Exclusion of duty of care*

The duty of care does not apply if or in so far as it appears from the trust instrument that the duty is not meant to apply.

COUNCIL REGULATION (EC) NO 2201/2003
of 27 November 2003

concerning jurisdiction and the recognition and enforcement of judgments in matrimonial matters and the matters of parental responsibility, repealing Regulation (EC) No 1347/2000

The Council of the European Union,

Having regard to the Treaty establishing the European Community, and in particular Article 61(c) and Article 67(1) thereof,

Having regard to the proposal from the Commission,

Having regard to the opinion of the European Parliament,

Having regard to the opinion of the European Economic and Social Committee,

Whereas:

(1) The European Community has set the objective of creating an area of freedom, security and justice, in which the free movement of persons is ensured. To this end, the Community is to adopt, among others, measures in the field of judicial cooperation in civil matters that are necessary for the proper functioning of the internal market.

(2) The Tampere European Council endorsed the principle of mutual recognition of judicial decisions as the cornerstone for the creation of a genuine judicial area, and identified visiting rights as a priority.

(3) Council Regulation (EC) No 1347/2000 sets out rules on jurisdiction, recognition and enforcement of judgments in matrimonial matters and matters of parental responsibility for the children of both spouses rendered on the occasion of the matrimonial proceedings. The content of this Regulation was substantially taken over from the Convention of 28 May 1998 on the same subject matter.

(4) On 3 July 2000 France presented an initiative for a Council Regulation on the mutual enforcement of judgments on rights of access to children.

(5) In order to ensure equality for all children, this Regulation covers all decisions on parental responsibility, including measures for the protection of the child, independently of any link with a matrimonial proceeding.

(6) Since the application of the rules on parental responsibility often arises in the context of matrimonial proceedings, it is more appropriate to have a single instrument for matters of divorce and parental responsibility.

(7) The scope of this Regulation covers civil matters, whatever the nature of the court or tribunal.

(8) As regards judgments on divorce, legal separation or marriage annulment, this Regulation should apply only to the dissolution of matrimonial ties and should not deal with issues such as the grounds for divorce, property consequences of the marriage or any other ancillary measures.

(9) As regards the property of the child, this Regulation should apply only to measures for the protection of the child, i.e. (i) the designation and functions of a person or body having charge of the child's property, representing or assisting the child, and (ii) the administration, conservation or disposal of the child's property. In this context, this Regulation should, for instance, apply in cases where the parents are in dispute as regards the administration of the child's property. Measures relating to the child's property which do not concern the protection of the child should continue to be governed by Council Regulation (EC) No 44/2001 of 22 December 2000 on jurisdiction and the recognition and enforcement of judgments in civil and commercial matters.

(10) This Regulation is not intended to apply to matters relating to social security, public measures of a general nature in matters of education or health or to decisions on the right of asylum and on immigration. In addition it does not apply to the establishment of parenthood, since this is a different matter from the attribution of parental responsibility, nor to other questions linked to the status of persons. Moreover, it does not apply to measures taken as a result of criminal offences committed by children.

(11) Maintenance obligations are excluded from the scope of this Regulation as these are already covered by Council Regulation No 44/2001. The courts having jurisdiction under this Regulation will generally have jurisdiction to rule on maintenance obligations by application of Article 5(2) of Council Regulation No 44/2001.

(12) The grounds of jurisdiction in matters of parental responsibility established in the present Regulation are shaped in the light of the best interests of the child, in particular on the criterion of proximity. This means that jurisdiction should lie in the first place with the Member State of the child's habitual residence, except for certain cases of a change in the child's residence or pursuant to an agreement between the holders of parental responsibility.

(13) In the interest of the child, this Regulation allows, by way of exception and under certain conditions, that the court having jurisdiction may transfer a case to a court of another Member State if this court is better placed to hear the case. However, in this case the second court should not be allowed to transfer the case to a third court.

(14) This Regulation should have effect without prejudice to the application of public international law concerning diplomatic immunities. Where jurisdiction under this Regulation cannot be exercised by reason of the existence of diplomatic immunity in accordance with international law, jurisdiction should be exercised in accordance with national law in a Member State in which the person concerned does not enjoy such immunity.

(15) Council Regulation (EC) No 1348/2000 of 29 May 2000 on the service in the Member States of judicial and extrajudicial documents in civil or commercial matters should apply to the service of documents in proceedings instituted pursuant to this Regulation.

(16) This Regulation should not prevent the courts of a Member State from taking provisional, including protective measures, in urgent cases, with regard to persons or property situated in that State.

(17) In cases of wrongful removal or retention of a child, the return of the child should be obtained without delay, and to this end the Hague Convention of 25 October 1980 would continue to apply as complemented by the provisions of this Regulation, in particular Article 11. The courts of the Member State to or in which the child has been wrongfully removed or retained should be able to oppose his or her return in specific, duly justified cases. However, such a decision could be replaced by a subsequent decision by the court of the Member State of habitual residence of the child prior to the wrongful removal or retention. Should that judgment entail the return of the child, the return should take place without any special procedure being required for recognition and enforcement of that judgment in the Member State to or in which the child has been removed or retained.

(18) Where a court has decided not to return a child on the basis of Article 13 of the 1980 Hague Convention, it should inform the court having jurisdiction or central authority in the Member State where the child was habitually resident prior to the wrongful removal or retention. Unless the court in the latter Member State has been seised, this court or the central authority should notify the parties. This obligation should not prevent the central authority from also notifying the relevant public authorities in accordance with national law.

(19) The hearing of the child plays an important role in the application of this Regulation, although this instrument is not intended to modify national procedures applicable.

(20) The hearing of a child in another Member State may take place under the arrangements laid down in Council Regulation (EC) No 1206/2001 of 28 May 2001 on cooperation between the courts of the Member States in the taking of evidence in civil or commercial matters.

(21) The recognition and enforcement of judgments given in a Member State should be based on the principle of mutual trust and the grounds for non-recognition should be kept to the minimum required.

(22) Authentic instruments and agreements between parties that are enforceable in one Member State should be treated as equivalent to 'judgments' for the purpose of the application of the rules on recognition and enforcement.

(23) The Tampere European Council considered in its conclusions (point 34) that judgments in the field of family litigation should be 'automatically recognised throughout the Union without any intermediate proceedings or grounds for refusal of enforcement'. This is why judgments on rights of access and judgments on return that have been certified in the Member State of origin in accordance with the provisions of this Regulation should be recognised and enforceable in all other Member States without any

further procedure being required. Arrangements for the enforcement of such judgments continue to be governed by national law.

(24) The certificate issued to facilitate enforcement of the judgment should not be subject to appeal. It should be rectified only where there is a material error, i.e. where it does not correctly reflect the judgment.

(25) Central authorities should cooperate both in general matter and in specific cases, including for purposes of promoting the amicable resolution of family disputes, in matters of parental responsibility. To this end central authorities shall participate in the European Judicial Network in civil and commercial matters created by Council Decision 2001/470/EC of 28 May 2001 establishing a European Judicial Network in civil and commercial matters.

(26) The Commission should make publicly available and update the lists of courts and redress procedures communicated by the Member States.

(27) The measures necessary for the implementation of this Regulation should be adopted in accordance with Council Decision 1999/468/EC of 28 June 1999 laying down the procedures for the exercise of implementing powers conferred on the Commission.

(28) This Regulation replaces Regulation (EC) No 1347/2000 which is consequently repealed.

(29) For the proper functioning of this Regulation, the Commission should review its application and propose such amendments as may appear necessary.

(30) The United Kingdom and Ireland, in accordance with Article 3 of the Protocol on the position of the United Kingdom and Ireland annexed to the Treaty on European Union and the Treaty establishing the European Community, have given notice of their wish to take part in the adoption and application of this Regulation.

(31) Denmark, in accordance with Articles 1 and 2 of the Protocol on the position of Denmark annexed to the Treaty on European Union and the Treaty establishing the European Community, is not participating in the adoption of this Regulation and is therefore not bound by it nor subject to its application.

(32) Since the objectives of this Regulation cannot be sufficiently achieved by the Member States and can therefore be better achieved at Community level, the Community may adopt measures, in accordance with the principle of subsidiarity as set out in Article 5 of the Treaty. In accordance with the principle of proportionality, as set out in that Article, this Regulation does not go beyond what is necessary in order to achieve those objectives.

(33) This Regulation recognises the fundamental rights and observes the principles of the Charter of Fundamental Rights of the European Union. In particular, it seeks to ensure respect for the fundamental rights of the

child as set out in Article 24 of the Charter of Fundamental Rights of the European Union,

Has adopted the present Regulation:

CHAPTER I
SCOPE AND DEFINITIONS

Article 1
Scope

1. This Regulation shall apply, whatever the nature of the court or tribunal, in civil matters relating to:
   (a) divorce, legal separation or marriage annulment;
   (b) the attribution, exercise, delegation, restriction or termination of parental responsibility.

2. The matters referred to in paragraph 1(b) may, in particular, deal with:
   (a) rights of custody and rights of access;
   (b) guardianship, curatorship and similar institutions;
   (c) the designation and functions of any person or body having charge of the child's person or property, representing or assisting the child;
   (d) the placement of the child in a foster family or in institutional care;
   (e) measures for the protection of the child relating to the administration, conservation or disposal of the child's property.

3. This Regulation shall not apply to:
   (a) the establishment or contesting of a parent-child relationship;
   (b) decisions on adoption, measures preparatory to adoption, or the annulment or revocation of adoption;
   (c) the name and forenames of the child;
   (d) emancipation;
   (e) maintenance obligations;
   (f) trusts or succession;
   (g) measures taken as a result of criminal offences committed by children.

Article 2
Definitions

For the purposes of this Regulation:

1. the term 'court' shall cover all the authorities in the Member States with jurisdiction in the matters falling within the scope of this Regulation pursuant to Article 1;

2. the term 'judge' shall mean the judge or an official having powers equivalent to those of a judge in the matters falling within the scope of the Regulation;

3. the term 'Member State' shall mean all Member States with the exception of Denmark;

4. the term 'judgment' shall mean a divorce, legal separation or marriage annulment, as well as a judgment relating to parental responsibility, pronounced by a court of a Member State, whatever the judgment may be called, including a decree, order or decision;

5. the term 'Member State of origin' shall mean the Member State where the judgment to be enforced was issued;

6. the term 'Member State of enforcement' shall mean the Member State where enforcement of the judgment is sought;

7. the term 'parental responsibility' shall mean all rights and duties relating to the person or the property of a child which are given to a natural or legal person by judgment, by operation of law or by an agreement having legal effect. The term shall include rights of custody and rights of access;

8. the term 'holder of parental responsibility' shall mean any person having parental responsibility over a child;

9. the term 'rights of custody' shall include rights and duties relating to the care of the person of a child, and in particular the right to determine the child's place of residence;

10. the term 'rights of access' shall include in particular the right to take a child to a place other than his or her habitual residence for a limited period of time;

11. the term 'wrongful removal or retention' shall mean a child's removal or retention where:
    (a) it is in breach of rights of custody acquired by judgment or by operation of law or by an agreement having legal effect under the law of the Member State where the child was habitually resident immediately before the removal or retention; and
    (b) provided that, at the time of removal or retention, the rights of custody were actually exercised, either jointly or alone, or would have been so exercised but for the removal or retention. Custody shall be considered to be exercised jointly when, pursuant to a judgment or by operation of law, one holder of parental responsibility cannot decide on the child's place of residence without the consent of another holder of parental responsibility.

CHAPTER II
JURISDICTION

Section 1
Divorce, legal separation and marriage annulment

Article 3
General jurisdiction

1. In matters relating to divorce, legal separation or marriage annulment, jurisdiction shall lie with the courts of the Member State

(a) in whose territory:
- the spouses are habitually resident, or
- the spouses were last habitually resident, insofar as one of them still resides there, or
- the respondent is habitually resident, or
- in the event of a joint application, either of the spouses is habitually resident, or
- the applicant is habitually resident if he or she resided there for at least a year immediately before the application was made, or
- the applicant is habitually resident if he or she resided there for at least six months immediately before the application was made and is either a national of the Member State in question or, in the case of the United Kingdom and Ireland, has his or her 'domicile' there;

(b) of the nationality of both spouses or, in the case of the United Kingdom and Ireland, of the 'domicile' of both spouses.

2. For the purpose of this Regulation, 'domicile' shall have the same meaning as it has under the legal systems of the United Kingdom and Ireland.

Article 4
Counterclaim
The court in which proceedings are pending on the basis of Article 3 shall also have jurisdiction to examine a counterclaim, insofar as the latter comes within the scope of this Regulation.

Article 5
Conversion of legal separation into divorce
Without prejudice to Article 3, a court of a Member State that has given a judgment on a legal separation shall also have jurisdiction for converting that judgment into a divorce, if the law of that Member State so provides.

Article 6
Exclusive nature of jurisdiction under Articles 3, 4 and 5
A spouse who:

(a) is habitually resident in the territory of a Member State; or

(b) is a national of a Member State, or, in the case of the United Kingdom and Ireland, has his or her 'domicile' in the territory of one of the latter Member States,

may be sued in another Member State only in accordance with Articles 3, 4 and 5.

Article 7
Residual jurisdiction

1. Where no court of a Member State has jurisdiction pursuant to Articles 3, 4 and 5, jurisdiction shall be determined, in each Member State, by the laws of that State.

2. As against a respondent who is not habitually resident and is not either a national of a Member State or, in the case of the United Kingdom and Ireland, does not have his 'domicile' within the territory of one of the latter Member States, any national of a Member State who is habitually resident within the territory of another Member State may, like the nationals of that State, avail himself of the rules of jurisdiction applicable in that State.

Section 2
Parental responsibility

Article 8
General jurisdiction

1. The courts of a Member State shall have jurisdiction in matters of parental responsibility over a child who is habitually resident in that Member State at the time the court is seised.

2. Paragraph 1 shall be subject to the provisions of Articles 9, 10 and 12.

Article 9
Continuing jurisdiction of the child's former habitual residence

1. Where a child moves lawfully from one Member State to another and acquires a new habitual residence there, the courts of the Member State of the child's former habitual residence shall, by way of exception to Article 8, retain jurisdiction during a three-month period following the move for the purpose of modifying a judgment on access rights issued in that Member State before the child moved, where the holder of access rights pursuant to the judgment on access rights continues to have his or her habitual residence in the Member State of the child's former habitual residence.

2. Paragraph 1 shall not apply if the holder of access rights referred to in paragraph 1 has accepted the jurisdiction of the courts of the Member State of the child's new habitual residence by participating in proceedings before those courts without contesting their jurisdiction.

Article 10
Jurisdiction in cases of child abduction

In case of wrongful removal or retention of the child, the courts of the Member State where the child was habitually resident immediately before the wrongful removal or retention shall retain their jurisdiction until the child has acquired a habitual residence in another Member State and:

(a) each person, institution or other body having rights of custody has acquiesced in the removal or retention; or

(b) the child has resided in that other Member State for a period of at least one year after the person, institution or other body having rights of custody has had or should have had knowledge of the whereabouts of the child and the child is settled in his or her new environment and at least one of the following conditions is met:

(i) within one year after the holder of rights of custody has had or should have had knowledge of the whereabouts of the child, no request for return has been lodged before the competent authorities of the Member State where the child has been removed or is being retained;

(ii) a request for return lodged by the holder of rights of custody has been withdrawn and no new request has been lodged within the time limit set in paragraph (i);

(iii) a case before the court in the Member State where the child was habitually resident immediately before the wrongful removal or retention has been closed pursuant to Article 11(7);

(iv) a judgment on custody that does not entail the return of the child has been issued by the courts of the Member State where the child was habitually resident immediately before the wrongful removal or retention.

Article 11

Return of the child

1. Where a person, institution or other body having rights of custody applies to the competent authorities in a Member State to deliver a judgment on the basis of the Hague Convention of 25 October 1980 on the Civil Aspects of International Child Abduction (hereinafter 'the 1980 Hague Convention'), in order to obtain the return of a child that has been wrongfully removed or retained in a Member State other than the Member State where the child was habitually resident immediately before the wrongful removal or retention, paragraphs 2 to 8 shall apply.

2. When applying Articles 12 and 13 of the 1980 Hague Convention, it shall be ensured that the child is given the opportunity to be heard during the proceedings unless this appears inappropriate having regard to his or her age or degree of maturity.

3. A court to which an application for return of a child is made as mentioned in paragraph 1 shall act expeditiously in proceedings on the application, using the most expeditious procedures available in national law.

   Without prejudice to the first subparagraph, the court shall, except where exceptional circumstances make this impossible, issue its judgment no later than six weeks after the application is lodged.

4. A court cannot refuse to return a child on the basis of Article 13b of the 1980 Hague Convention if it is established that adequate arrangements have been made to secure the protection of the child after his or her return.

5. A court cannot refuse to return a child unless the person who requested the return of the child has been given an opportunity to be heard.

6. If a court has issued an order on non-return pursuant to Article 13 of the 1980 Hague Convention, the court must immediately either directly or through its central authority, transmit a copy of the court order on non-return and of the relevant documents, in particular a transcript of the hearings before the court, to the court with jurisdiction or central authority in the Member State where the child was habitually resident immediately before the wrongful removal or retention, as determined by national law. The court shall receive all the mentioned documents within one month of the date of the non-return order.

7. Unless the courts in the Member State where the child was habitually resident immediately before the wrongful removal or retention have already been seised by one of the parties, the court or central authority that receives the information mentioned in paragraph 6 must notify it to the parties and invite them to make submissions to the court, in accordance with national law, within three months of the date of notification so that the court can examine the question of custody of the child.

   Without prejudice to the rules on jurisdiction contained in this Regulation, the court shall close the case if no submissions have been received by the court within the time limit.

8. Notwithstanding a judgment of non-return pursuant to Article 13 of the 1980 Hague Convention, any subsequent judgment which requires the return of the child issued by a court having jurisdiction under this Regulation shall be enforceable in accordance with Section 4 of Chapter III below in order to secure the return of the child.

Article 12
Prorogation of jurisdiction

1. The courts of a Member State exercising jurisdiction by virtue of Article 3 on an application for divorce, legal separation or marriage annulment shall have jurisdiction in any matter relating to parental responsibility connected with that application where:
   (a) at least one of the spouses has parental responsibility in relation to the child; and
   (b) the jurisdiction of the courts has been accepted expressly or otherwise in an unequivocal manner by the spouses and by the holders of parental responsibility, at the time the court is seised, and is in the superior interests of the child.

2. The jurisdiction conferred in paragraph 1 shall cease as soon as:
   (a) the judgment allowing or refusing the application for divorce, legal separation or marriage annulment has become final;
   (b) in those cases where proceedings in relation to parental responsibility are still pending on the date referred to in (a), a judgment in these proceedings has become final;
   (c) the proceedings referred to in (a) and (b) have come to an end for another reason.

3. The courts of a Member State shall also have jurisdiction in relation to parental responsibility in proceedings other than those referred to in paragraph 1 where:
   (a) the child has a substantial connection with that Member State, in particular by virtue of the fact that one of the holders of parental responsibility is habitually resident in that Member State or that the child is a national of that Member State; and
   (b) the jurisdiction of the courts has been accepted expressly or otherwise in an unequivocal manner by all the parties to the proceedings at the time the court is seised and is in the best interests of the child.

4. Where the child has his or her habitual residence in the territory of a third State which is not a contracting party to the Hague Convention of 19 October 1996 on jurisdiction, applicable law, recognition, enforcement and cooperation in respect of parental responsibility and measures for the protection of children, jurisdiction under this Article shall be deemed to be in the child's interest, in particular if it is found impossible to hold proceedings in the third State in question.

Article 13
Jurisdiction based on the child's presence

1. Where a child's habitual residence cannot be established and jurisdiction cannot be determined on the basis of Article 12, the courts of the Member State where the child is present shall have jurisdiction.

2. Paragraph 1 shall also apply to refugee children or children internationally displaced because of disturbances occurring in their country.

Article 14
Residual jurisdiction
Where no court of a Member State has jurisdiction pursuant to Articles 8 to 13, jurisdiction shall be determined, in each Member State, by the laws of that State.

Article 15
Transfer to a court better placed to hear the case

1. By way of exception, the courts of a Member State having jurisdiction as to the substance of the matter may, if they consider that a court of another Member State, with which the child has a particular connection, would be better placed to hear the case, or a specific part thereof, and where this is in the best interests of the child:
   (a) stay the case or the part thereof in question and invite the parties to introduce a request before the court of that other Member State in accordance with paragraph 4; or
   (b) request a court of another Member State to assume jurisdiction in accordance with paragraph 5.

2. Paragraph 1 shall apply:
   (a) upon application from a party; or

(b) of the court's own motion; or
(c) upon application from a court of another Member State with which the child has a particular connection, in accordance with paragraph 3.

A transfer made of the court's own motion or by application of a court of another Member State must be accepted by at least one of the parties.

3. The child shall be considered to have a particular connection to a Member State as mentioned in paragraph 1, if that Member State:
(a) has become the habitual residence of the child after the court referred to in paragraph 1 was seised; or
(b) is the former habitual residence of the child; or
(c) is the place of the child's nationality; or
(d) is the habitual residence of a holder of parental responsibility; or
(e) is the place where property of the child is located and the case concerns measures for the protection of the child relating to the administration, conservation or disposal of this property.

4. The court of the Member State having jurisdiction as to the substance of the matter shall set a time limit by which the courts of that other Member State shall be seised in accordance with paragraph 1.

If the courts are not seised by that time, the court which has been seised shall continue to exercise jurisdiction in accordance with Articles 8 to 14.

5. The courts of that other Member State may, where due to the specific circumstances of the case, this is in the best interests of the child, accept jurisdiction within six weeks of their seisure in accordance with paragraph 1(a) or 1(b). In this case, the court first seised shall decline jurisdiction. Otherwise, the court first seised shall continue to exercise jurisdiction in accordance with Articles 8 to 14.

6. The courts shall cooperate for the purposes of this Article, either directly or through the central authorities designated pursuant to Article 53.

Section 3
Common provisions

Article 16
Seising of a Court

1. A court shall be deemed to be seised:
(a) at the time when the document instituting the proceedings or an equivalent document is lodged with the court, provided that the applicant has not subsequently failed to take the steps he was required to take to have service effected on the respondent; or
(b) if the document has to be served before being lodged with the court, at the time when it is received by the authority responsible for service, provided that the applicant has not subsequently failed to take the steps he was required to take to have the document lodged with the court.

Article 17

Examination as to jurisdiction

Where a court of a Member State is seised of a case over which it has no jurisdiction under this Regulation and over which a court of another Member State has jurisdiction by virtue of this Regulation, it shall declare of its own motion that it has no jurisdiction.

Article 18

Examination as to admissibility

1. Where a respondent habitually resident in a State other than the Member State where the action was brought does not enter an appearance, the court with jurisdiction shall stay the proceedings so long as it is not shown that the respondent has been able to receive the document instituting the proceedings or an equivalent document in sufficient time to enable him to arrange for his defence, or that all necessary steps have been taken to this end.

2. Article 19 of Regulation (EC) No 1348/2000 shall apply instead of the provisions of paragraph 1 of this Article if the document instituting the proceedings or an equivalent document had to be transmitted from one Member State to another pursuant to that Regulation.

3. Where the provisions of Regulation (EC) No 1348/2000 are not applicable, Article 15 of the Hague Convention of 15 November 1965 on the service abroad of judicial and extrajudicial documents in civil or commercial matters shall apply if the document instituting the proceedings or an equivalent document had to be transmitted abroad pursuant to that Convention.

Article 19

Lis pendens and dependent actions

1. Where proceedings relating to divorce, legal separation or marriage annulment between the same parties are brought before courts of different Member States, the court second seised shall of its own motion stay its proceedings until such time as the jurisdiction of the court first seised is established.

2. Where proceedings relating to parental responsibility relating to the same child and involving the same cause of action are brought before courts of different Member States, the court second seised shall of its own motion stay its proceedings until such time as the jurisdiction of the court first seised is established.

3. Where the jurisdiction of the court first seised is established, the court second seised shall decline jurisdiction in favour of that court.

   In that case, the party who brought the relevant action before the court second seised may bring that action before the court first seised.

Article 20
Provisional, including protective, measures

1. In urgent cases, the provisions of this Regulation shall not prevent the courts of a Member State from taking such provisional, including protective, measures in respect of persons or assets in that State as may be available under the law of that Member State, even if, under this Regulation, the court of another Member State has jurisdiction as to the substance of the matter.

2. The measures referred to in paragraph 1 shall cease to apply when the court of the Member State having jurisdiction under this Regulation as to the substance of the matter has taken the measures it considers appropriate.

COUNCIL REGULATION (EC) NO 4/2009
of 18 December 2008

on jurisdiction, applicable law, recognition and enforcement of decisions and cooperation in matters relating to maintenance obligations

The Council of the European Union,

Having regard to the Treaty establishing the European Community, and in particular Article 61(c) and Article 67(2) thereof,

Having regard to the proposal from the Commission,

Having regard to the opinion of the European Parliament,

Having regard to the opinion of the European Economic and Social Committee,

Whereas:

(1) The Community has set itself the objective of maintaining and developing an area of freedom, security and justice, in which the free movement of persons is ensured. For the gradual establishment of such an area, the Community is to adopt, among others, measures relating to judicial cooperation in civil matters having cross-border implications, in so far as necessary for the proper functioning of the internal market.

(2) In accordance with Article 65(b) of the Treaty, these measures must aim, inter alia, to promote the compatibility of the rules applicable in the Member States concerning the conflict of laws and of jurisdiction.

(3) In this respect, the Community has among other measures already adopted Council Regulation (EC) No 44/2001 of 22 December 2000 on jurisdiction and the recognition and enforcement of judgments in civil and commercial matters, Council Decision 2001/470/EC of 28 May 2001 establishing a European Judicial Network in civil and commercial matters, Council Regulation (EC) No 1206/2001 of 28 May 2001 on cooperation between the courts of the Member States in the taking of evidence in civil or commercial matters, Council Directive 2003/8/EC of 27 January 2003 to improve access to justice in cross-border disputes by establishing minimum common rules relating to legal aid for such disputes, Council Regulation (EC) No 2201/2003 of 27 November 2003 on jurisdiction and the recognition and enforcement of judgments in matrimonial matters and in matters of parental responsibility, Regulation (EC) No 805/2004 of the European Parliament and of the Council of 21 April 2004 creating a European Enforcement Order for uncontested claims, and Regulation (EC) No 1393/2007 of the European Parliament and of the Council of 13 November 2007 on the service in the Member States of judicial and extrajudicial documents in civil or commercial matters (service of documents).

(4) The European Council in Tampere on 15 and 16 October 1999 invited the Council and the Commission to establish special common procedural rules to simplify and accelerate the settlement of cross-border disputes

concerning, inter alia, maintenance claims. It also called for the abolition of intermediate measures required for the recognition and enforcement in the requested State of a decision given in another Member State, particularly a decision relating to a maintenance claim.

(5) A programme of measures for the enforcement of the principle of mutual recognition of decisions in civil and commercial matters, common to the Commission and to the Council, was adopted on 30 November 2000. That programme provides for the abolition of the exequatur procedure for maintenance claims in order to boost the effectiveness of the means by which maintenance creditors safeguard their rights.

(6) The European Council meeting in Brussels on 4 and 5 November 2004 adopted a new programme called 'The Hague Programme: strengthening freedom, security and justice in the European Union' (hereinafter referred to as The Hague Programme).

(7) At its meeting on 2 and 3 June 2005, the Council adopted a Council and Commission Action Plan which implements The Hague Programme in concrete actions and which mentions the necessity of adopting proposals on maintenance obligations.

(8) In the framework of The Hague Conference on Private International Law, the Community and its Member States took part in negotiations which led to the adoption on 23 November 2007 of the Convention on the International Recovery of Child Support and other Forms of Family Maintenance (hereinafter referred to as the 2007 Hague Convention) and the Protocol on the Law Applicable to Maintenance Obligations (hereinafter referred to as the 2007 Hague Protocol). Both those instruments should therefore be taken into account in this Regulation.

(9) A maintenance creditor should be able to obtain easily, in a Member State, a decision which will be automatically enforceable in another Member State without further formalities.

(10) In order to achieve this goal, it is advisable to create a Community instrument in matters relating to maintenance obligations bringing together provisions on jurisdiction, conflict of laws, recognition and enforceability, enforcement, legal aid and cooperation between Central Authorities.

(11) The scope of this Regulation should cover all maintenance obligations arising from a family relationship, parentage, marriage or affinity, in order to guarantee equal treatment of all maintenance creditors. For the purposes of this Regulation, the term 'maintenance obligation' should be interpreted autonomously.

(12) In order to take account of the various ways of resolving maintenance obligation issues in the Member States, this Regulation should apply both to court decisions and to decisions given by administrative authorities, provided that the latter offer guarantees with regard to, in particular, their impartiality and the right of all parties to be heard. Those authorities should therefore apply all the rules of this Regulation.

(13) For the reasons set out above, this Regulation should also ensure the recognition and enforcement of court settlements and authentic instruments without affecting the right of either party to such a settlement or instrument to challenge the settlement or instrument before the courts of the Member State of origin.

(14) It should be provided in this Regulation that for the purposes of an application for the recognition and enforcement of a decision relating to maintenance obligations the term 'creditor' includes public bodies which are entitled to act in place of a person to whom maintenance is owed or to claim reimbursement of benefits provided to the creditor in place of maintenance. Where a public body acts in this capacity, it should be entitled to the same services and the same legal aid as a creditor.

(15) In order to preserve the interests of maintenance creditors and to promote the proper administration of justice within the European Union, the rules on jurisdiction as they result from Regulation (EC) No 44/2001 should be adapted. The circumstance that the defendant is habitually resident in a third State should no longer entail the non-application of Community rules on jurisdiction, and there should no longer be any referral to national law. This Regulation should therefore determine the cases in which a court in a Member State may exercise subsidiary jurisdiction.

(16) In order to remedy, in particular, situations of denial of justice this Regulation should provide a forum necessitatis allowing a court of a Member State, on an exceptional basis, to hear a case which is closely connected with a third State. Such an exceptional basis may be deemed to exist when proceedings prove impossible in the third State in question, for example because of civil war, or when an applicant cannot reasonably be expected to initiate or conduct proceedings in that State. Jurisdiction based on the forum necessitatisshould, however, be exercised only if the dispute has a sufficient connection with the Member State of the court seised, for instance the nationality of one of the parties.

(17) An additional rule of jurisdiction should provide that, except under specific conditions, proceedings to modify an existing maintenance decision or to have a new decision given can be brought by the debtor only in the State in which the creditor was habitually resident at the time the decision was given and in which he remains habitually resident. To ensure proper symmetry between the 2007 Hague Convention and this Regulation, this rule should also apply as regards decisions given in a third State which is party to the said Convention in so far as that Convention is in force between that State and the Community and covers the same maintenance obligations in that State and in the Community.

(18) For the purposes of this Regulation, it should be provided that in Ireland the concept of 'domicile' replaces the concept of 'nationality' which is also the case in the United Kingdom, subject to this Regulation being applicable in the latter Member State in accordance with Article 4 of the Protocol on

the position of the United Kingdom and Ireland annexed to the Treaty on European Union and the Treaty establishing the European Community.

(19) In order to increase legal certainty, predictability and the autonomy of the parties, this Regulation should enable the parties to choose the competent court by agreement on the basis of specific connecting factors. To protect the weaker party, such a choice of court should not be allowed in the case of maintenance obligations towards a child under the age of 18.

(20) It should be provided in this Regulation that, for Member States bound by the 2007 Hague Protocol, the rules on conflict of laws in respect of maintenance obligations will be those set out in that Protocol. To that end, a provision referring to the said Protocol should be inserted. The 2007 Hague Protocol will be concluded by the Community in time to enable this Regulation to apply. To take account of a scenario in which the 2007 Hague Protocol does not apply to all the Member States a distinction for the purposes of recognition, enforceability and enforcement of decisions needs to be made in this Regulation between the Member States bound by the 2007 Hague Protocol and those not bound by it.

(21) It needs to be made clear in this Regulation that these rules on conflict of laws determine only the law applicable to maintenance obligations and do not determine the law applicable to the establishment of the family relationships on which the maintenance obligations are based. The establishment of family relationships continues to be covered by the national law of the Member States, including their rules of private international law.

(22) In order to ensure swift and efficient recovery of a maintenance obligation and to prevent delaying actions, decisions in matters relating to maintenance obligations given in a Member State should in principle be provisionally enforceable. This Regulation should therefore provide that the court of origin should be able to declare the decision provisionally enforceable even if the national law does not provide for enforceability by operation of law and even if an appeal has been or could still be lodged against the decision under national law.

(23) To limit the costs of proceedings subject to this Regulation, the greatest possible use of modern communications technologies, particularly for hearing parties, would be helpful.

(24) The guarantees provided by the application of rules on conflict of laws should provide the justification for having decisions relating to maintenance obligations given in a Member State bound by the 2007 Hague Protocol recognised and regarded as enforceable in all the other Member States without any procedure being necessary and without any form of control on the substance in the Member State of enforcement.

(25) Recognition in a Member State of a decision relating to maintenance obligations has as its only object to allow the recovery of the maintenance claim determined in the decision. It does not imply the recognition by that

Member State of the family relationship, parentage, marriage or affinity underlying the maintenance obligations which gave rise to the decision.

(26) For decisions on maintenance obligations given in a Member State not bound by the 2007 Hague Protocol, there should be provision in this Regulation for a procedure for recognition and declaration of enforceability. That procedure should be modelled on the procedure and the grounds for refusing recognition set out in Regulation (EC) No 44/2001. To accelerate proceedings and enable the creditor to recover his claim quickly, the court seised should be required to give its decision within a set time, unless there are exceptional circumstances.

(27) It would also be appropriate to limit as far as possible the formal enforcement requirements likely to increase the costs to be borne by the maintenance creditor. To that end, this Regulation should provide that a maintenance creditor ought not to be required to have a postal address or an authorised representative in the Member State of enforcement, without this otherwise affecting the internal organisation of the Member States in matters relating to enforcement proceedings.

(28) In order to limit the costs of enforcement proceedings, no translation should be required unless enforcement is contested, and without prejudice to the rules applicable to service of documents.

(29) In order to guarantee compliance with the requirements of a fair trial, this Regulation should provide for the right of a defendant who did not enter an appearance in the court of origin of a Member State bound by the 2007 Hague Protocol to apply for a review of the decision given against him at the stage of enforcement. However, the defendant must apply for this review within a set period which should start no later than the day on which, in the enforcement proceedings, his property was first made non-disposable in whole or in part. That right to apply for a review should be an extraordinary remedy granted to the defendant in default and not affecting the application of any extraordinary remedies laid down in the law of the Member State of origin provided that those remedies are not incompatible with the right to a review under this Regulation.

(30) In order to speed up the enforcement in another Member State of a decision given in a Member State bound by the 2007 Hague Protocol it is necessary to limit the grounds of refusal or of suspension of enforcement which may be invoked by the debtor on account of the cross-border nature of the maintenance claim. This limitation should not affect the grounds of refusal or of suspension laid down in national law which are not incompatible with those listed in this Regulation, such as the debtor's discharge of his debt at the time of enforcement or the unattachable nature of certain assets.

(31) To facilitate cross-border recovery of maintenance claims, provision should be made for a system of cooperation between Central Authorities designated by the Member States. These Authorities should assist maintenance creditors and debtors in asserting their rights in another Member State by submitting applications for recognition, enforceability and enforcement

of existing decisions, for the modification of such decisions or for the establishment of a decision. They should also exchange information in order to locate debtors and creditors, and identify their income and assets, as necessary. Lastly, they should cooperate with each other by exchanging general information and promoting cooperation amongst the competent authorities in their Member States.

(32) A Central Authority designated under this Regulation should bear its own costs, except in specifically determined cases, and should provide assistance for all applicants residing in its Member State. The criterion for determining a person's right to request assistance from a Central Authority should be less strict than the connecting factor of 'habitual residence' used elsewhere in this Regulation. However, the 'residence' criterion should exclude mere presence.

(33) In order to provide full assistance to maintenance creditors and debtors and to facilitate as much as possible cross-border recovery of maintenance, the Central Authorities should be able to obtain a certain amount of personal information. This Regulation should therefore oblige the Member States to ensure that their Central Authorities have access to such information through the public authorities or administrations which hold the information concerned in the course of their ordinary activities. It should however be left to each Member State to decide on the arrangements for such access. Accordingly, a Member State should be able to designate the public authorities or administrations which will be required to supply the information to the Central Authority in accordance with this Regulation, including, if appropriate, public authorities or administrations already designated in the context of other systems for access to information. Where a Member State designates public authorities or administrations, it should ensure that its Central Authority is able to access the requisite information held by those bodies as provided for in this Regulation. A Member State should also be able to allow its Central Authority to access requisite information from any other legal person which holds it and controls its processing.

(34) In the context of access to personal data and the use and transmission thereof, the requirements of Directive 95/46/EC of the European Parliament and of the Council of 24 October 1995 on the protection of individuals with regard to the processing of personal data and on the free movement of such data, as transposed into the national law of the Member States, should be complied with.

(35) For the purposes of the application of this Regulation it is however necessary to define the specific conditions of access to personal data and of the use and transmission of such data. In this context, the opinion of the European Data Protection Supervisor has been taken into consideration. Notification of the data subject should take place in accordance with national law. It should however be possible to defer the notification to prevent the debtor from transferring his assets and thus jeopardising the recovery of the maintenance claim.

(36) On account of the costs of proceedings it is appropriate to provide for a very favourable legal aid scheme, that is, full coverage of the costs relating to proceedings concerning maintenance obligations in respect of children under the age of 21 initiated via the Central Authorities. Specific rules should therefore be added to the current rules on legal aid in the European Union which exist by virtue of Directive 2003/8/EC thus setting up a special legal aid scheme for maintenance obligations. In this context, the competent authority of the requested Member State should be able, exceptionally, to recover costs from an applicant having received free legal aid and lost the case, provided that the person's financial situation so permits. This would apply, in particular, where someone well-off had acted in bad faith.

(37) In addition, for maintenance obligations other than those referred to in the preceding recital, all parties should be guaranteed the same treatment in terms of legal aid at the time of enforcement of a decision in another Member State. Accordingly, the provisions of this Regulation on continuity of legal aid should be understood as also granting such aid to a party who, while not having received legal aid in the proceedings to obtain or amend a decision in the Member State of origin, did then benefit from such aid in that State in the context of an application for enforcement of the decision. Similarly, a party who benefited from free proceedings before an administrative authority listed in Annex X should, in the Member State of enforcement, benefit from the most favourable legal aid or the most extensive exemption from costs or expenses, provided that he shows that he would have so benefited in the Member State of origin.

(38) In order to minimise the costs of translating supporting documents the court seised should only require a translation of such documents when this is necessary, without prejudice to the rights of the defence and the rules applicable concerning service of documents.

(39) To facilitate the application of this Regulation, Member States should be obliged to provide the Commission with the names and contact details of their Central Authorities and with other information. That information should be made available to practitioners and to the public through publication in the Official Journal of the European Union or through electronic access to the European Judicial Network in civil and commercial matters established by Decision 2001/470/EC. Furthermore, the use of forms provided for in this Regulation should facilitate and speed up communication between the Central Authorities and make it possible to submit applications electronically.

(40) The relationship between this Regulation and the bilateral or multilateral conventions and agreements on maintenance obligations to which the Member States are party should be specified. In this context it should be stipulated that Member States which are party to the Convention of 23 March 1962 between Sweden, Denmark, Finland, Iceland and Norway on the recovery of maintenance by the Member States may continue to apply that Convention since it contains more favourable rules on recognition and enforcement than those in this Regulation. As regards the conclusion of

future bilateral agreements on maintenance obligations with third States, the procedures and conditions under which Member States would be authorised to negotiate and conclude such agreements on their own behalf should be determined in the course of discussions relating to a Commission proposal on the subject.

(41) In calculating the periods and time limits provided for in this Regulation, Regulation (EEC, Euratom) No 1182/71 of the Council of 3 June 1971 determining the rules applicable to periods, dates and time limits should apply.

(42) The measures necessary for the implementation of this Regulation should be adopted in accordance with Council Decision 1999/468/EC of 28 June 1999 laying down the procedures for the exercise of implementing powers conferred on the Commission.

(43) In particular, the Commission should be empowered to adopt any amendments to the forms provided for in this Regulation in accordance with the advisory procedure provided for in Article 3 of Decision 1999/468/EC. For the establishment of the list of the administrative authorities falling within the scope of this Regulation, and the list of authorities competent to certify the right to legal aid, the Commission should be empowered to act in accordance with the management procedure provided for in Article 4 of that Decision.

(44) This Regulation should amend Regulation (EC) No 44/2001 by replacing the provisions of that Regulation applicable to maintenance obligations. Subject to the transitional provisions of this Regulation, Member States should, in matters relating to maintenance obligations, apply the provisions of this Regulation on jurisdiction, recognition, enforceability and enforcement of decisions and on legal aid instead of those of Regulation (EC) No 44/2001 as from the date on which this Regulation becomes applicable.

(45) Since the objectives of this Regulation, namely the introduction of a series of measures to ensure the effective recovery of maintenance claims in cross-border situations and thus to facilitate the free movement of persons within the European Union, cannot be sufficiently achieved by the Member States and can therefore, by reason of the scale and effects of this Regulation, be better achieved at Community level, the Community may adopt measures in accordance with the principle of subsidiarity as set out in Article 5 of the Treaty. In accordance with the principle of proportionality as set out in that Article this Regulation does not go beyond what is necessary to achieve those objectives.

(46) In accordance with Article 3 of the Protocol on the position of the United Kingdom and Ireland, annexed to the Treaty on European Union and to the Treaty establishing the European Community, Ireland has given notice of its wish to take part in the adoption and application of this Regulation.

(47) In accordance with Articles 1 and 2 of the Protocol on the position of the United Kingdom and Ireland, annexed to the Treaty on European Union and to the Treaty establishing the European Community, the United Kingdom is not taking part in the adoption of this Regulation and is not bound by it or subject to its application. This is, however, without prejudice to the possibility for the United Kingdom of notifying its intention of accepting this Regulation after its adoption in accordance with Article 4 of the said Protocol.

(48) In accordance with Articles 1 and 2 of the Protocol on the position of Denmark annexed to the Treaty on European Union and the Treaty establishing the European Community, Denmark is not taking part in the adoption of this Regulation and is not bound by it or subject to its application, without prejudice to the possibility for Denmark of applying the amendments made here to Regulation (EC) No 44/2001 pursuant to Article 3 of the Agreement of 19 October 2005 between the European Community and the Kingdom of Denmark on jurisdiction and the recognition and enforcement of judgments in civil and commercial matters,

Has adopted this Regulation:

CHAPTER I
SCOPE AND DEFINITIONS

Article 1
Scope of application

1. This Regulation shall apply to maintenance obligations arising from a family relationship, parentage, marriage or affinity.

2. In this Regulation, the term 'Member State' shall mean Member States to which this Regulation applies.

Article 2
Definitions

1 For the purposes of this Regulation:

   1. the term 'decision' shall mean a decision in matters relating to maintenance obligations given by a court of a Member State, whatever the decision may be called, including a decree, order, judgment or writ of execution, as well as a decision by an officer of the court determining the costs or expenses. For the purposes of Chapters VII and VIII, the term 'decision' shall also mean a decision in matters relating to maintenance obligations given in a third State;
   2. the term 'court settlement' shall mean a settlement in matters relating to maintenance obligations which has been approved by a court or concluded before a court in the course of proceedings;
   3. the term 'authentic instrument' shall mean:

(a) a document in matters relating to maintenance obligations which has been formally drawn up or registered as an authentic instrument in the Member State of origin and the authenticity of which:

(i) relates to the signature and the content of the instrument, and

(ii) has been established by a public authority or other authority empowered for that purpose; or,

(b) an arrangement relating to maintenance obligations concluded with administrative authorities of the Member State of origin or authenticated by them;

4. the term 'Member State of origin' shall mean the Member State in which, as the case may be, the decision has been given, the court settlement has been approved or concluded, or the authentic instrument has been established;

5. the term 'Member State of enforcement' shall mean the Member State in which the enforcement of the decision, the court settlement or the authentic instrument is sought;

6. the term 'requesting Member State' shall mean the Member State whose Central Authority transmits an application pursuant to Chapter VII;

7. the term 'requested Member State' shall mean the Member State whose Central Authority receives an application pursuant to Chapter VII;

8. the term '2007 Hague Convention Contracting State' shall mean a State which is a contracting party to the Hague Convention of 23 November 2007 on the International Recovery of Child Support and other Forms of Family Maintenance (hereinafter referred to as the 2007 Hague Convention) to the extent that the said Convention applies between the Community and that State;

9. the term 'court of origin' shall mean the court which has given the decision to be enforced;

10. the term 'creditor' shall mean any individual to whom maintenance is owed or is alleged to be owed;

11. the term 'debtor' shall mean any individual who owes or who is alleged to owe maintenance.

2. For the purposes of this Regulation, the term 'court' shall include administrative authorities of the Member States with competence in matters relating to maintenance obligations provided that such authorities offer guarantees with regard to impartiality and the right of all parties to be heard and provided that their decisions under the law of the Member State where they are established:

(i) may be made the subject of an appeal to or review by a judicial authority; and

(ii) have a similar force and effect as a decision of a judicial authority on the same matter.

These administrative authorities shall be listed in Annex X. That Annex shall be established and amended in accordance with the management procedu re referred to in Article 73(2) at the request of the Member State in which the administrative authority concerned is established.

3. For the purposes of Articles 3, 4 and 6, the concept of 'domicile' shall replace that of 'nationality' in those Member States which use this concept as a connecting factor in family matters.

For the purposes of Article 6, parties which have their 'domicile' in different territorial units of the same Member State shall be deemed to have their common 'domicile' in that Member State.

CHAPTER II
JURISDICTION

Article 3
General provisions

In matters relating to maintenance obligations in Member States, jurisdiction shall lie with:

(a) the court for the place where the defendant is habitually resident, or

(b) the court for the place where the creditor is habitually resident, or

(c) the court which, according to its own law, has jurisdiction to entertain proceedings concerning the status of a person if the matter relating to maintenance is ancillary to those proceedings, unless that jurisdiction is based solely on the nationality of one of the parties, or

(d) the court which, according to its own law, has jurisdiction to entertain proceedings concerning parental responsibility if the matter relating to maintenance is ancillary to those proceedings, unless that jurisdiction is based solely on the nationality of one of the parties.

Article 4
Choice of court

1. The parties may agree that the following court or courts of a Member State shall have jurisdiction to settle any disputes in matters relating to a maintenance obligation which have arisen or may arise between them:
   (a) a court or the courts of a Member State in which one of the parties is habitually resident;
   (b) a court or the courts of a Member State of which one of the parties has the nationality;
   (c) in the case of maintenance obligations between spouses or former spouses:
      (i) the court which has jurisdiction to settle their dispute in matrimonial matters; or

(ii) a court or the courts of the Member State which was the Member State of the spouses' last common habitual residence for a period of at least one year.

The conditions referred to in points (a), (b) or (c) have to be met at the time the choice of court agreement is concluded or at the time the court is seised.

The jurisdiction conferred by agreement shall be exclusive unless the parties have agreed otherwise.

2. A choice of court agreement shall be in writing. Any communication by electronic means which provides a durable record of the agreement shall be equivalent to 'writing'.

3. This Article shall not apply to a dispute relating to a maintenance obligation towards a child under the age of 18.

4. If the parties have agreed to attribute exclusive jurisdiction to a court or courts of a State party to the Convention on jurisdiction and the recognition and enforcement of judgments in civil and commercial matters, signed on 30 October 2007 in Lugano (hereinafter referred to as the Lugano Convention), where that State is not a Member State, the said Convention shall apply except in the case of the disputes referred to in paragraph 3.

Article 5
Jurisdiction based on the appearance of the defendant

Apart from jurisdiction derived from other provisions of this Regulation, a court of a Member State before which a defendant enters an appearance shall have jurisdiction. This rule shall not apply where appearance was entered to contest the jurisdiction.

Article 6
Subsidiary jurisdiction

Where no court of a Member State has jurisdiction pursuant to Articles 3, 4 and 5 and no court of a State party to the Lugano Convention which is not a Member State has jurisdiction pursuant to the provisions of that Convention, the courts of the Member State of the common nationality of the parties shall have jurisdiction.

Article 7
Forum necessitatis

Where no court of a Member State has jurisdiction pursuant to Articles 3, 4, 5 and 6, the courts of a Member State may, on an exceptional basis, hear the case if proceedings cannot reasonably be brought or conducted or would be impossible in a third State with which the dispute is closely connected.

The dispute must have a sufficient connection with the Member State of the court seised.

Article 8
Limit on proceedings

1. Where a decision is given in a Member State or a 2007 Hague Convention Contracting State where the creditor is habitually resident, proceedings to modify the decision or to have a new decision given cannot be brought by the debtor in any other Member State as long as the creditor remains habitually resident in the State in which the decision was given.

2. Paragraph 1 shall not apply:
   (a) where the parties have agreed in accordance with Article 4 to the jurisdiction of the courts of that other Member State;
   (b) where the creditor submits to the jurisdiction of the courts of that other Member State pursuant to Article 5;
   (c) where the competent authority in the 2007 Hague Convention Contracting State of origin cannot, or refuses to, exercise jurisdiction to modify the decision or give a new decision; or
   (d) where the decision given in the 2007 Hague Convention Contracting State of origin cannot be recognised or declared enforceable in the Member State where proceedings to modify the decision or to have a new decision given are contemplated.

Article 9
Seising of a court

For the purposes of this Chapter, a court shall be deemed to be seised:

(a) at the time when the document instituting the proceedings or an equivalent document is lodged with the court, provided that the claimant has not subsequently failed to take the steps he was required to take to have service effected on the defendant; or

(b) if the document has to be served before being lodged with the court, at the time when it is received by the authority responsible for service, provided that the claimant has not subsequently failed to take the steps he was required to take to have the document lodged with the court.

Article 10
Examination as to jurisdiction

Where a court of a Member State is seised of a case over which it has no jurisdiction under this Regulation it shall declare of its own motion that it has no jurisdiction.

Article 11
Examination as to admissibility

1. Where a defendant habitually resident in a State other than the Member State where the action was brought does not enter an appearance, the court with jurisdiction shall stay the proceedings so long as it is not shown that the defendant has been able to receive the document instituting the

proceedings or an equivalent document in sufficient time to enable him to arrange for his defence, or that all necessary steps have been taken to this end.

2. Article 19 of Regulation (EC) No 1393/2007 shall apply instead of the provisions of paragraph 1 of this Article if the document instituting the proceedings or an equivalent document had to be transmitted from one Member State to another pursuant to that Regulation.

3. Where the provisions of Regulation (EC) No 1393/2007 are not applicable, Article 15 of the Hague Convention of 15 November 1965 on the service abroad of judicial and extrajudicial documents in civil or commercial matters shall apply if the document instituting the proceedings or an equivalent document had to be transmitted abroad pursuant to that Convention.

Article 12
Lis pendens

1. Where proceedings involving the same cause of action and between the same parties are brought in the courts of different Member States, any court other than the court first seised shall of its own motion stay its proceedings until such time as the jurisdiction of the court first seised is established.

2. Where the jurisdiction of the court first seised is established, any court other than the court first seised shall decline jurisdiction in favour of that court.

Article 13
Related actions

1. Where related actions are pending in the courts of different Member States, any court other than the court first seised may stay its proceedings.

2. Where these actions are pending at first instance, any court other than the court first seised may also, on the application of one of the parties, decline jurisdiction if the court first seised has jurisdiction over the actions in question and its law permits the consolidation thereof.

3. For the purposes of this Article, actions are deemed to be related where they are so closely connected that it is expedient to hear and determine them together to avoid the risk of irreconcilable judgments resulting from separate proceedings.

Article 14
Provisional, including protective, measures

Application may be made to the courts of a Member State for such provisional, including protective, measures as may be available under the law of that State, even if, under this Regulation, the courts of another Member State have jurisdiction as to the substance of the matter.

1985 HAGUE CONVENTION ON THE LAW APPLICABLE TO TRUSTS AND ON THEIR RECOGNITION

The States signatory to the present Convention,

Considering that the trust, as developed in courts of equity in common law jurisdictions and adopted with some modifications in other jurisdictions, is a unique legal institution,

Desiring to establish common provisions on the law applicable to trusts and to deal with the most important issues concerning the recognition of trusts,

Have resolved to conclude a Convention to this effect, and have agreed upon the following provisions—

CHAPTER I
SCOPE

Article 1
This Convention specifies the law applicable to trusts and governs their recognition.

Article 2
For the purposes of this Convention, the term 'trust' refers to the legal relationships created – inter vivos or on death – by a person, the settlor, when assets have been placed under the control of a trustee for the benefit of a beneficiary or for a specified purpose.

A trust has the following characteristics—

a) the assets constitute a separate fund and are not a part of the trustee's own estate;

b) title to the trust assets stands in the name of the trustee or in the name of another person on behalf of the trustee;

c) the trustee has the power and the duty, in respect of which he is accountable, to manage, employ or dispose of the assets in accordance with the terms of the trust and the special duties imposed upon him by law.

The reservation by the settlor of certain rights and powers, and the fact that the trustee may himself have rights as a beneficiary, are not necessarily inconsistent with the existence of a trust.

Article 3
The Convention applies only to trusts created voluntarily and evidenced in writing.

Article 4
The Convention does not apply to preliminary issues relating to the validity of wills or of other acts by virtue of which assets are transferred to the trustee.

Article 5
The Convention does not apply to the extent that the law specified by Chapter II does not provide for trusts or the category of trusts involved.

CHAPTER II
APPLICABLE LAW

Article 6
A trust shall be governed by the law chosen by the settlor. The choice must be express or be implied in the terms of the instrument creating or the writing evidencing the trust, interpreted, if necessary, in the light of the circumstances of the case.

Where the law chosen under the previous paragraph does not provide for trusts or the category of trust involved, the choice shall not be effective and the law specified in Article 7 shall apply.

Article 7
Where no applicable law has been chosen, a trust shall be governed by the law with which it is most closely connected.

In ascertaining the law with which a trust is most closely connected reference shall be made in particular to—

a) the place of administration of the trust designated by the settlor;

b) the situs of the assets of the trust;

c) the place of residence or business of the trustee;

d) the objects of the trust and the places where they are to be fulfilled.

Article 8
The law specified by Article 6 or 7 shall govern the validity of the trust, its construction, its effects, and the administration of the trust.

In particular that law shall govern—

a) the appointment, resignation and removal of trustees, the capacity to act as a trustee, and the devolution of the office of trustee;

b) the rights and duties of trustees among themselves;

c) the right of trustees to delegate in whole or in part the discharge of their duties or the exercise of their powers;

d) the power of trustees to administer or to dispose of trust assets, to create security interests in the trust assets, or to acquire new assets;

e) the powers of investment of trustees;

f) restrictions upon the duration of the trust, and upon the power to accumulate the income of the trust;

g) the relationships between the trustees and the beneficiaries including the personal liability of the trustees to the beneficiaries;

h) the variation or termination of the trust;

i) the distribution of the trust assets;

j) the duty of trustees to account for their administration.

Article 9
In applying this Chapter a severable aspect of the trust, particularly matters of administration, may be governed by a different law.

Article 10
The law applicable to the validity of the trust shall determine whether that law or the law governing a severable aspect of the trust may be replaced by another law.

CHAPTER III
RECOGNITION

Article 11

A trust created in accordance with the law specified by the preceding Chapter shall be recognised as a trust.

Such recognition shall imply, as a minimum, that the trust property constitutes a separate fund, that the trustee may sue and be sued in his capacity as trustee, and that he may appear or act in this capacity before a notary or any person acting in an official capacity.

In so far as the law applicable to the trust requires or provides, such recognition shall imply, in particular—

a) that personal creditors of the trustee shall have no recourse against the trust assets;

b) that the trust assets shall not form part of the trustee's estate upon his insolvency or bankruptcy;

c) that the trust assets shall not form part of the matrimonial property of the trustee or his spouse nor part of the trustee's estate upon his death;

d) that the trust assets may be recovered when the trustee, in breach of trust, has mingled trust assets with his own property or has alienated trust assets. However, the rights and obligations of any third party holder of the assets shall remain subject to the law determined by the choice of law rules of the forum.

Article 12
Where the trustee desires to register assets, movable or immovable, or documents of title to them, he shall be entitled, in so far as this is not prohibited

by or inconsistent with the law of the State where registration is sought, to do so in his capacity as trustee or in such other way that the existence of the trust is disclosed.

Article 13
No State shall be bound to recognise a trust the significant elements of which, except for the choice of the applicable law, the place of administration and the habitual residence of the trustee, are more closely connected with States which do not have the institution of the trust or the category of trust involved.

Article 14
The Convention shall not prevent the application of rules of law more favourable to the recognition of trusts.

CHAPTER IV
GENERAL CLAUSES

Article 15
The Convention does not prevent the application of provisions of the law designated by the conflicts rules of the forum, in so far as those provisions cannot be derogated from by voluntary act, relating in particular to the following matters—

a) the protection of minors and incapable parties;

b) the personal and proprietary effects of marriage;

c) succession rights, testate and intestate, especially the indefeasible shares of spouses and relatives;

d) the transfer of title to property and security interests in property;

e) the protection of creditors in matters of insolvency;

f) the protection, in other respects, of third parties acting in good faith.

If recognition of a trust is prevented by application of the preceding paragraph, the court shall try to give effect to the objects of the trust by other means.

Article 16
The Convention does not prevent the application of those provisions of the law of the forum which must be applied even to international situations, irrespective of rules of conflict of laws.

If another State has a sufficiently close connection with a case then, in exceptional circumstances, effect may also be given to rules of that State which have the same character as mentioned in the preceding paragraph.

Any Contracting State may, by way of reservation, declare that it will not apply the second paragraph of this Article.

Article 17
In the Convention the word 'law' means the rules of law in force in a State other than its rules of conflict of laws.

Article 18
The provisions of the Convention may be disregarded when their application would be manifestly incompatible with public policy (ordre public).

Article 19
Nothing in the Convention shall prejudice the powers of States in fiscal matters.

Article 20
Any Contracting State may, at any time, declare that the provisions of the Convention will be extended to trusts declared by judicial decisions.

This declaration shall be notified to the Ministry of Foreign Affairs of the Kingdom of the Netherlands and will come into effect on the day when this notification is received.

Article 31 is applicable to the withdrawal of this declaration in the same way as it applies to a denunciation of the Convention.

Article 21
Any Contracting State may reserve the right to apply the provisions of Chapter III only to trusts the validity of which is governed by the law of a Contracting State.

Article 22
The Convention applies to trusts regardless of the date on which they were created.

However, a Contracting State may reserve the right not to apply the Convention to trusts created before the date on which, in relation to that State, the Convention enters into force.

Article 23
For the purpose of identifying the law applicable under the Convention, where a State comprises several territorial units each of which has its own rules of law in respect of trusts, any reference to the law of that State is to be construed as referring to the law in force in the territorial unit in question.

Article 24
A State within which different territorial units have their own rules of law in respect of trusts is not bound to apply the Convention to conflicts solely between the laws of such units.

Article 25
The Convention shall not affect any other international instrument containing provisions on matters governed by this Convention to which a Contracting State is, or becomes, a Party.

CHAPTER V
FINAL CLAUSES

Article 26

Any State may, at the time of signature, ratification, acceptance, approval or accession, or at the time of making a declaration in terms of Article 29, make the reservations provided for in Articles 16, 21 and 22.

No other reservation shall be permitted.

Any Contracting State may at any time withdraw a reservation which it has made; the reservation shall cease to have effect on the first day of the third calendar month after notification of the withdrawal.

Article 27

The Convention shall be open for signature by the States which were Members of the Hague Conference on Private International Law at the time of its Fifteenth Session.

It shall be ratified, accepted or approved and the instruments of ratification, acceptance or approval shall be deposited with the Ministry of Foreign Affairs of the Kingdom of the Netherlands.

Article 28

Any other State may accede to the Convention after it has entered into force in accordance with Article 30, paragraph 1.

The instrument of accession shall be deposited with the Ministry of Foreign Affairs of the Kingdom of the Netherlands.

The accession shall have effect only as regards the relations between the acceding State and those Contracting States which have not raised an objection to its accession in the twelve months after the receipt of the notification referred to in Article 32. Such an objection may also be raised by Member States at the time when they ratify, accept or approve the Convention after an accession. Any such objection shall be notified to the Ministry of Foreign Affairs of the Kingdom of the Netherlands.

Article 29

If a State has two or more territorial units in which different systems of law are applicable, it may at the time of signature, ratification, acceptance, approval or accession declare that this Convention shall extend to all of its territorial units or only to one or more of them and may modify this declaration by submitting another declaration at any time.

Any such declaration shall be notified to the Ministry of Foreign Affairs of the Kingdom of the Netherlands and shall state expressly the territorial units to which the Convention applies.

If a State makes no declaration under this Article, the Convention is to extend to all territorial units of that State.

Article 30
The Convention shall enter into force on the first day of the third calendar month after the deposit of the third instrument of ratification, acceptance or approval referred to in Article 27.

Thereafter the Convention shall enter into force—

a) for each State ratifying, accepting or approving it subsequently, on the first day of the third calendar month after the deposit of its instrument of ratification, acceptance or approval;

b) for each acceding State, on the first day of the third calendar month after the expiry of the period referred to in Article 28;

c) for a territorial unit to which the Convention has been extended in conformity with Article 29, on the first day of the third calendar month after the notification referred to in that Article.

Article 31
Any Contracting State may denounce this Convention by a formal notification in writing addressed to the Ministry of Foreign Affairs of the Kingdom of the Netherlands, depositary of the Convention.

The denunciation takes effect on the first day of the month following the expiration of six months after the notification is received by the depositary or on such later date as is specified in the notification.

Article 32
The Ministry of Foreign Affairs of the Kingdom of the Netherlands shall notify the States Members of the Conference, and the States which have acceded in accordance with Article 28, of the following—

a) the signatures and ratifications, acceptances or approvals referred to in Article 27;

b) the date on which the Convention enters into force in accordance with Article 30;

c) the accessions and the objections raised to accessions referred to in Article 28;

d) the extensions referred to in Article 29;

e) the declarations referred to in Article 20;

f) the reservation or withdrawals referred to in Article 26;

g) the denunciations referred to in Article 31.

In witness whereof the undersigned, being duly authorised thereto, have signed this Convention.

Done at The Hague, on the first day of July, 1985, in English and French, both texts being equally authentic, in a single copy which shall be deposited in the archives of the Government of the Kingdom of the Netherlands, and of which a certified copy shall be sent, through diplomatic channels, to each of the States Members of the Hague Conference on Private International Law at the date of its Fifteenth Session.

TRUSTS LAW (2017 REVISION) – CAYMAN ISLANDS

PART VII
TRUSTS-FOREIGN ELEMENT

87 *Definitions in this Part*

In this Part-

'dispose' and 'disposition', in relation to property, connote every form of conveyance, transfer, assignment, lease, mortgage, pledge or other transaction by which any legal or equitable interest in property is created, transferred or extinguished;

'formalities', in relation to a disposition of property, means the documentary and other actions required generally by the laws of a relevant jurisdiction for all dispositions of like form concerning property of like nature, without regard to-

(a) the fact that the particular disposition is made in trust;

(b) the terms of the trust;

(c) the circumstances of the parties to the disposition; or

(d) any other particular circumstances,

but include any special formalities required by reason that the party effecting the disposition is not of full age, is subject to a mental or bodily infirmity or is a corporation.

'heirship right' means any right, claim or interest in, against or to property of a person arising, accruing or existing in consequence of, or in anticipation of, that person's death, other than any such right, claim or interest created by will or other voluntary disposition by such person or resulting from an express limitation in the disposition of the property to such person;

'personal relationship' includes every form of relationship by blood or marriage, including former marriage, and in particular a personal relationship between two persons exists if-

(a) one is the child of the other, natural or adopted (whether or not the adoption is recognised by law), legitimate or illegitimate;

(b) one is married to the other (whether or not the marriage is recognised by law);

(c) one cohabits with the other or so conducts himself or herself in relation to the other as to give rise in any jurisdiction to any rights, obligations or responsibilities analogous to those of parent and child or husband and wife; or

(d) personal relationships exist between each of them and a third person, but no change in circumstances causes a personal relationship, once established, to terminate; and 'settlor', in relation to a trust, means and includes each and every person who, directly or indirectly, on behalf of himself or on behalf of any other or others, as owner or as the holder of a power in that behalf, disposes of property to be held in such trust or declares or otherwise creates such trust.

88 *Application of this Part*

This Part applies to every trust and every disposition of property in trust made before, on or after the 31st May, 1987, whether such property is situate in the Islands or elsewhere.

89 *Governing law*

(1) In determining the governing law of a trust, regard is first to be had to the terms of the trust and to any evidence therein as to the intention of the parties; and the other circumstances of the trust are to be taken into account only if the terms of the trust fail to provide such evidence.

(2) A term of the trust expressly selecting the laws of the Islands to govern the trust is valid, effective and conclusive regardless of any other circumstances.

(3) A term of the trust that the laws of the Islands are to govern a particular aspect of the trust or that the Islands or the courts of the Islands are the forum for the administration of the trust or any like provision is conclusive evidence, subject to any contrary term of the trust, that the parties intended the laws of the Islands to be the governing law of the trust and is valid and effective accordingly.

(4) If the terms of a trust so provide, the governing law of the trust may be changed to or from the laws of the Islands provided that-
   (a) in the case of a change to the laws of the Islands, such change is recognised by the governing law of the trust previously in effect; or
   (b) in the case of a change from the laws of the Islands, the new governing law would recognise the validity of the trust and the respective interests of the beneficiaries.

(5) A change in governing law shall not affect the legality or validity of, or render any person liable for, any thing done before the change.

90 *Matters determined by governing law*

All questions arising in regard to a trust which is for the time being governed by the laws of the Islands or in regard to any disposition of property upon the trusts thereof including questions as to-

(a) the capacity of any settlor;

(b) any aspect of the validity of the trust or disposition or the interpretation or effect thereof;

(c) the administration of the trust, whether the administration be conducted in the Islands or elsewhere, including questions as to the powers, obligations, liabilities and rights of trustees and their appointment and removal; or

(d) the existence and extent of powers, conferred or retained, including powers of variation or revocation of the trust and powers of appointment, and the validity of any exercise thereof,

are to be determined according to the laws of the Islands, without reference to the laws of any other jurisdictions with which the trust or disposition may be connected:

Provided that this section-

(i) does not validate any disposition of property which is neither owned by the settlor nor the subject of a power in that behalf vested in the settlor, nor does this section affect the recognition of foreign laws in determining whether the settlor is the owner of such property or the holder of such a power;

(ii) takes effect subject to any express contrary term of the trust or disposition;

(iii) does not, as regards the capacity of a corporation, affect the recognition of the laws of its place of incorporation;

(iv) does not affect the recognition of foreign laws prescribing generally (without reference to the existence or terms of the trust) the formalities for the disposition of property;

(v) does not validate any trust or disposition of immovable property situate in a jurisdiction other than the Islands which is invalid according to the laws of such jurisdiction; and

(vi) does not validate any testamentary trust or disposition which is invalid according to the laws of the testator's domicile.

91 Exclusion of foreign law

Subject to the same provisos as are set out in paragraphs (i) to (vi) of section 90, it is expressly declared that no trust governed by the laws of the Islands and no disposition of property to be held upon the trusts thereof is void, voidable, liable to be set aside or defective in any fashion, nor is the capacity of any settlor to be questioned, nor is the trustee, any beneficiary or any other person to be subjected to any liability or deprived of any right, by reason that-

(a) the laws of any foreign jurisdiction prohibit or do not recognise the concept of a trust; or

(b) the trust or disposition avoids or defeats rights, claims or interests conferred by foreign law upon any person by reason of a personal relationship to the settlor or by way of heirship rights, or contravenes any rule of foreign law or any foreign judicial or administrative order or action intended to recognise, protect, enforce or give effect to any such rights, claims or interests.

92 *Heirship rights*

An heirship right conferred by foreign law in relation to the property of a living person shall not be recognised as-

(a) affecting the ownership of immovable property in the Islands or movable property wherever situate for the purposes of paragraph (i) of section 90 or for any other purpose; or

(b) constituting an obligation or liability for the purposes of the Fraudulent Dispositions Law (1996 Revision) or for any other purpose.

93 *Foreign judgments*

A foreign judgment shall not be recognised, enforced or give rise to any estoppel insofar as it is inconsistent with section 91 or 92.

94 *Application of this Part*

(1) This Part does not render any person liable for any thing done before 31st May, 1987.

(2) Sections 91, 92 and 93 apply to every trust and every disposition of property in trust made before, on or after the 7th August, 1995, whether such property is situate in the Islands or elsewhere.

TRUSTS (JERSEY) LAW 1984

PART 2
PROVISIONS APPLICABLE ONLY TO A JERSEY TRUST

Creation, validity and duration of Jersey trusts

9 *Extent of application of law of Jersey to creation, etc. of a trust*

(1) Subject to paragraph (3), any question concerning –
(a) the validity or interpretation of a trust;
(b) the validity or effect of any transfer or other disposition of property to a trust;
(c) the capacity of a settlor;
(d) the administration of the trust, whether the administration be conducted in Jersey or elsewhere, including questions as to the powers, obligations, liabilities and rights of trustees and their appointment or removal;
(e) the existence and extent of powers, conferred or retained, including powers of variation or revocation of the trust and powers of appointment and the validity of any exercise of such powers;
(f) the exercise or purported exercise by a foreign court of any statutory or non-statutory power to vary the terms of a trust; or
(g) the nature and extent of any beneficial rights or interests in the property,

shall be determined in accordance with the law of Jersey and no rule of foreign law shall affect such question.

(2) Without prejudice to the generality of paragraph (1), any question mentioned in that paragraph shall be determined without consideration of whether or not –
(a) any foreign law prohibits or does not recognise the concept of a trust; or
(b) the trust or disposition avoids or defeats rights, claims, or interests conferred by any foreign law upon any person by reason of a personal relationship or by way of heirship rights, or contravenes any rule of foreign law or any foreign judicial or administrative order or action intended to recognize, protect, enforce or give effect to any such rights, claims or interests.

(2A) Subject to paragraph (2), paragraph (1) –
(a) does not validate any disposition of property which is neither owned by the settlor nor the subject of a power of disposition vested in the settlor;
(b) does not affect the recognition of the law of any other jurisdiction in determining whether the settlor is the owner of any property or the holder of any such power;
(c) is subject to any express provision to the contrary in the terms of the trust or disposition;

(d) does not, in determining the capacity of a corporation, affect the recognition of the law of its place of incorporation;

(e) does not affect the recognition of the law of any other jurisdiction prescribing the formalities for the disposition of property;

(f) does not validate any trust or disposition of immovable property situate in a jurisdiction other than Jersey which is invalid under the law of that jurisdiction; and

(g) does not validate any testamentary disposition which is invalid under the law of the testator's domicile at the time of his death.

(3) The law of Jersey relating to légitime shall not apply to the determination of any question mentioned in paragraph (1) unless the settlor is domiciled in Jersey.

(3A) The law of Jersey relating to conflict of laws (other than this Article) shall not apply to the determination of any question mentioned in paragraph (1).

(4) No –

(a) judgment of a foreign court; or

(b) decision of any other foreign tribunal (whether in an arbitration or otherwise),

with respect to a trust shall be enforceable, or given effect, to the extent that it is inconsistent with this Article, irrespective of any applicable law relating to conflict of laws.

(5) The rule donner et retenir ne vaut shall not apply to any question concerning the validity, effect or administration of a trust, or a transfer or other disposition of property to a trust.

(6) In this Article –

'foreign' refers to any jurisdiction other than Jersey;

'heirship rights' means rights, claims or interests in, against or to property of a person arising or accruing in consequence of his or her death, other than rights, claims or interests created by will or other voluntary disposition by such person or resulting from an express limitation in the disposition of his or her property;

'légitime' and 'donner et retenir ne vaut' have the meanings assigned to them by Jersey customary law;

'personal relationship' includes the situation where there exists, or has in the past existed, any of the following relationships –

(a) any relationship between a person and the settlor or a beneficiary, by blood, marriage, civil partnership or adoption (whether or not the marriage, civil partnership or adoption is recognised by law);

(b) any arrangement between a person and the settlor or a beneficiary such as to give rise in any jurisdiction to any rights, obligations or responsibilities analogous to those of parent and child, husband and wife or civil partners; or

(c) any relationship between –
   (i) a person who has a relationship mentioned in either of paragraphs (a) and (b) with the settlor or a beneficiary, and
   (ii) a third person who does not have a relationship mentioned in either of paragraphs (a) and (b) with the settlor or a beneficiary.

(7) Despite Article 59, this Article applies to trusts whenever constituted or created.

TRUSTS (GUERNSEY) LAW 2007

PART II
PROVISIONS APPLICABLE ONLY TO GUERNSEY TRUSTS

Creation, validity and duration of Guernsey trusts

14 Application of Guernsey law to questions of validity.

(1) Subject to the terms of the trust, all questions arising in relation to a Guernsey trust or any disposition of property to or upon such a trust, including (without limitation) questions as to –

(a) the capacity of the settlor,

(b) the validity, interpretation or effect of the trust or disposition or any variation or termination thereof,

(c) the administration of the trust, whether it is conducted in Guernsey or elsewhere, including (without limitation) questions as to the functions, appointment and removal of trustees and enforcers,

(d) the existence and extent of any functions in respect of the trust, including (without limitation) powers of variation, revocation and appointment, and the validity of the exercise of any such function,

(e) the distribution of the trust property,

are to be determined according to the law of Guernsey without reference to the law of any other jurisdiction.

For these purposes 'the law of Guernsey' does not include the Guernsey rules of private international law, except those set out in this section.

(2) Subsection (1) –

(a) does not validate any disposition of property which is neither owned by the settlor nor the subject of a power of disposition vested in the settlor,

(b) does not affect the recognition of the law of any other jurisdiction in determining whether the settlor is the owner of any property or the holder of any such power,

(c) is subject to any express provision to the contrary in the terms of the trust or disposition,

(d) does not, in determining the capacity of a corporation, affect the recognition of the law of its place of incorporation,

(e) does not affect the recognition of the law of any other jurisdiction prescribing the formalities for the disposition of property,

(f) subject to subsection 3, does not validate any trust or disposition of real property situate in a jurisdiction other than Guernsey which is invalid under the law of that jurisdiction, and

(g) subject to subsection 3, does not validate any testamentary disposition which is invalid under the law of the testator's domicile at the time of his death.

(3) No Guernsey trust, and no disposition of property to or upon such a trust, is void, voidable, liable to be set aside, invalid or subject to any implied

condition, nor is the capacity of any settlor, trustee, enforcer, trust official or beneficiary to be questioned, nor is any settlor, trustee, enforcer, trust official, beneficiary or third party to be subjected to any obligation or liability or deprived of any right, claim or interest, by reason that –

(a) the laws of any other jurisdiction prohibit or do not recognise the concept of a trust, or

(b) the trust or disposition –

(i) avoids or defeats or potentially avoids or defeats rights, claims, interests, obligations or liabilities conferred or imposed by the law of any other jurisdiction on any person –

(A) by reason of a personal relationship to a settlor or any beneficiary, or

(B) by way of foreign heirship rights, or

(ii) contravenes or potentially contravenes any rule of law, judgment, order or action of any other jurisdiction intended to recognise, protect, enforce or give effect to any such rights, claims, interests, obligations or liabilities.

(4) Notwithstanding any legislation or other rule of law for the time being in force in relation to the recognition or enforcement of judgments, no judgment or order of a court of a jurisdiction outside Guernsey shall be recognised or enforced or give rise to any right, obligation or liability or raise any estoppel if and to the extent that –

(a) it is inconsistent with this Law, or

(b) the Royal Court, for the purposes of protecting the interests of the beneficiaries or in the interests of the proper administration of the trust, so orders.

(5) This section applies –

(a) whenever the trust or disposition arose or was made,

(b) notwithstanding any other provision of this Law.

(6) In relation to a Guernsey trust of personal property or any disposition of such property to or upon such a trust, the law of Guernsey relating to légitime and the rights of a surviving spouse apply only where the settlor is domiciled there at the time of his death.

Index

[*All references are to paragraph numbers*]

www.ingramcontent.com/pod-product-compliance
Ingram Content Group UK Ltd.
Pitfield, Milton Keynes, MK11 3LW, UK
UKHW051416150926
475561UK00005B/192

9 781526 508058